PRESSED FOR ALL TIME

Pressed for All Time

PRODUCING THE GREAT JAZZ ALBUMS

FROM LOUIS ARMSTRONG AND BILLIE HOLIDAY

TO MILES DAVIS AND DIANA KRALL

MICHAEL JARRETT

THE UNIVERSITY OF

NORTH CAROLINA PRESS

Chapel Hill

This book was published with the assistance of the Anniversary Fund of the University of North Carolina Press.

The University of North Carolina Press has been a member of the Green Press Initiative since 2003.

Cover illustration:
istock.com/© Elaineitalia

Library of Congress Cataloging-in-Publication Data
Names: Jarrett, Michael, 1953– interviewer.
Title: Pressed for all time : producing the great jazz albums from Louis Armstrong and Billie Holiday to Miles Davis and Diana Krall / [interviews by] Michael Jarrett.
Description: Chapel Hill : The University of North Carolina Press, [2016] | Includes bibliographical references and index.
Identifiers: LCCN 2016019245|
ISBN 9781469630588 (cloth : alk. paper) |
ISBN 9781469630595 (ebook)
Subjects: LCSH: Jazz—Production and direction—History. | Sound recording executives and producers—United States—Interviews. | Sound recordings—United States—History.
Classification: LCC ML3508 .P74 2016 |
DDC 781.65/149—dc23 LC record available at https://lccn.loc.gov/2016019245

Significant portions of the interviews with George Avakian, Ornette Coleman, Michael Cuscuna, Tom Dowd, Orrin Keepnews, Teo Macero, Sonny Rollins, Creed Taylor, James Blood Ulmer, and Tom Dowd were excerpted from Michael Jarrett, *Sound Tracks: A Musical ABC, Vols. 1–3* (Philadelphia: Temple University Press, 1998). I gratefully acknowledge permission to reprint. Portions of the interviews with several producers appeared in Michael Jarrett, "The Self-Effacing Producer: Absence Summons Presence," in *The Art of Record Production: An Introductory Reader for a New Academic Field*, ed. Simon Frith and Simon Zagorski-Thomas (Burlington, Vt.: Ashgate, 2012), 129–48. Reprinted by permission. Interview material from several other producers appeared in Michael Jarrett, "Cutting Sides: Jazz Record Producers and Improvisation," in *The Other Side of Nowhere: Jazz, Improvisation, and Communities in Dialogue*, ed. Daniel Fischlin and Ajay Heble (Middletown, Conn.: Wesleyan University Press/New England Press, 2004), 319–49. Reprinted by permission. Photographer William Claxton's comments on Sonny Rollins's *Way out West* appeared in Michael Jarrett, *Drifting on a Read: Jazz as a Model for Writing* (Albany: SUNY Press, 1999), 199. Reprinted by permission. Portions of comments by Leo Feigin, Carla Bley, and Steve Swallow originally appeared in *Jazziz*. They are reprinted by permission.

For the

Chattanooga and Tampa

Public Libraries,

for lending me lots of

great jazz albums

CONTENTS

INTRODUCTION

....

I f every word in this book did not come from interviews I conducted over the last twenty-five years, if I'd invented instead of organized its words, you could think I was taking a crack at writing the great jazz novel: experimental, sure; postmodern, maybe. It's a book you can, if you like, hopscotch your way through, but read conventionally, from beginning to end, it is something of a metaepic. Instead of focusing on heroic deeds of iconic jazz artists—the amazing but true adventures of Pops, Duke, Bird, Mingus, and Miles—it tells stories behind those stories. Imagine a companion to *The Odyssey* that cobbled together fascinating, but less testosterone-fueled, behind-the-scenes anecdotes of jugglers, housewives, thieves, weavers, cooks, rope makers, stable boys, and black-smiths: all told in their own words. You'd have, as is the case here, a weave of many voices: a rhapsody—songs strung together.

In this story of jazz albums, fifty-seven people talk about their work on more than two hundred records. With few exceptions, they spoke with me by telephone, but I've begun to hear their voices collectively as a surround-sound mix. Everyone I spoke with for these pages—except for an engineer (John Palladino) and a photographer (William Claxton)—has sat in the producer's chair of a recording booth. For most of them, production was (or still is) their main gig. A few are known primarily as musicians, but they've produced records for themselves and in some cases for others. Their comments included here speak to issues of record production. And since I've used the word *record*, let me clarify its use in these pages. As a noun, *records* can refer to wax cylinders, 10- or 12-inch vinyl discs, multitrack tapes, cassettes, CDs, mp3 downloads, and any other medium used to mechanically or electronically encode sound. In other words, we'll always have records—in some form or another.

This book focuses almost exclusively on American music, despite the global reach of jazz. It tells the seventy-five-year history of jazz record albums. That story has reached a point of resolution because the album format evolved. Don't get me wrong. I am in no way restating the tired claim that jazz—the music—is dead. On that topic, I have no idea and little interest, but I notice that astonishing jazz albums—records—are still being issued, and they are selling. Rather, I'm saying the story of the jazz album has concluded. The album as a format—a way of organizing a program of music, analogous to narrative organizing movies—is what we might call morphologically stable. Inevitably, new mediums for recording music will emerge (cranial implants, anyone?), but while the album shows no sign of disappearing, it also shows no sign of further development. However debatable this opinion may be, it's most useful for the historical perspective it affords. We can see or, better, we can hear that behind the story of the album format is an untold narrative of jazz production: how producers developed different practices for making, organizing, and presenting jazz recordings. Sharing those practices as they played out in specific instances is the reason for this book. Its talking heads explain their working methods, their contributions to a lot of great albums. But again, it's been a long time since a new way to organize musical material has emerged, or a new way to produce jazz records. Today, the music remains vital, but it is produced and presented in time-honored ways described in this oral history.

To demonstrate the contributions this book's fifty-five producers made to the albums that defined jazz, I've arranged interview material around specific recordings ordered chronologically by release dates. It's an organizing device. Even when producers' comments are general, they are paired with exemplary albums in order to give readers concrete points of reference. Please note, I am not declaring that producers were actually referring to highlighted albums even when they weren't mentioned by name. For example, Teo Macero never spoke with me about his postproduction work on *Kind of Blue*, yet I group comments he made under that album title. Why? Whenever possible, I want to direct the attention of readers to career-defining productions. Mostly, producers speak exclusively of their own projects, delivering informal case studies, or they provide historical contexts for their work. Occasionally, I've used the observations of producers to give the larger narrative more continuity and cohesion, though I'm fond of picturing this book as, itself, a kind of record album, a massive box set. With a few exceptions—where someone died before I could speak with him—I was able to interview the producers who created and developed the jazz album. Who did I miss? Five of the greats: John Hammond at Columbia Records, Alfred Lion and Francis Wolff at Blue Note, Lester Koenig at Contemporary, and Nesuhi Ertegun at Atlantic. In my defense, I will say that Hammond—whose contributions to American music are inestimable—is a fairly marginal figure in the story of jazz albums. He made records (what we'd think of as singles), and though his career was long and distinguished, he left an indelible mark on jazz before the arrival of long-playing albums. I will also add that he, Lion and Wolff, Koenig, and

Ertegun evoke lots of interesting commentary in these pages, from producers who knew them well. Lester Koenig is described by his son John, who is also a musician (a master cellist) and record producer. All of the major producers I missed are in some way included in this book, if only as they are evoked by their peers.

To record most of the interviews that formed the raw material from which this book was built, I used a Wollensak cassette recorder and a small microphone with a suction cup that fit on the back of my telephone's receiver. Occasionally, I conducted interviews in person. For example, I talked with Ornette Coleman in the late 1980s, when his original quartet reunited to play a concert in Atlanta. Interviewing Carla Bley and Steve Swallow at their home in Woodstock, New York, was my response to a magazine assignment given by my editor at *Jazziz*. Tower Records' magazine *Pulse!* sent me to Sony Music for a piece on Louis Armstrong. There I spoke with a team of engineers and producers reissuing, more or less, the jazz canon. I recorded all of the above mentioned interviews onto cassettes that are now archived in the Southern Folklife Collection at the Wilson Library of the University of North Carolina, Chapel Hill.

My editors at *Pulse!* indulged me from the late 1980s until the magazine (and, shortly thereafter, Tower's stores) shut down in 2002. I pitched them several articles on the production of jazz albums: first, because I was (and still am) passionate about the music and, second, because I was mystified by production. What did jazz producers actually do? I started interviewing people in the mid-1980s, spoke with a lot more in the mid-1990s, and in the past couple of years I caught up with some people I'd missed. Only a small fraction of the interview material I gathered made it into magazine articles. For one thing, the published pieces were short, but, mainly, there was another explanation. Early on, during those mid-1990s interviews, I envisioned this book, and slightly altered my tactics by enlarging the scope of conversations. I'd telephone a legendary producer—say, Milt Gabler. (His number was in the phone book.) I'd introduce myself, describe my assignment or the story I hoped to pitch, and say that I wanted to talk more than was, perhaps, required because I was pulling together material for a possible book. Every single producer with whom I spoke was a model of graciousness, and I spoke with many of them more than once—pretty much anytime a new assignment gave me an excuse to call. After telling Gabler that I was recording our conversation for use in print (or, if I forgot, having him ask if I was taping), I explained that I had two lines of questions. First, "Did you have a philosophy of production, what it should and should not be?" Second, "What about your contributions to specific recordings?" From my transcription of the conversation, I'd write the article and, once published, mail copies to my interview subjects. Although it nagged at me, I did little or nothing about writing that promised book.

Maybe my antidepressant started working. But just as likely the obituary of a producer—on whose work I'd doted—served as a memento mori, reminding me of not just the obvious but also, and more important, why I'd started talking to jazz record producers in the first place. Once I managed to figure out what and how much producers actually did, I was even more convinced that their stories needed to be told. The crucial role that producers played in the history of jazz albums wasn't so much underappreciated as it was largely unknown. Besides, why keep so many great stories all to myself?

The overarching narrative told in these pages begins in the mid-1930s, with a bit of prehistory: that's less than five years before the first 78-rpm jazz album (of new music); a little more than ten years before record albums became 10-inch discs played at 33⅓ rpm; and almost twenty years before albums meant 12-inch discs tucked inside paper sleeves and cardboard jackets, featuring really cool cover art by such favorites as Alex Steinweiss, Jim Flora, David Stone Martin, and Reid Miles. In the 1930s, record albums—very much the musical equivalent of photograph albums—were multidisc collections of 78-rpm records. Seventy-eight revolutions per minute gave listeners a whopping five minutes of music per side for 12-inch discs—the size reserved for classical music and operatic arias—and a paltry three minutes per side for 10-inch discs. In the history of jazz, there is no better example of the medium constraining the music.

Inviting a host of jazz musicians to a downtown club in 1938, Milt Gabler, owner of New York's Commodore Record Shop, took the initiative to record the resulting jam sessions, which he then issued as 12-inch, 78-rpm jazz records. At about that same time, a college sophomore at Yale named George Avakian convinced Decca Records to let him record a group of Chicago musicians. The records he produced were issued as a set: the first jazz album of newly recorded music. Gabler and Avakian's ideas were innovative but hardly unthinkable. They were in the air. More significant, they revealed a keen awareness of an emergent audience for jazz—for hot jazz, to be specific. More than any other single factor, the audience for this music came to shape the development of jazz as its patterns of consumption operated like artificial selection. No record producer could long afford to ignore what people wanted. Why would they? Gabler and Avakian initiated a pattern for jazz production that still endures: select—invest in—musicians that you enjoy and hope that a respectable number of fans agree with your choices. Successful producers are the avant-garde of public tastes.

Artists-and-repertoire (A & R) men were close to what we call producers. (Jazz production was and still is a white, male-dominated field.) They worked for the big record labels, then as now an oligopoly analogous to Hollywood's studios. A & R men chose and, therefore, by default rejected which artists to record. Plus, they chose and, therefore, rejected which songs to record. They functioned as the gatekeepers of an art form. Beginning in the 1950s, A & R men could evolve into full-fledged producers as magnetic tape became a widespread, economical recording medium. Eventually, tape afforded control over all phases of record making. Producers could even "go independent": build studios or, more typically, rent them (room, equipment, and engineers) from the major labels. Because independent producers and independent record labels were necessarily dependent on the pressing plants and distribution networks of the major labels, they emerged slowly. Self-produced artists—Lennie Tristano is a prime example—remained the rarest of rare birds. Even in the twenty-first century, with the advent of digital-audio workstations (DAWs), big-label producers (or producers who have deals with the major labels) are still powerful figures in the creation of records.

The four chapters of this book mark significant shifts in the development of recording technology and, therefore, in the story of jazz albums. Chapter 1 (1936–49) starts the clock in the pretape, prealbum era, when music was recorded to acetate or lacquer masters. Music taken up in chapter 2 (1950–66) and chapter 3 (1967–90) was mastered to tape—monophonic, stereo, or multitrack—and sold as singles and albums. Whether or not the recordings featured in chapter 4 (1991–present) were mastered to hard drives—and many weren't—they were produced during the digital era, when albums meant CDs, digital downloads, and vinyl for enthusiasts.

At the head of each chapter, I name a recording that exemplifies production during a particular era. Consider it a point of reference. Taken together, they suggest a basic reality of jazz production. Jazz records are, almost without exception, records of jazz performances, despite a history of fairly regular changes in recording mediums. This is the case even in an era, such as the present one, when many pop records are layers of discrete musical moments—corrected and composited—and the role of pop producer blurs with that of engineer. The process of producing jazz albums focuses, primarily, on ensuring (by any means necessary) that musicians will create great performances captured by engineers. This is why jazz producers honor no fixed method of working. It turns out that making a jazz album, like playing jazz, is an art of improvisation.

It is no exaggeration to declare that, while musicians make music, producers make records. That observation, however, carries with it a distinct risk. It practically stakes out the possibility of an auteur theory of record production as a way to underscore and simplify the contributions of people such as those interviewed for this book. Part of me dearly wishes I could in good conscience claim, "If you want to know who actually made the great jazz records, meet the producers," or, "If you're looking for the real author of *Louis Armstrong Plays W. C. Handy* (1954), the album, contact its producer George Avakian." I know full well that Avakian's role in the creation of this album was essential. Of course, Armstrong created the music (though Handy wrote the tunes), but, put bluntly, without Avakian there would be no album.

It's necessary, then, to explain why I refuse to take what looks like the audacious step of installing producers as the authors of jazz albums, and why this book—despite turning a spotlight on record production—is not meant to imply any such theory. My first reason is theoretical. As an analytical term, "author" has become less than useful, even when quick reflection on contemporary anxieties over "intellectual property" suggests that our culture is obsessed with determining authorship. Continuing debates pitting evolution against intelligent design provide a good example of what I mean. Imagining a single, omnipotent creator—an author of the universe, for example—solves lots of problems by instituting a simple metaphysical solution. Nowadays, we're anxious because, in an age of mechanical and, more recently, digital reproduction, authorship feels like an unsustainable concept. That's why so much cultural work goes into shoring it up. Authorship has gigantic material—that is to say, financial—consequences. My question becomes, *What happens to a culture or, rather, what has happened to our culture if and when another concept replaces author?* I have a hunch that "record producer" signifies one such early attempt to designate or to conceive of such a concept. "Music" as Jacques Attali claimed, "is prophecy. Its styles and economic organization are ahead of the rest of society."[1]

My second reason for rejecting auteur theory is ideological. Jazz production as practiced for more than seventy-five years is an art form of

---

1. Jacques Attali, *Noise: The Political Economy of Music*, trans. Brian Massumi (Minneapolis: University of Minnesota Press, 1985), 11.

self-effacement. But the self-effacing producer doesn't so much thwart the notion of authorship as he eliminates any possibility of an author except the musician whose name is featured conspicuously on an album's cover. Invariably, the producer recedes, and this move toward invisibility, transparency, or, better, toward inaudibility foregrounds the principal performer as an artist, making him or her the obvious author of the record. The musical vision or personality of the jazz producer is, perhaps, latent in the sound of every album he produces, but it is almost never manifest. The producer covers his tracks. That's his job. He strives (most likely unconsciously) to leave no trace of his presence. Conventionally, he labors to craft an album that sounds like the only people who worked hard in its making were the musicians. The same argument applies to engineers.

Q: How many producers does it take to screw in a lightbulb?
A: I don't know. What do you think?

Jazz musician and producer Bob Belden told me that joke, perhaps to emphasize that the long history of jazz neither boasts nor bemoans figures comparable to such producers as Phil Spector, Billy Sherrill, Baby Face, Timbaland, Pharrell Williams, and next year's award-winning pop Svengali. Jazz production does, though, have its fair share of megalomaniacs (you'll figure out who I mean), but without exception they have happily subordinated their madness to the greater madness of featured artists. In this book you'll have confirmed what you already know: making a jazz album is a collaborative process. But you'll learn about noteworthy collaborations and about the wide range of roles played by producers.

All of which begs the original question: What, exactly, do jazz producers do? What is the answer to the question that motivated my interviews? Had I but world enough, and time, I'd categorize, analyze, and theorize all of the material I gathered. But that would require another book. Instead, I'll reduce all of the talk—everything that follows—to one point. Jazz record producers are best understood as a distinct group of highly sophisticated listeners—a special class of artists, really—who are the direct, historical result of an active, widely distributed connoisseur culture devoted to jazz. They're enthusiasts, attuned to the finest nuances of jazz, elevating taste to the level of an art form. But instead of limiting their critical responses to the development of a heightened form of consumption and becoming hipster aesthetes, they've responded to what they've heard by making (more of) what they want to hear. That said, I'll emulate a certain admirable tendency of record producers. I'll get out of the way and let the artists blow so you can listen to what they have to say.

BIOGRAPHICAL SKETCHES

Jazz producers are not household names. As I've explained above, that's not how the business of jazz works. *Pressed for All Time* was built from my interviews with the following people. They are its soloists. Below, I've provided thumbnail sketches.

Jean-Philippe Allard—Even though Allard is a record company executive—he's general director of both Polydor Records and Universal Music Publishing in France—he has produced some of the best jazz of the past twenty-five years. He is responsible for extending the recording careers of J. J. Johnson, Helen Merrill, Abbey Lincoln, Stan Getz, Charlie Haden, Randy Weston, and John McLaughlin to great effect.

George Avakian—Very much the Platonic ideal of a jazz record producer. As staff producer at Columbia, Avakian more or less invented the jazz album (as a recorded concept). To that record label he brought Louis Armstrong, Dave Brubeck, Erroll Garner, and Miles Davis.

Brian Bacchus—Bacchus was an A & R man for Verve, Antilles, RCA, and Blue Note before moving into production and doing stellar work with Randy Weston, Patricia Barber, and Gregory Porter. His A & R work with Norah Jones contributed mightily to her debut, one of the biggest-selling albums in history.

Steve Backer—Primarily a record company executive. While working as general manager at Impulse, Backer signed Keith Jarrett and Gato Barbieri. Later, working for Clive Davis at Arista, he executive-produced some of the 1970s' most significant jazz and, then, for BMG in the 1980s and 1990s, a series of reissues on the Bluebird label.

Bob Belden—A saxophonist, composer, recording artist, and historian, Belden used his production expertise to create high-concept albums of bands he led and to reissue electric jazz from Sony Music's catalog.

Steve Berkowitz—The senior vice president of Sony's Legacy records, Berkowitz has, for years, superintended one of popular music's most vital reissue programs.

Carla Bley—A composer, bandleader, and pianist, Bley has produced her recordings for her own label—Watt Records—since the 1970s.

Michael Brooks—Music archivist—and something of an epic bard—at Sony Music.

Matt Cavaluzzo—An archival audio engineer at Sony Music, significant in establishing that company's digital-archive program.

William Claxton—A photographer most recognized in jazz circles for his contributions to Contemporary Records, which is to say, the "look" of West Coast cool.

Ornette Coleman—Known primarily as an alto saxophonist and composer, Coleman was the great iconoclast of jazz.

Marilyn Crispell—A pianist and composer, Crispell has produced several of her many albums.

Michael Cuscuna—Though Cuscuna produced some of the 1970s' most significant jazz albums (for Atlantic and, especially, Arista), he has become the most important reissue producer in jazz history and, therefore, an archivist of great significance. He is the eminence behind Mosaic Records—the premier label issuing historic multidisc collections.

Joel Dorn—The last of Atlantic's free-range producers, Dorn was comfortable and conversant with all forms of American vernacular music.

Tom Dowd—As one of popular music's most celebrated engineers, Dowd recorded virtually all of Atlantic Records' canonical jazz titles. He was inducted into the Rock and Roll Hall of Fame in 2012.

Esmond Edwards—Jazz production is a white-dominated field. An African American, Edwards stands out, especially for his exceptional work at Prestige, Argo (Chess), and Impulse.

Leo Feigin—For close to forty years, Feigin has kept the free-improvisation flame burning. The massive catalog of his London-based label, Leo Records, is an accomplishment of Herculean proportions.

Sid Feller—When Ray Charles left Atlantic Records for ABC-Paramount, his producer became Feller.

Joe Fields—During a long career, spent primarily as a record company executive, Fields has founded, bought, sold, and been associated with a great many labels, most notably Muse, Arista, Savoy, HighNote, and Savant.

Milt Gabler—One of America's most distinguished record men, a true pioneer. The music Gabler produced for Decca and his own company, Commodore, is the sound of classic jazz.

Kip Hanrahan—The producer as architect. Hanrahan consistently brings together players of distinction to realize his visions. Either that or the distinctive creations of the musicians he brings together conjure a producer of rare vision.

Nat Hentoff—Known primarily as a writer and critic, Hentoff also produced several excellent albums for Candid Records, where he was director of A & R. Many of those records featured friends such as Charles Mingus, Cecil Taylor, and Max Roach.

Charlie Haden—Haden figures in this history of record production because he coproduced *Beyond the Missouri Sky (Short Stories)* with Pat Metheny, but his contributions to jazz, as a bassist, composer, and bandleader, are vast.

Dave Holland—Nowadays, this legendary bassist and bandleader produces his own albums (distributed by ECM), though his comments in these pages primarily concern his tenure with Miles Davis.

Wayne Horvitz—Horvitz has produced albums by Bill Frisell, Marty Ehrlich, Bern Nix, the World Saxophone Quartet, Robin Holcomb, and the President. He is also a widely admired keyboardist and composer.

Bob Johnston—Most lauded for his 1960s work with Bob Dylan, Johnston also produced a single, "Cabaret," for Louis Armstrong.

Herb Jordan—Jordan has, most notably, produced albums for pianist Geri Allen and singer Andy Bey.

Stanley Jordan—*Magic Touch*, Jordan's major-label debut, brought the guitarist much attention. He self-produced his second album for Blue Note, *Standards, Volume 1*.

Helen Keane—Though Keane produced artists other than Bill Evans, the albums she made with the pianist are perennials.

Orrin Keepnews—Keepnews founded three jazz record labels— Riverside, Milestone, and Landmark—at which he produced albums by some of the music's most notable figures.

Marc Kirkeby—An archivist for Sony Music.

John Koenig—A cellist with the Jerusalem Symphony and the Swedish Radio Symphony, and a record producer at Atlantic and Contemporary, the latter label founded by his father—Lester Koenig—in 1949.

Bob Koester—Runs a shrine for record lovers: Chicago's Jazz Record Mart. Koester is also the founder and owner of Delmark Records.

Steve Lake—Lake went from writing about music (notably for *The Wire*) to producing high-quality albums of free improvisation for ECM.

Bill Laswell—Laswell's music rarely honors stylistic boundaries. His bass playing—for Material, Praxis, Last Exit, and many other bands— and his production work—for his label, Axiom, and many other imprints—are visionary.

Tommy LiPuma—LiPuma produced thirty-five albums certified gold or platinum by the Recording Industry Association of America, which makes him probably the most popular jazz producer ever. For example, one of his productions, George Benson's *Breezin'*, went triple platinum: that's 3 million units sold.

Teo Macero—While a staff producer at Columbia, Macero did much more than produce Miles, Monk, and Mingus, but that was enough to make him legendary. He was also a composer, arranger, and musician.

Pat Metheny—Best known as an exceptionally adventurous guitarist, Metheny has also (meticulously) produced his own recordings since leaving ECM in the mid-1980s.

Ed Michel—It is no overstatement to say that the sizable, deserved reputation enjoyed by Impulse Records was a consequence of productions by Bob Thiele (1961–68) and Ed Michel (1969–75).

Sue Mingus—The widow of Charles Mingus and, with Gunther Schuller and John McClure, the producer of *Epitaph*, her late husband's masterwork.

Jay Newland—A producer and a greatly admired engineer. To date, he has won nine Grammy Awards.

John Palladino—A pioneering engineer, Palladino did early work for Contemporary Records (and brought engineer Roy DuNann to that label) but was primarily a mainstay at Capitol Records.

Bob Porter—A walking encyclopedia of jazz, Porter produced a series of soul-influenced recordings for Prestige. He has also played a central role in reissuing historically significant jazz.

Bobby Previte—Drummer, composer, bandleader, and (almost always) a self-produced artist.

Ken Robertson—A mastering engineer at Sony Legacy.

Sonny Rollins—A jazz colossus and national treasure: for years, Rollins has been largely a self-produced artist (with his late wife, Lucille).

Don Schlitten—Before creating Xanadu Records, Schlitten had already produced a distinguished body of work at Signal, Cobblestone, Prestige, RCA, Muse, and Onyx Records.

John Snyder—Work at CTI, Horizon, Atlantic, A&M, Denon, and Artists House defines Snyder as one the most significant producers of the last quarter of the twentieth century.

Craig Street—Crisscrossing musical boundaries, Street made his
reputation producing career-defining albums for Cassandra Wilson.

Steve Swallow—In partnership with Carla Bley, Swallow has produced
a number of albums for Watt Records. He is also a bass player and
composer of great renown.

Creed Taylor—One of the most financially successful producers in jazz
history, Taylor created Impulse Records for ABC Paramount and,
later, his own label, CTI (Creed Taylor International).

Bob Thiele—For eight incredibly productive years (1961–68), Thiele ran
the creative side of Impulse Records: the house that Trane built.

Lee Townsend—His many productions—for example, of guitarists
Bill Frisell, Charlie Hunter, John Scofield, Pat Metheny, and John
Abercrombie—are most distinguished by Townsend's exquisite taste.

James Blood Ulmer—A guitarist and self-produced artist, Ulmer has a
playing style that is sui generis, though associated with the music of
Ornette Coleman.

Bob Weinstock—The founder of Prestige Records (1949) and several
affiliated labels, Weinstock was a legendary nonobtrusive record
producer.

Hal Willner—Working across a variety of media (recordings, live
concerts, TV, and movies), Willner is the ringleader of a musical circus
with constantly shifting personnel.

Joe Zawinul—Zawinul and Wayne Shorter founded the seminal jazz-
fusion band Weather Report, and they produced its albums. Both
musicians played in bands led by Miles Davis. Zawinul had earlier
played keyboards for Dinah Washington and Cannonball Adderley,
for whom he wrote "Mercy, Mercy, Mercy."

EDITOR'S NOTE

Unless otherwise indicated, names listed under album titles refer to the original producers of the albums. As needed, I indicate "reissue producers." A number of times, people's names are followed by information in parenthesis: for example, Orrin Keepnews (Riverside) or William Claxton (photographer). In these cases the talking head is there to provide orientation or context, to ensure continuity, or to provide specific information about an album he did not produce or about another producer.

PRESSED FOR ALL TIME

CADENZA
Don Schlitten on Producing Jazz Records
....

I n one respect, Don Schlitten is like everyone interviewed for this book. Despite vast individual differences, the folks who have made jazz albums share one characteristic. They've been—to a person— jazz fans. Whatever else they are or have been—bluebloods, musicians, entrepreneurs, critics, recording engineers, and entertainment lawyers—they're connoisseurs. Their exquisite taste—or their taste for the exquisite—motivates and guides their work as record producers. They record and release albums they love, made by musicians they love. Sometimes, as in the exceptional cases of Norman Granz and Creed Taylor, jazz producers make a lot of money. Most of the time, they don't.

They understand producing jazz as a vocation or calling, although no one with whom I've spoken would own up to motivations that lofty or noble. Take Don Schlitten. Early on, he recognized record production as an art. While the musicians he produced were routinely of the highest caliber- masters of their art—none had the slightest clue how to create a record album, much less get it distributed. That wasn't part of their skill sets. They knew how to make music.

Schlitten worked as a journeyman producer in the 1950s and 1960s, during which time he started a couple of record labels, Signal and Cobblestone, and served as head of production at Prestige Records, working for the founder and owner of the label, Bob Weinstock. All told, Schlitten produced more than 300 albums. In the 1970s, after producing records for Joe Fields at Muse, Schlitten formed his own company, Xanadu Records, where he eventually created a catalog of over 200 albums, which he steadfastly refused to digitize. His comments are included here because they provide a concise and perceptive overview of jazz record production.

DON SCHLITTEN
First off, I think the word *producer* is very confusing. In the old days, you weren't anything. Then you became an A & R man, which is short for "artist and repertoire." You worked for a large company because there were no small companies. You were in charge of talking to people who were plugging songs and getting the artists who were under contract to the company to record those songs.

The Jazz World of Don Schlitten

Later, in the forties, when independent labels started to appear, the word changed because nobody wanted to deal with song pluggers, for lots of reasons. You supervised recordings. Rock 'n' roll appeared in the fifties and, all of a sudden, the producer became a very important cog in the wheel. Anyone who was an A & R man or a supervisor was now a producer.

You ask, "What did he do?" In truth, if you use the analogy of film, a producer is the guy with the money, and the director is the guy who tells everybody what to do and how to do it. So what is the producer of a record? Is he the guy who's paying for it, or does he have some kind of musical input? It all becomes very confusing.

When I started Xanadu Records—and nobody ever asked me about it, although every once in a while I would catch somebody copying me—I decided to put "reissued by" on the album cover, if I, obviously, put out a reissue. If I put together a new record, but made up of material that I didn't actually go into the studio and help create, then I would call myself a "producer." But if I was really in charge of the whole shooting match, then I called myself a "director." When I put out a record that I'd just done in the studio—from concept to finished product—I put "produced and directed by." It made me look like some kind of big shot in Hollywood. I don't know whether it confused people more or confused them less, but that's how I got around that business.

It is interesting. You look at a record, let's say one by Charlie Parker, and it will say "produced by so and so," and "so and so" wasn't even born when that music was recorded. I don't know how other to explain it than everybody needs to see their names in print, no matter what. But I do believe it's very deceiving to somebody who comes into a store, looks at that record, and does not know that Charlie Parker died in 1955, and this guy listed as the "producer" was born in 1979.

When I started producing, which was way back in the fifties, I had to work with somebody who was putting up the money. But at Xanadu I put up my own money. It changed around for me that way, but in truth what a producer is supposed to do—assuming you've got all of your money and nobody's telling you what to do or how to do it—what you're really supposed to do is come up with a concept and see it through to the end. Going back to primitive times, that includes selecting the artist and the repertoire. In today's world, it also includes being a psychiatrist, a mother, a friend, a boss, and a lot of other things. But most importantly, I think a producer has to know music. He has to be on good terms with the artists; they're not afraid of him. They're not coming in to do a job but rather joining with the producer to help create music. To me that's the most important thing.

You really have to create the proper environment in which the artist can play his best. In a world other than jazz, if you are producing Glenn Gould, you have to make sure that the piano keys are all oiled properly so that they can slide off his fingers; you have to use the proper amount of Vaseline on the black keys. But really, I find that it's most important to have a good relationship with all of the artists and with the engineer—who I consider to be one of the artists—and for everyone to have the same goal in mind, which is to create some beautiful music. It's not as simple as it sounds. One guy had a fight with his wife that morning. Another guy, his hemorrhoids are bothering him. When you decide that this [record production] is what you want to do, from the get-go you've got to make sure that you have the right concept for the artist, and that these are the right players to work with the leader on this concept. You've got to make sure that all the musicians respect each other, and that they're not coming to do a record date; they're coming to play music.

When you call up a guy and say, "Would you like to do a session?" and he says, "How much?" or "Who's it with?" that's one way of doing it. Or you can ask, "Would you like to do a session with so and so?" And he says, "Of course!" He doesn't even mention the money, because it's secondary. But of course, this is a new world, and money is the name of the game, which is why I am slipping back into the shadows. I can't deal with this mentality. I don't think it has anything to do with the music I've given my life for. I've seen all of the inspiration, the love and the fun, the things that went into it and helped make it what it was, rapidly disintegrate. I find that very sad.

Even though my first sessions were done in the fifties on tape, rather than on acetate or wire, which certainly preceded me, recording was done primarily the same way as it had always been done. There was no mixing. You got a balance and captured the performance. Whatever you got, you got. In those days, some engineers working for small independent companies didn't even have the proper technique for splicing and editing tape. The only difference, when I started, was music went to tape instead of discs. Otherwise, things were the same. The idea was to get a proper balance and go for a take, make sure it wasn't too short or too long.

When you moved into stereo and, later on, to multitrack tape—to four-track, eight-track, sixteen, and all the way up—you then had options to play around with. Multitracking changed around a lot of things. Way back when, on some sessions that I did, a musician would come in, and he'd be totally confused about what was going on. He wasn't used to that sort of stuff. He didn't believe that you could do this and you could do that. Multitracking did create a lot of short cuts. It made the musician aware that, in many cases, if he fucked up, somebody could un-fuck him up.

I believe that discipline is very, very important in life. Once you throw away discipline, you start to throw away yourself. Which is to say, you need to adhere to certain ways of working, and you need to do things right. You can't say, "Okay, he'll fix it later," or "We'll do that later." Things ought to be done right—right then. A lot of that discipline changed with the possibilities of tape, but it did change gradually because the first sessions were done direct to tape. I remember in 1978 or '79, somebody came up with this "new" discovery called direct-to-disc, which is really what people were doing in the thirties and forties. Some genius came up with this "new concept." It didn't last very long, but it was interesting that somebody discovered something that they thought was very important.

Mixing and all that [postproduction] stuff is very important today, not only because it helps clean up mistakes, but [also] because it allows you to do certain things you couldn't do before. But I produce—how to describe it?—pretty honestly and acoustically. There's not too much of what they call sweetening, adding echo, or let's put strings on tomorrow; or this is no good, we'll erase it and put somebody else on top. I have used some of those techniques on rare occasions, but I'd say 95 percent of my work is pretty much getting the right sound from an engineer who understands that this saxophone player needs one mike and this bass player needs another mike. Everybody needs a different mike, because they have different sounds. I had a trumpet player once, who I watched very carefully. I discovered that, whenever he got very emotional, he'd bend over and play with the bell of his horn pointed towards the floor. Now, that's awkward to record. Noticing this, I put another microphone on the floor so that, just in case he did that, I'd still get him. Of course, you can do that only if you're multitracking. In other words, that guy could not have recorded in 1945. He would've gotten lost someplace.

I've never used multitrack technology as a safety net. I've used it only where I thought it would help the situation. I recorded or produced or directed—whatever you want to call it—a young cat in the late seventies by the name of Peter Sprague, a guitar player. He was very interested in Indian music, and in combining Indian music with jazz. I heard him as a jazz player and was very impressed. When we started to talk, I realized where he was trying to go with his music. In that situation, you're going to use multitracking because he's going to record with the rhythm section swinging, and then you're going to add on top of it the sitar, the tabla, or whatever else you want—maybe a Chinese gong here and there. You certainly couldn't do all of that at one time. So there was an instance where, if I really wanted to capture this person's music, I needed the technology to go with it.

With somebody else—if I did a solo piano album—the idea was to create an atmosphere where the artist was most comfortable. Some guys feel very comfortable in the dark, and so you turn off all the lights. If it's a big studio, maybe you'll put up some walls to make it more intimate, but not to where he feels too lonely. Then there are people who like an audience. They're very insecure if there aren't one hundred people in the control room screaming for them. Other guys want quiet. They want to be left alone.

I always try to place everybody physically close together into as intimate a surrounding as possible. Otherwise, it's not real. If you need to take a trolley car or a bus to get to the drummer and tell him to use brushes, that's silly. He should be right there. I strive to put everybody as close together as humanly possible so that they can feel that intimacy and warmth from each other.

If somebody is in the thick of creating something, and something happens with the technology, you don't want to blow his mind. You very gently turn up or turn down the lights, so it's not an abrupt bang in the head. You've got to understand all these things, because everybody is a different kind of screwball. Everybody's got a different kind of a problem. You have to understand who your guy is, who you're working with. You need to have a good relationship with him, have his respect, and know that your engineer knows what to do and what the room can do, which is very important. If I were to go look for a new studio now, I'd be in a lot of trouble because I couldn't find an all-wooden studio. They don't exist anymore because they're not necessary for the new world. So there are a bunch of tiny little things that go into making an album that you really have to feel secure with.

What I did was find myself an engineer and stay with him for twenty years. When I say we're recording so-and-so today with just a rhythm section, he'll say, "Who's the pianist?"

I'll tell him, "We're using Barry Harris today."

He'll know what to do, because Barry has a softer touch than, let's say, Wynton Kelly. He'll know what mike to use and where to place it. Let's say I'm doing [saxophonist] Al Cohn. You have to know him: what he sounds like, how he moves, what he does when he overblows—which sometimes cats do when they get excited. You have to make sure that you have the right microphone in the right spot to take care of all those things. You could have seven different microphones for seven different saxophone players. With bass players, all of them use amps and mikes and stuff like that. Some guys like the mike inside their bass; some guys like it in front. What I like to do, and this is an advantage that technology gave me, is to record them both ways: both through the amplifier and through the instrument. Then I can mix it so that it comes out as one sound. It's a more penetrating sound, but it's still an acoustic sound. Technology has helped out in some areas; in other areas, it's just a cop-out for somebody. You're painting a picture. With this kind of music, if you're really into it, you're also improvising. I can be improvising even when I'm mixing the record.

1

CUTTING SIDES
Producing 78-RPM Discs,
1936–1949

....

EXEMPLARY RECORDING—BILLIE HOLIDAY, "STRANGE FRUIT"
Long before magnetic tape—which was one of the spoils of World War II—
record-company managers called "recording directors" controlled the
preproduction phase of record making. They chose artists to record, and
they paired songs from the music-publishing firms of Tin Pan Alley with
those artists. Thus, these early record producers came to be more generally known as A & R men—short for "artists and repertoire." In the studio,
during and after supervising the recording of 10-inch, 78-rpm discs, they
could do very little that, by today's standards, would qualify as production
(and nothing resembling postproduction). Artists could do even less. Back
then, in order to stamp records, steam-powered machines—housed inside large pressing plants—were fitted with molds derived from the masters cut in the studio. The very same process is used today to press vinyl
records, but with one huge difference. Stampers are derived by a process
that begins with taped or digital masters. Before the invention of tape,
masters of wax and, later, lacquer or acetate—discs with one song per
side—made it physically next to impossible for artists to own the actual
products of their labor. To fall back on a Marxist phrase, they had no access to the means of production. Consequently, the record industry was
highly concentrated, especially after the Depression. Material conditions
practically assured that it would take the form of an oligopoly.

As Milt Gabler tells the story, Billie Holiday was in a serious bind when
she complained to him in 1939. Columbia Records would not permit her
to record "Strange Fruit." The song had been a hit with the left-leaning
crowd at Café Society, a racially integrated Greenwich Village club where
the singer enjoyed a regular gig. Gabler solved her problem. After successfully obtaining an exception to Holiday's contract, he recorded Lady
Day singing "Strange Fruit" for Commodore, his own record label. The
record was pressed (mass produced as shellac discs) by Vocalion, a company owned by CBS which, not so coincidentally, owned Columbia.

Again, Gabler cut "Strange Fruit"—straight to a lacquer or acetate disc.

All of the records described in this chapter, focusing on the 78-rpm era, were recorded to exactly the same medium. Thus, at that time "records" meant what we'd call "singles," and "albums" meant multidisc sets of "singles" devoted to classical music. The first jazz albums, at least of newly recorded music, originated when Decca Records bought a college sophomore's idea: issue three multidisc packages of hot music from Chicago, New Orleans, and Kansas City. The college kid, George Avakian, produced the *Chicago Jazz Album* (1940), the first installment of this projected series and, therefore, the first jazz album. It was a set of six 10-inch records, again, recorded at 78 rpm.

Jazz albums as we know them—programs of music taped and then reproduced on 12-inch LPs or "long-playing records" played at 33⅓ rpm— would have to wait more than ten years, until Avakian, back from World War II and employed by Columbia Records, would score another of many "firsts."

Orrin Keepnews (Riverside)

Until you get into the LP period—and I make no particular distinction between the 10-inch and the 12-inch LP—and the automatic-album approach that the long-playing record ushered in, the producer, as such, was not a terribly noticeable figure. But there were exceptions: above all, Milt Gabler and John Hammond. They were fairly unique—noticeable and influential producers—in the days when you were dealing, primarily, with individual records, 78-rpm singles.

Go back to the days of the 78, and that really was a vastly different approach to recording. Even though some records did come out in groups— two or three 78s as an album—you didn't have the benefit of the kind of album thinking that we later had. The ability of Gabler and Hammond to transition into the contemporary world, to come into the LP world, was a tremendous accomplishment. It was as if D. W. Griffith had been able to make talkies.

Next week, I'm going to be in the studio editing and sequencing a CD. The fact that it was recorded digitally, which is very different from early LPs, does not impact my work in the studio. Technology changes but, with jazz, neither the product nor the vocabulary has changed that much. Today, with reissues we use computerized noise-removal techniques. Years ago, we used industrial razor blades and spliced tapes to do noise removal. The technologies are very different, but the reason why it's being done and the effect that we're trying to accomplish is exactly the same.

As a record producer who, in 1956, was producing Thelonious Monk, I frankly don't think any challenge anybody can throw at me today is going to be any more demanding than that challenge was then. I am saying that the key element in jazz is, as it always has been, the artist. The key challenge to the producer is to establish a successful relationship with the artist. Technological differences between present and past are secondary to that.

BILLY BANKS' RHYTHMAKERS, "MARGIE" (1936, UNITED HOT CLUBS OF AMERICA; ORIGINALLY ISSUED, 1932, ARC)
Milt Gabler (UHCA Reissues)

After World War I, after 1918, there were hot records of orchestras that people danced to. There were solos on them, and that's what collectors were looking for [in the thirties]. The solos were the interesting parts. They were jazz. Dance music came out of jazz. The soloists on those dance records—that went back as far as the Original Dixieland Jazz Band and Red Nichols and His Five Pennies—were mostly white musicians, but the black artists were the ones who were really putting down the right music.

I started to reissue records in the middle thirties at my Commodore Music Shop [which opened in New York in 1926]. Mostly, they were jazz records [recorded in the twenties]. I put out some Bessie Smith. I never put out Ethel Waters. I should have. There was Louis Armstrong, the Hot Fives and Sevens, and there was Duke Ellington. There were a lot of hot records, but the greatest tool for selling them was Charles Delaunay's *Hot Discography* [1936]. I used to import them from Europe and sell them in my store. I started the United Hot Clubs of America with Marshall Stearns. I put out the UHCA label. I wanted people to join the Hot Club in order to buy the original Hot Clubs of America records.

To build up my discography and record label, I used to lease the masters from the major companies. There was no tape; you couldn't copy them. You had to have shellac records or mothers. You could play the mothers like records. Stampers were negatives of the mothers. I had to buy the pressings from the company that owned the masters. You couldn't copy them and make your own masters. That would be bootlegging. You had to go back to the company to press the records on shellac. It took steam and pressure and a cooling system. They had the masters, the mothers, and the stampers—everything.[1]

1. Very briefly, the music is recorded—etched or cut—to a lacquer or acetate disc. This master disc is electroplated with nickel. Peeled off, this metal foil is called the

We developed a following. Guys like John Hammond, the Erteguns, and Jerry Wexler, they were all my customers. They used to come in and collect records in my store. [French jazz critic] Hugues Panassié used to buy records from me through the mail. My UHCA reissues started to work so well that the record labels, who used to lease me the masters, decided that they would put out the records themselves. After we'd built up the market, John Hammond went to Columbia and got the job of reissuing their catalog. "That's the end of my Hot Club records," I said. "We built up the market, and now the major companies—Victor, Columbia, and Brunswick—they're putting out the records themselves with a special label." I could see that the Commodore Music Shop and the Hot Club label couldn't compete with the majors.

I was the first one ever to put the personnel and the history of the recording on the label. I used to sell the reissues that I put out on UHCA for seventy-five cents and for a dollar. Even the rarer ones—where I had to make masters, mothers, and stampers—sold for a dollar and a half. When the labels started to put out their own reissues, they could sell records for a normal price [i.e., at the same price as a new record]. The handwriting was on the wall. That was the end of my UHCA label—or almost the end. I did start to reissue Gennett and labels like that.

"I better make my own label," I said. That's when I started Commodore Records. By 1938, I'd started to record my own records.

George Avakian (Columbia)

When Louis [Armstrong] came back from Europe in 1933, Joe Glaser took over his business affairs entirely and immediately got his career started again with a contract at Decca Records. That was a natural for Jack Kapp, who had been the head of Brunswick. He hadn't recorded Louis, but Kapp was from Chicago. He and Glaser knew each other.

Glaser saw that the Decca label might take off under Kapp. Their price for records was half of that charged by the other popular lines, of which there were really only two. There was the Brunswick label which, later, became part of the Columbia/CBS operation and the Victor label, both

---

"master matrix." As a negative of the original positive, the master matrix is also designated as the "negative master." From this matrix (a flimsy sort of mold), another positive is made (a sturdy sort of record)—this one of metal. A copy of the original master disc, it is called a "mother," and from it yet another negative—the "stamper"—is fashioned. The stamper is the mold used in mass producing records. If it wears out, additional stampers are made from the mother.

selling for seventy-five cents. Decca was selling for thirty-five cents. I remember buying three for eighty-eight cents at Macy's whenever my mother took me shopping with her.

I'd head for the record department on, I believe, the fifth floor and get lost there for a half hour or so listening to the latest records. I'd end up buying three Deccas or one Brunswick. There weren't very many Victors that I liked. I think Ellington was the only person who I bought on that label for quite a while.

Milt Gabler (Decca/Commodore)

In those days, if you sold Victor—before it was RCA Victor, it was the Victor Talking Machine Company—if you got a license to sell Caruso, you couldn't sell Columbia records. It was like an automobile franchise. When I went into the record business, I couldn't get Victor records because there was a dealer around the corner. I had to wait until he went out of business, and then I got the Victors. Before that, I had records on Columbia, Brunswick, Harmony, and Perfect. Perfect sold records for twenty-five cents. There was even a paper record, sold at newsstands, for fifteen cents. It bombed, but they did have them. Jack Kapp decided that Decca would break the main record line. He thought records were too expensive for the times. It was just coming out of the Depression. They were in business in '34.

BILLIE HOLIDAY, *BILLIE'S BLUES* (1936, VOCALION)
George Avakian (Columbia)

John Hammond produced Benny Goodman studio recordings in '31. In 1936, I was in college, thinking of John as a veteran. Incidentally, I must tell you I don't like talking about John. I liked him very much, but many times he was a remarkably insensitive and dishonest person.

None of us ever talked about it, but John did some really terrible things, which you couldn't do much about. He was a powerful and rich man. In an interview with Chris Albertson, I finally broke down and talked. When I did, Chris—who worked at Columbia when John came back to the company in the sixties—Chris called me and said, "Am I glad you did that! I've been bottling up all this stuff about what Hammond did, and not talking about it. I feel released." Then he told me some things that were just about as shocking as what I had experienced.

There was a conspiracy not to talk, and besides John had the remarkable ability to tell a whopping lie, looking you in the eye, which left you with the feeling that, if you ever tried to fight this lie, he had the power to get away with a bigger whopper. So leave it alone. It was quite incredible what he was able to do.

There was a behind-his-back joke that collectors used to repeat [that] at first I thought was a little unfair and then I realized no, it's true. One collector meets another. To make a point stick, he says, "Well, I was in the studio at the time." The other collector would know he was hearing one of John Hammond's pet phrases, which simply meant, "I am positive that what I say is so." John would constantly—even in print—talk about how he was "in the studio at the time." You could mention somebody by name in a conversation, and John would cut in and say, "I discovered him." Sometimes it was true, but he said that all the time. That was a great need that he had, reflected in this attitude where he wanted it to be his thing. It was embarrassing and overrode other considerations.

Sadly, you're not a Vanderbilt. Such power makes "discovery" problematic. As often as not, the artists are doing the looking. They're the bears actively seeking a honeypot.

John always had a feeling that he had enormous power. He really did, I guess, but he hurt so many people. Take Billie Holiday, for example. John is generally credited—and he grabbed the credit all the time—with discovering and promoting Billie.[2] But Billie herself—in [*Lady Sings the Blues*] the book that was written through interviews with her by Bill Dufty and his wife—talks about Bernie Hanighen as the really important person in her early record career. He was a songwriter who wrote the lyrics to Thelonious Monk's "'Round Midnight," among other things. Bernie was a freelancer in the record business. He produced for the Vocalion label and was thus the producer of Billie's first records under her own name. She thought the world of him, and said so. By doing that, she didn't come out and say that John Hammond exaggerated his role, but everybody understood that was what she meant.

VARIOUS, *THE COMMODORE STORY* (ORIGINAL RECORDINGS, 1938–1943; COMPILATION, 1997, GRP/COMMODORE)
Milt Gabler

I didn't distribute Commodore records. I sold them just in the store. We got write-ups. Dealers wrote, and I would sell records at dealer's discount directly from my store. We didn't go after it to make hit records. I did it

---

2. Hammond produced Billie Holiday's "Billie's Blues" (1936).

to make jazz records, to preserve the music and to show the next [generation of] musicians that were learning to blow their noses how it should be played. I tried to be a teacher: tell you what to collect, what to listen for.

I used particular musicians or artists—they were definitely artists—because they had a style that I was familiar with from their earlier work. I chose specific artists for the jam sessions because of the way they played, the way they enjoyed playing, and who they liked working with. They were freestyle recordings. I never told them what to blow! I might tell them when I wanted them to play. "You take the first chorus after the theme is stated." They'd follow in a certain progression due to what horn they were playing and how they spoke on their instruments.

I might pick some standard tune that we were going to play and then tell them about it on the job the night before. Sometimes, I guess they would woodshed it, but there were almost never written arrangements. Sometimes, there were some sketches. But I never had arrangements on those first records.

The jam sessions were on Fifty-Second Street, a couple were down in the Village, but mostly they were on Fifty-Second Street at Jimmy Ryan's [jazz club]. When I got busy up at Decca producing records and traveling to record in Chicago and L.A., I turned it over to my brother-in-law, Jack Crystal [comedian Billy Crystal's father]. He was running the shop, the Commodore Music Shop, at the time. He took over my jazz concerts on Fifty-Second and eventually moved them down to Second Avenue.

LESTER YOUNG, *THE "KANSAS CITY" SESSIONS* (ORIGINAL RECORDING, 1938; REISSUE, 1997, COMMODORE)
Milt Gabler

With Lester Young, we used the guys from Basie's Band. I had Lester play clarinet. Well, he played tenor on a date, too. Of course, they were working together every night. The arranger was Eddie Durham, the first guy to play electric guitar. He had written little parts.

Sometimes, if you were just doing a blues—like I named "Countless Blues"—they worked a little figure out by head, and then they set the riff, took three solos after that. Everybody knew the chords of the blues. All they did was pick a key.

I'd tell them: "Buck [Clayton] will take the first chorus and Lester the second one—take it on in, come back to the riff."

You know what the scale was on Fifty-Second Street for a three-hour [jam] session? Ten dollars—double for the leader and contract. They'd come every week. I'd have some jugs there in the back near Zooty's drums. Be the bartender. Boy, they used to have a ball. They were so successful. When they closed the clubs on Sunday afternoons, the Hickory Club and the other ones, they all started to run jam sessions. Then they started to broadcast them. It grew from that.

That's where George Wein and Norman Granz got the idea of jazz concerts: from Jimmy Ryan's on Fifty-Second Street. Granz came in from the Coast once, I remember, on a Saturday night. He said, "Milt, this is the greatest! I'm going back to California and do the same thing." The next thing you know, he had JATP [Jazz at the Philharmonic]. Wein is still doing it [the Newport Jazz Festival].

Don't forget there was no tape. Records ran, mostly, anywhere from 2'40" to 3'15". That's the most you could get on a [10-inch] 78-rpm record before you'd run into the cut-off groove. Everything had to be laid out in front. I was the first one to make 12-inch [78-rpm] jazz recordings. You couldn't get enough playing time to let the guy really blow on a three-minute record. I could make it four minutes on a 12-inch [record].

During the war we were cutting directly to lacquer; acetate records were developed.[3] You could cut directly to a lacquer disc. Before that, we cut on wax.

Did you record the Basie Decca sessions?

No. The Basie Band left [in 1939] just before I went to Decca [in 1941]. John [Hammond] took them to Columbia. The story was the Decca men—who had been doing those sessions—didn't like John telling them how to record the band. They barred him from the studio because he was butting in on the dates. When Basie's contract was up, John took the band to Columbia. Anyway, he'd gotten a job at Columbia producing records and recording, so he took them over there.

EDDIE CONDON AND HIS BAND, "BALLIN' THE JACK" (1938), *BALLIN' THE JACK* (REISSUE, 1989, COMMODORE)
Milt Gabler

I used to do Eddie Condon's sessions in a normal studio. The first one, I did up at Brunswick. Then I moved to the Decca Studio. They were nor-

---

3. "Lacquer" and "acetate" are used as synonyms.

mal studios, with flats and baffles—things like that. When I wanted a great sound for the Condon band, I took them to Liederkranz Hall, where even the New York Philharmonic recorded. It was a studio owned by Columbia, or used by Columbia. It was like a dance hall, with a live wooden floor and a high ceiling. I'd put the band in the middle of that. But it's the way you placed the mikes. Those records have a fantastic sound, "Ballin' the Jack" and those things that I did with Condon with Fats Waller on them. That was natural reverb on those records, the Pythian Temple, no, Liederkranz Hall, had. But Pythian Temple was also a ballroom on Seventieth Street. We made a studio out of that. That's where I made [Peggy Lee's] "Lover" and Bill Haley's "Rock around the Clock."

BILLIE HOLIDAY, "STRANGE FRUIT" (1939), *STRANGE FRUIT* (COMMODORE)
Milt Gabler

She [Billie Holiday] came to me and wanted to use strings. I knew the jazz magazines would jump on me for doing that. But I did it anyway. I just used them to play like an organ background. They weren't way out, written in a jazz sense. They were used to give the record sweetness.

Billie Holiday wanted to record "Strange Fruit," but Columbia wouldn't let her, right?

That's right. She came to me almost in tears one day when I had the store on Fifty-Second Street. I said, "What's a matter, Billie?" Columbia Records was a block away.

"They won't let me record 'Strange Fruit,' my biggest number."

"I know," I said. I hear it in the club. You go back and tell them ..." I had just started to record the year before, to make Commodore Records, and I always made instrumentals. I let the musicians sing the vocals, like [Jack] Teagarden or Lips Page.

I said, "You go back and tell them that I'll record it. I'm only a little record label. I just make records for my store," which was true. "I'll record that thing in a second. Go up there and get permission."

I recorded it at one of Columbia's studios. I used a club band led by Frankie Newton. I picked the other tunes. I said, "We'll do a blues." She'd made that great "Billie's Blues" on Vocalion [in 1936], and I wanted to get a blues. We did "I've Got a Right to Sing the Blues" and "Yesterdays," Jerome Kern. "Fine and Mellow" was a blues. I helped her get some lyrics together on that.

I would acquiesce to anything that Billie had her mind on making. She liked to do stuff for friends. Sometimes I liked the material; sometimes I didn't. But I knew that she was trying to help some songwriters. She knew it was good for them, and she'd help them by doing the song.

The writers would come to me. They'd write a Billie Holiday–type song. Some of those writers were darn good. I accepted their material. Some of them were published by Decca Publishing Company; many were published by big publishers. The first ones, E. B. Marx [for example], got a lot of the copyrights.

But that never was the reason I did it or gave it to those publishers. They romanced the artists on their own. They all hung around Fifty-Second Street. You were a good publisher if you were able to get something at the source, like "Lover Man" was a Fifty-Second Street song. The songwriters came to Billie to sing the song at the club she was in.

VARIOUS, *CHICAGO JAZZ ALBUM* (1940, DECCA)
George Avakian

The first jazz album anybody ever recorded—and by that I mean new recordings, not a collection of 78-rpm reissue sides packaged into an album—was 1939.[4] [The album was recorded in 1939; released in 1940.] I was a sophomore at Yale and a record collector, writing for *Tempo* magazine, which was later bought by *DownBeat*. I did the "Collector's Corner" column. I got to be pretty well known as—I hate to use the word—an "expert." None of us were experts at that time. I was one of the early people who really delved into the history of out-of-print recorded jazz.

I got the idea of bringing together the old, white Chicago musicians, the first white group that really picked up on the New Orleans jazz guys who had moved to Chicago. One reason for doing the album was because, at age nineteen, I was aware that those guys were getting very old, and "By

---

4. In 1936, Victor released *The Bix Beiderbecke Memorial Album*, the first record set "devoted to a nonclassical artist." Elijah Wald, *How the Beatles Destroyed Rock 'n' Roll: An Alternative History of American Popular Music* (New York: Oxford University Press, 2009), 121.

God, they drink so much, they're going to die early," the way Bix already had done. I thought, "If the old Chicago style is ever going to be revived, it'd better be done fast." Some of those people were thirty-five, thirty-six years old!

They created a style of their own, which didn't stay put. It was in flux. I wanted these guys to go back to the way they had been playing ten, twelve years earlier, as evidenced on the group of records which had earned the name "Chicago Style." A French author named Hugues Panassié, who wrote the first good book on jazz, called it "le style Chicago." The name stuck, but it is forgotten now. These were people whose names you're probably familiar with: Eddie Condon, Bud Freeman, Pee Wee Russell, Dave Tough—that crowd of young musicians who came up in the twenties.

So right from the beginning, a creative idea resulted in an album rather than a recording simply supervised by a producer. I set up three sessions for three different groups, reviving several of the tunes that they had played, in much the same style they had kind of dropped. I'll give you one good reason. One of these groups' characteristics was the explosive way by which they kept up the tension throughout their performances. Among the devices used was that of everybody joining in on the last two bars of each solo to create a springboard for the next soloist. Jelly Roll Morton used it, for example, and the Chicagoans used it fairly well. The excitement created on the few records that they made was quite terrific.

I said to Eddie Condon one day, "Eddie, how come you don't do that anymore?" He looked at me. "George, you mean night after night after night after night?" I realized that this was fine for record sessions and occasional performances, but those guys were used to playing six nights a week from nine P.M. to four A.M., except on Sundays, when they had to stop at three A.M. because of the New York Blue Law the churches put through.

Decca bought the idea from me. They paid me seventy-five dollars [to produce the album], which didn't even cover my expenses to go to Chicago. Really, though, I would have been glad to do it for nothing. Shortly after that, Columbia Records asked me to come in and research their factory files and produce a series of singles and albums called *The Hot Jazz Classics*. That was the first series of reissues that ever came out, but that project ended when the war came along, and there was a big shellac shortage. The Japanese had taken over Malaysia, source of about 98 percent of the world's supply of shellac. I got drafted right after I graduated in '41. That stopped the clock until I got back to New York five years later.

During the period we're talking about, just before and after World

War II, the term "A&R man" hadn't been used. Generally, the recording director—that was the title used—was the person who made a contact with music publishers. The publishers called most of the shots regarding what was going to be recorded, because they controlled the advertising and promotion. Through their own radio-station contact people, they got a lot of air exposure for new songs. These were, often, songs which were in movies. That was the biggest exposure.

Oddly enough, the Broadway shows didn't produce any real hits at that time. After all, very few people could get to Broadway. There were no planes flying across the country. People didn't fly in for a weekend in New York to catch the shows and that sort of thing. Let's face it, only rich people could afford those high prices. Even though I'd gone to Yale, I was the immigrant son of a father who came to America without knowing a word of English. In those days, Broadway shows cost something like five dollars a seat! I can remember when they broke the ten-dollar barrier. I think that might have been with *Camelot* [1960]. Ten dollars was a sensationally high price. It occasioned a big story in the *New York Times*. I'm giving you background more than anything else.

Joel Dorn (Atlantic)

All the jazz record companies were reflections of the guys who owned them. Take a look.

Verve: Norman Granz ran the JATP [Jazz at the Philharmonic] concerts. He had the artists, had them do combinations, and put those combinations on record.

Blue Note: that was Alfred Lion and Francis Wolff. They were Germans, who captured the purest real jazz. I think Blue Note was the best real jazz label, ever. It was like a Mercedes. Form followed function. They didn't add strings. They got the real shit. [Rudy] Van Gelder was the perfect engineer for them. If you needed a surgeon—a guy with a surgeon's cool look—Rudy was it. He was one of the first guys where you heard people talking about an engineer having a sound. Those Blue Note and Prestige records, they were the standard.

[Orrin] Keepnews at Riverside ran a Blue-Note type operation. They did quality stuff. Cannonball [Adderley] was the core of their label—even though they had Monk, Bill Evans, and little bits and pieces: Johnny Griffin, Lockjaw Davis, and Wes Montgomery at the beginning. But Keepnews and Cannon together, their simultaneous run! As a producer, without Cannon, he made brilliant records, but when he and Cannon got together, that's when they made that great combination: real jazz, yet it was commercial.

Atlantic, when Nesuhi [Ertegun] ran jazz there, didn't have that cold look. He was from Turkey. He was a more poetic guy than the German guys at Blue Note. He had a little exotica, more warmth to him. He got together one of the greatest collections of musicians ever and did absolutely documentary work.

LOU WATTERS' YERBA BUENA JAZZ BAND, *LOU WATTERS' YERBA BUENA JAZZ BAND* (1942, GOOD TIME JAZZ)
John Koenig (Contemporary/Good Time Jazz)

When my father [Lester Koenig] was a boy in New York in the twenties and thirties, he was a jazz record collector and that was a small community of people. One of the people he befriended and who befriended him was John Hammond, who was seven years older than my father. John took him under his wing and brought him along to sessions he was producing. My father kind of got the bug.

George Avakian (Columbia)

I was an Armstrong fan from my last year in high school. Lester, the older brother of a classmate of mine, Julian Koenig, at the Horace Mann School, played me some old, out-of-print records. I thought, "Gee whiz, I had no idea that Louis Armstrong could do this." I realized he was much more than the flashy entertainer I'd heard on the current records of 1937. I very quickly realized that he was the greatest individual influence, performer, and innovator in jazz.

John Koenig (Contemporary/Good Time Jazz)

I don't know that *classmate* is the correct word, but while at Dartmouth, Bud Schulberg befriended my father. Bud Schulberg's father was B. P. Schulberg, the head of production at Paramount [Studios in Hollywood].

My father was the music and movie critic for the Dartmouth paper, which B. P. subscribed to as a dutiful father. He liked my father's reviews, and my father spent some holidays with the Schulberg family here [in Los Angeles]. My father went to Yale Law School, because his father was a judge, but when his father died, he had to quit. He went to work for WNEW in New York—for Martin Block and *Make Believe Ballroom*, a radio program that also staged concerts.

After about a year, he got a telegram from B. P. Schulberg saying, "Come to Hollywood. I'm going to set you up as a writer here at Paramount." He would have been nineteen or twenty in 1937. He was born in December of 1917. He graduated from college quite young, went to law school quite young, and quit law school quite young. So he came to L.A.

On Melrose Avenue, near the front gate to Paramount, there was a store called the Jazz Man Record Shop owned by David Stuart and his wife, Marili Morden. Dave later became a noted art dealer; Marili was a music promoter. I think her favorite artist was T-Bone Walker. She was bound and determined to take him from Central Avenue to the Sunset Strip. That was her mission. Among the things they did, other than sell records, was produce new records. David and some confederates went and rediscovered Bunk Johnson working in a rice field in New Iberia, Louisiana. They bought him some new false teeth and recorded him in 1942.

Dave was the first person to hire my father to make records on his own. There was a San Francisco revival of New Orleans style music: Bob Scoby, Turk Murphy, Lou Watters, and so on. The first records my father recorded as a producer were of Lou Watters at the Dawn Club [in San Francisco]. This would have been 1941.

The war happened, and my father went in the film unit of the Army Air Corps, which is how he ended up associated with [film director William] Wyler. He wrote the original war documentary *The Memphis Belle*, which was enormously successful. By the time he got out and came back to L.A., David and Marili had divorced, and Marili had married Nesuhi Ertegun, who had connected up with Kid Ory and made some wonderful records in '45 on the Jazz Man or the Crescent label. They had two labels. I forget how one distinguished which records were on what label. Eventually, they all ended up on my father's label, Good Time Jazz. When Nesuhi and Marili got divorced, they sold the masters to my father, and that became the foundation of his traditional jazz label. Interestingly, both exes of Marili Morden—David and Nesuhi—eventually came to work at Contemporary/Good Time Jazz and became company vice presidents.

My father had observed John [Hammond] producing, and by being on the set with Wyler, from *The Best Years of Our Lives* [1946] through *Roman Holiday* [1953], he learned a lot about how to get good performances. He brought that kind of sensitivity to producing records.

COLEMAN HAWKINS, LESTER YOUNG, DON BYAS, AND BEN WEBSTER, *TENOR SAX* (1942, SAVOY)
Bob Porter (Savoy Reissues)

Herman Lubinsky was not a music guy. He was a business guy. Lubinsky got into music from a store called United Radio, which sold radios

and electronic parts, things like that. The black customers that he served bought records, and so he put a record section in United Radio. That's how he started to learn who and what to record.

He got into recording in 1942, just before the recording ban [when he created Savoy Records]. Once the ban was over in late '44, he picked up and went wild. The next five years or so were wonderful years for Savoy Jazz. Much of that stuff was recorded by Teddy Reig, who started at Savoy in 1945. Teddy was the main guy—not the only guy. He did most of the key recordings during that time, though Gil Fuller and Bobby Shad also did some. At that time Savoy was acquiring recordings from other labels. After a while, Lee Magid replaced Teddy, and Ozzie Cadena arrived in '54. He was there for about six years and did most of Savoy's LP-era jazz.

So Teddy Reig in the forties, Ozzie Cadena in the fifties, and Lee Magid in between: they were really the guys. Freddie Mendelsohn did some jazz recording, mostly avant-garde jazz in the sixties, but it was poorly recorded, and it wasn't very good.

CHARLIE PARKER, "KO KO" (1945, SAVOY)
Bob Porter (Savoy Reissues)

Teddy Reig found guys. He made the first Charlie Parker records. He made the first Dexter Gordon records. Stan Getz. You can go on and on. You can say, "A lot of those guys didn't make a lot of records for Savoy." That was because of Lubinsky and how cheap he was, but Teddy really knew how to make records, and his track record was terrific. Roost was his label before it got sold to Roulette.

2

ROLLING TAPE
Producing Jazz LPs, 1950–1966

....

EXEMPLARY RECORDING—DUKE ELLINGTON, *ELLINGTON AT NEWPORT*

In 1947, Bing Crosby, who had invested heavily in the newly established Ampex Company, recorded his nationally syndicated radio show—not to standard 16-inch transcription discs (cut at 33⅓ rpm) but to magnetic tape. (Allied troops had "discovered" tape machines when they liberated Berlin.) Then, a year later, Columbia Records introduced the vinyl LP or "long-playing record." Discs that used this new medium played quietly at 33⅓ revolutions per minute, and they began to replace the shellac 78-rpm record, which had been the industry standard for half a century. A 10-inch LP—the format initially reserved for popular music—could now hold thirty-five total minutes of music; both sides of a 10-inch, 78-rpm disc held a grand total of five and a half minutes. Call it a revolution in recording technology. That's exactly what it was—but one with a caveat. Producers could now capture for reproduction and sale on records music that had routinely happened for many years only on various stages. Recording technology had, at long last, caught up with the actual practice of making jazz music. It therefore utterly transformed how jazz was formatted to records, though it scarcely affected how jazz musicians made music outside recording studios.

No one was better positioned to take advantage of the revolution in recording technology than George Avakian, head of Columbia's Popular Album Department. In 1948, he produced *The Voice of Frank Sinatra*, the first 10-inch LP. In 1950—after transferring Benny Goodman's 1938 Carnegie Hall Concert to tape (from a stack of transcription discs)—Avakian produced the first 12-inch LP, a double album, of that historic concert.[1] For

---

1. Pressing Goodman's 1938 concert onto two LPs, in the 12-inch format reserved for classical music and Broadway shows, allowed Columbia to sell the album on its Masterworks label at a higher price than that charged for pop LPs. It still sold 1 million copies. The album was, therefore, an exception to a rule that held force well into

Louis Armstrong Plays W. C. Handy (1954), Avakian—working with one-track or monophonic tape—had Armstrong sing and, at the same time, accompany himself on trumpet. When the Ellington Orchestra played Newport in 1956, Avakian employed the still-new medium of tape, not only to record on location but to capture soloists—such as Paul Gonsalves on "Diminuendo and Crescendo in Blue"—in full flight. The resulting album exemplified new possibilities for the jazz album. A year later, with Miles Davis's *Miles Ahead* (1957), Avakian exploited the artistic possibilities of cut-and-paste editing to create (or to enable) an ideal performance. And, of course, he used tape splicing to fix the occasional mistake—the flubbed note. With the above and other LPs—by Erroll Garner, Dave Brubeck, and Buck Clayton—Avakian, in effect, created the jazz album as a format commensurate with jazz as an art form.

Which means, with Avakian as the great exemplar, the jazz record producer came into his own as something much more than the A & R man of the 78-rpm era. The technology that introduced new mediums (tape and the LP) enabled the development of a new format (the record album) and the arrival of a new kind of artist (the record producer). Foiling any theory of technological determinism, the new recording mediums and formats didn't bring about significant new performance practices for jazz musicians. Rather, for at least thirty years—since the 1917 recordings of the Original Dixieland Jazz Band—there had been a distinct lack of fit between jazz as performed onstage and jazz as retooled for the recording of 78-rpm records. Certainly, musicians had accommodated the old recording medium. Indeed, by formatting their music to meet its severe restrictions, they had developed an art form: the jazz record. For example, Ellington wrote compositions specifically for 78s, and improvisers—Coleman Hawkins and Lester Young, for example—learned to work brilliantly within the 78's time limitations. But such adaptations resembled a forced exercise: something like requiring epic poets to write only in haikus printed singly on index cards. Great poetry could result, but at a substantial cost.

Tape and the long-playing album arrived, therefore, as a wish fulfillment. Jazz could be recorded as it was actually made on stages and in jam sessions. But realizing and developing the potential of new mediums and new formats is no small thing, and that is why Gabler, Avakian, Bob Weinstock (at Prestige Records), and the musicians they produced were so innovative. To coin a tautology, they made jazz more what it already was.

the mid-fifties, at which time the major labels finally discontinued the 10-inch pop LP, standardized albums as 12-inch discs, and stopped manufacturing 78-rpm records.

If the album is understood as a form for organizing music on LP (an electronic medium)—analogous to the sonata form organizing music on a score (a literary medium) for performance in symphony halls—then its development divides fairly neatly into the two eras surveyed in this chapter and the next. The period of one- and two-track recording can be regarded as the jazz album's classical era (1950–66); the period of multitrack recording as its baroque era (1967–90). Although I wouldn't live or die by these distinctions, they do align the story of the jazz album with a conventional opposition used to conceptualize art history, and they make sense of the stylistic gulf that separates, for instance, Miles Davis's 'Round about Midnight (1957) and his album Get Up with It (1974).

Tom Dowd (Atlantic Engineer)

Back in '47, '48, '49, '50, with Parker, Lester Young, Dizzy, Lenny Tristano, Shearing, you were limited to like two minutes and thirty-five seconds, two minutes and forty seconds. That's all you could get on a damn 10-inch, 78-rpm record. Every once in a while you'd get a jazz nut who made a 12-inch [78-rpm] record, and it ran to three minutes and forty seconds or something like that. But you didn't find people running to the store buying it. So we were handicapped and limited by time. As we got into the longer playing mediums—even the initial 10-inch LPs—all of a sudden you could have two or three songs on one side that ran four minutes each, which is like a 60 percent gain on what you had on the 78-rpm version. Oh, hello there! We can make the solos longer. It's a different world, different culture.

BENNY GOODMAN, *THE FAMOUS 1938 CARNEGIE HALL JAZZ CONCERT* (1950, COLUMBIA)
George Avakian

Even though I'd produced that one album for Decca Records [*Chicago Jazz Album*, 1940], when I returned to Columbia after the war, I didn't have much opportunity to create projects. I was low man on the A & R totem pole. Joe Higgins was the head of the department, Morty Palitz was his right-hand man and the house arranger/conductor, and then Manny Saks came in over Joe. This sounds ridiculous, but all the pop work was done by us, and I didn't do that much of it because Joe and Morty, later replaced by Mitchell Ayres, handled most of the sessions.

I'd go along: observe and sharpen whatever it took to produce a record. Very often, they'd leave before the end of a session. I ended up finishing sessions for people—such as Frank Sinatra—which was fun.

Finally I started doing sessions of my own. I became head of the international department simply because I was the only person in the New York office who spoke a foreign language. That's a silly reason, but nobody else wanted to do it, and there was nobody else to do it. Which was great! The business became international very quickly after that. There I was trying to do something with the foreign-language recordings, polka bands, and those sorts of things. It taught me an awful lot.

I did get to do a few sessions. Sidney Bechet, who I admired, was the first jazz artist that I recorded on 78 rpm at Columbia. But the real breakthrough came when the LP was invented. By then, I was in charge of the Popular Album Department, which meant very little in the 78-rpm days. But with the LP, that frankly became the department that brought in the most money. LPs simply took over the business. That had to be in 1949.

Incidentally, when I later joined RCA in 1960, one of the questions I asked was, "How did you guys come up with 45?" RCA's propaganda said it was the best speed for sound, and it was the best medium (that is, a 7-inch disc) for the most important money-earning aspect of classical music—namely, operatic arias, overtures, and the like, compositions that ran about five minutes or so. One of the guys laughed, "Oh, we decided we weren't going to follow Columbia. We had to be creators. So we simply subtracted 33 from 78 and came up with 45." I don't know if that's true, and I could never get anybody else to say it was true. But that one guy said, "George, it really is true, but nobody else would admit it." I can see why.

So here we were with 33⅓-rpm albums. The big breakthrough that came in building up sales was the 12-inch popular LP. It was more than just an extension of the old 78-rpm album with eight sides: four 10-inch discs translated into eight tracks on a 10-inch LP. What made the 12-inch LP really go was, first of all, you had better variety of material. Second, the price was right.

I'm going to tell you something else that wasn't written about, but it was a key to the success of the 12-inch pop LP. The first 12-inch pop LPs were priced at $4.95. (In those days, the magic numbers ended in five instead of eight—$4.95 instead of $4.98.) That was a little high. Jim Conkling was the president of Columbia Records. He never got the credit he deserved because the man who replaced him, Goddard Lieberson, got so much publicity. Jim was a brilliant guy who came up with the concept that put across the 12-inch popular LP on a big scale for everybody. He did it in a strange way which, at first, people thought Columbia was crazy to do. Jim figured we could drop the price by one dollar. How could we afford to do that? Everybody knew manufacturing costs, the union scale for musicians, advances that had to be paid, and royalties that had to be set up.

Jim came up with the idea that, if we could get publishers to lower the standard rate of two cents per composition to one and a half cents, they would earn much more money because the record company would sell that many more records. Saving six cents per disc would put Columbia in a position to make a profit. If we had big hits, we'd really make a profit. Without a change in the price structure, we'd be spinning our wheels, breaking even, trying to establish something.

Jim got practically every publisher to agree except one, who told him and me, when we had our meeting, "Fellows, I'm going to stick to two cents, and you know something? I'll still make much more money than you think, because, even though you don't want to use my stuff, you've got to." This was the publisher who had the bulk of Gershwin, Cole Porter, Richard Rogers, Jerome Kern, all the big names: an organization called Music Publishers Holding Corporation. It was owned by Warner Brothers, oddly enough a company that did musicals in movies on a pioneer basis, but not with any record-company ties. That's why, in 1958, Jim Conkling would leave Columbia to organize Warner Brothers Records, and I would go with him. It was a fantastic opportunity to start something new.

Columbia's competition didn't realize that we had these deals with the publishers. They thought we were crazy and figured we were losing money. We weren't. Finally, the word got out, and everybody else went the same way. But we had such a huge head start that it was unbelievable. Also, Jim conceived the idea of starting our own record club: the first big record club. There was only the Book of the Month Club and a couple of small mail-order operations before that. There again, the volume jumped like crazy.

I'll give you a statistic that's really scary, and it's true. In the middle of 1957, I remember a report that New York University and *Billboard* magazine were issuing every quarter. The [record] companies paid for this service. It was a confidential report which broke down all record sales in the United States, by company and by category. Then, it broke down each category within each company. This report crossed my desk and practically knocked me out of my chair. Columbia's pop LP department—again, partly thanks to the record club—was bringing in twenty-six cents of every dollar spent in the United States for records of all types and, within the company, eighty-two cents out of every dollar. You can imagine what that did to my insides. I was working like hell. I'd finally managed to get two assistants, who I stole from other departments because the budget didn't call for more people in my department. I realized, "I can't go on this way, killing myself and getting a raise and a bonus every year. It isn't worth it." That was when I left to go with Jim to form Warner Brothers Records.

You didn't get royalties from those early albums?

What money I had didn't come out of records. I never got royalties on that old stuff. We didn't get credit as producers. The only way people knew that I had done something was if I wrote an annotation for a record.

At the time, what did you think the 12-inch LP had accomplished in terms of creative possibilities?

Already, the concept that I used in making the 10-inch LPs—pop LPs—was, think of it as a radio program in which the entire package has a purpose. It's programmed. You start with something which catches the attention of the listener on the outside first track. In fact, I did this deliberately on both sides. I'd find a real attention-grabber. Then, I'd pace the program and end with something that made listeners want to turn the record over. I applied that to everything—including reissues from the old 78-rpm albums (which is how the 10-inch LPs really began). Gradually, I created more and more new product specifically for that type of recording.

But the 12-inch LP opened up something else again. In 1950, I transferred the Benny Goodman *Carnegie Hall Concert* [of 1938] from big, 16-inch acetates to a Fairchild tape recorder which went at 15 inches per second [ips]. Those were used for certain situations, but the standard had become Ampexes with 30 inches per second.[2]

ERROLL GARNER, *PIANO MOODS* (1950, COLUMBIA)
George Avakian

I realized, "Now we've got some real space. With jazz musicians, you can give them a chance to stretch out. You don't have to have a three-minute performance on every recording." The first artist that I did this with was

2. In my interview with Avakian (one of several), he mistakenly swapped the speeds of the Fairchild and the Ampex. I have corrected this error. The keen eye of one of my UNC Press–appointed readers caught the mistake. He wrote: "It was the Ampex that ran at 30 ips in 1950 and forced the Columbia engineers to use the Fairchild, which operated at 15 ips. I know this from the engineer, Bill Savory, who worked on the project (and who, incidentally, Avakian steered me to as the technical authority)." He further notes that the error illustrates the "limitations of oral testimony." I am indebted to his observations.

Erroll Garner. He was one who could do it. I deliberately told him, "Let's do some recordings where you play approximately six minutes for each track. We'll have six songs on the 12-inch LP instead of the usual twelve."

That worked marvelously, and then I went on, using Duke Ellington for long works [*Masterpieces by Ellington* (1951) and *Ellington Uptown* (1952)] and the Buck Clayton Jam Sessions, during which, for the first time, there were studio jam sessions that ran as long as, I believe, twenty-seven minutes for one continuous performance.

That was one way of creating an LP in a way that didn't exist previously. This went on into other things like recording dance bands on location, which had never been done deliberately. It was always accidental that somebody happened to record, say, the Benny Goodman Orchestra of 1937 off the air.

ELLA FITZGERALD, *ELLA SINGS GERSHWIN* (1950, DECCA); REISSUED ON *PURE ELLA* (1994, GRP/DECCA)
Michael Cuscuna (Mosaic)

Milt Gabler was very thoughtful, very methodical, and very good at planning and rehearsal. And talk about the quality of invisibility. He stayed with a major label [Decca], did children's records, polka records, and Bill Haley. In those days, when you were on a major label and the head of A & R, you did all sorts of records. I don't think he really got out there as an identity as much as he should have.[3]

Milt Gabler

As far as the record company was concerned, the man responsible for the sessions was the producer. They didn't use that term. It was just in the A & R department, artists and repertoire. I used to say, "I don't play the horses. I bet my job every day, by picking the songs and the people who are going to perform them."

3. Gabler joined Decca Records, as staff producer, in 1941. The following year, Ella Fitzgerald joined the label and Gabler recorded Lionel Hampton's proto–rock 'n' roll version of "Flying Home" (with Illinois Jacquet on tenor saxophone).

That [album] was my idea. Ellis [Larkins] was one of my favorite piano accompanists. The singers loved to have him play behind them. To keep it pure, I used just Ellis and Ella—not even a drummer.

My job was to get a proper balance between the two. Sometimes we got it [a master] in two takes, sometimes three, sometimes one. That's why the historians or those who go into the archives sometimes find more than one take of a tune. I had to like the performance, figure they couldn't do it better or determine that was the best they had that day. They never argued with me if I asked for another take, or if I made a suggestion. I very seldom had to tell Ella to go for another take. If you play different takes that she made in the studio on a particular session, the performances and the interpretations are almost identical on all of them. It was hard to choose. I chose the performances I liked the best at that instant in the studio and had them processed. I had stampers made and sample pressings. Then I had to approve which take was the master take—the first choice. When I left the studio, what was on those lacquers was what came out on records.

How did things change after tape arrived?

We didn't have to send two [lacquer] masters to the factory. If a third performance was just as good as the other two, I might send three masters. But most of the time, you'd send two masters in case one was damaged in the process of making [metal] masters [i.e., master matrices, "negatives" of the lacquer masters]. So in the studio you'd make two cuts direct-to-disc. Today, that's been a boon for reissues, because you've got two recorded performances of the artists.

When tape came in, you had to process only one performance. If they saved the tape, fine. And you could begin to edit, but I'd already edited on 16-inch discs. I'd play records on two machines and record to a third. I did that with "Rock around the Clock" [1954], Bill Haley. It's hard to think of the first time. But the Bill Haley records used overdubs. It was monaural, so I had to use three machines.

Additionally, when tape replaced acetates, producers became owners, lots of times, along with the artists. They formed little companies of their own, and there was a scramble for money. They controlled everything and dropped the good, talented songwriters for their own junk. Some of them were great. I won't mention the Beatles, but they were a perfect example. When you were an act as strong as the Beatles, or some others that came in at that time, you wanted to control all of your product. Presley was that way, too, with Hill and Range Publishing. He had to own 50 percent of the copyright on anything he recorded. That restricted some professional songwriters from going to him, if they didn't want to give away half of their copyright. That started to change the quality of songs. It became a gigantic business. The quality, not of musicianship, but of the material declined.

LOUIS ARMSTRONG AND ELLA FITZGERALD, "DREAM A LITTLE DREAM" (1950), *BILLY CRYSTAL PRESENTS THE MILT GABLER STORY* (ORIGINAL RECORDING, 1950, DECCA; COMPILATION, 2005, VERVE)
Milt Gabler

I knew Louis's work so well from his recorded repertoire and also from going to hear him, like at Basin Street. When I first recorded Louis, he had Luis Russell's Band.

Later, I'd give him copies of songs, and he did it his way with a small band. He was one of the greatest singers, the way he used to interpret lyrics. I don't just mean his riffing. I mean the way he phrased a song. You listen to some of those great old songs. They became standards because he made them.

I recorded Louis and Ella together [in this case with Sy Oliver's Orchestra] because I loved what they did. They went for it and improvised. All the great singers I did! At the time I had Ella Fitzgerald, I had Carmen McRae waiting in the wings. I knew Norman Granz was going to take Ella away from Decca.[4]

I wanted the record to sound like I was hearing the artist in the room. If it didn't have the proper balance, I'd go in and change it. Don't forget, we didn't have multimikes. The most we had was three or four mikes, and there was only one main mike really, and a vocal mike. One you'd crack for the rhythm section. But they all had to be picked up on the main mike. To get a proper balance, you had to move the horns back or closer. We used platforms. I won't get into the Guy Lombardo balance. His band was so successful they never wanted to change their sound. We had special platforms designed for different horn sections so they would be exactly the same distance from the one microphone every time they recorded. The engineers would come out with a tape and measure the height, the distance from the wall.

4. Impresario Norman Granz formed Verve Records in 1955. In 1956, he elaborated on Gabler's idea and recorded Ella Fitzgerald's *The Cole Porter Songbook*, her first album in a series of "songbooks."

STAN KENTON, *STAN KENTON CONDUCTS ROBERT GRAETTINGER'S CITY OF GLASS* (1951, CAPITOL)
John Palladino (Capitol Engineer)

At the time, there was no band that played as loud as Stan Kenton's. It was pretty powerful. He didn't spring things on you like giving you a solo and then the poor guy wouldn't blend in. When everybody starts playing loud, it's sometimes very difficult to hope for a solid band sound and have everybody pretty smooth—to have it come out right. But since the band was a performing band, they lived that music. They knew how to balance for the bandstand. So in the studio a lot of their balance had to be up to them. Stan could do that. If you got into trouble, you could try to balance it up a bit.

When Stan first came into our studio, I think he was a little amazed. He had heard some of our records. All of the studios tried to find old churches or big rooms in order to use the natural acoustics, which can be done, but it's a tough job. We recorded Stan in the same room that we did country and western. It was a small studio. But when we got through with a track, with all the tricks we did, it sounded like it was recorded in a big room. We extended the sound with the use of echo chambers.

We did, however, with some of the Kenton things, go to a larger space, like a motion-picture soundstage one time. And we did remotes. He was in the ballroom down on Long Beach or something. Sometimes, we'd go to universities where he was playing on a stage.[5]

---

5. Speaking of extending sound with echo chambers, Palladino told me: "They could be as dumb as a stairwell in a big building. Sometimes, especially when you had to go on remotes, you could put up an echo chamber, or you would try to find a little room—maybe, a tiled restroom—with very live walls. You had to put a mike in there, and you had to put a speaker in there. Then, you fed a portion of what you were picking up on your microphones into that chamber [through the speaker], and you balanced the amount of reverberation against the quality of sound that you were attempting. The echo chambers were on the roof at Radio Recorders and on the roof at [Capitol Records Studio on] Melrose. At the [Capitol Records] Tower, they were underground. You'll notice there's a great deal of difference between recordings by various companies because of the sounds of their chambers." Michael Jarrett, *Producing Country: The Inside Story of the Great Recordings* (Middletown, Conn.: Wesleyan University Press, 2014), 26.

MILES DAVIS, "DIG," RELEASED ON *THE NEW SOUNDS* (PRESTIGE 10-INCH LP, 1951); RELEASED ON *DIG* (PRESTIGE 12-INCH LP, 1956)

Ed Michel (Impulse)

For me, the first Miles Davis LP, where he played eight- and nine-minute tunes, was a mind boggler. Up to that point I'd thought of music in three-minute segments—as a consumer and as a listener. Those were the first things that made use of the medium in a different kind of way. After that, all bets were off. A piece could be as long as it had to be.

Bob Weinstock

I sensed that we were going to have LPs. I'd heard rumblings. And I did three sessions that were monumental. The first one was Miles Davis with Sonny Rollins and Jackie McLean. Art Blakey was on drums, and I had Walter Bishop Jr. [piano] and Tommy Potter [bass]. I said, "Miles, we're going to stretch out."

He said, "You mean we're just going to play?"

"As long as you want almost—within reason."

He said, "Okay, who should I use?"

"You seem to love Sonny Rollins." If you look at the early ones, Sonny's on a lot of them.

He asked, "What about this young guy, Jackie McLean? He's pretty good, too, if we're going to stretch out."

"Yeah, I've heard him," I said. "He's good."

That session [1951] we did "Dig" and "Blueing." Jackie doesn't play on some of the tunes. He wasn't really that great at the time. He was good.

So Miles and Sonny stretched out. That's how it went. We'd always talk about the personnel, what we were going to do. A lot of times they'd have tunes. Other times, I'd have tunes. Our main emphasis was just to play and stretch out. We accomplished that there.

Next, I did either Zoot Sims with a quartet or Gerry Mulligan's Tentet [*Swingin' with Zoot Sims* and *Mulligan Plays Mulligan*, both recorded in 1951]. On the Gerry thing I had him stretch out. He played a long solo, and then he and [tenor saxophonist] Allen Eager would play. If I wanted them to play more, they'd look at me, and I'd nod my head, "yeah" or "no." Then they'd switch. I'd sort of "cut my throat," and he'd know to go out at the end of the chorus.

One of the best Zoot albums ever made is called *Swingin' with Zoot Sims* [1951], where [on "Zoot Swings the Blues"] he just kept going on and on and on.

PEGGY LEE, "LOVER" (1952), *BLACK COFFEE AND OTHER DELIGHTS: THE DECCA ANTHOLOGY* (COMPILATION, 1994, MCA)
Milt Gabler

My favorite record that I did with her is "Lover." I had to do it twice. She wasn't out of tune. It was because, I've forgotten the drummer's name, but he had one of those large cymbals with little metal things coming through, a buzz cymbal. Peggy did that song in a very fast tempo. That was her interpretation [which she'd worked out with the Gordon Jenkins Orchestra]. It had never been done that way. It was originally a waltz. She wanted to give it that treatment as if she were angry. It was a salty interpretation.

We did it the first time. I couldn't get the ringing of that cymbal out. Her voice wasn't free enough. It was a big orchestra with crazy, fast strings. When we were listening to the playback of the choice of that day's performance, I vetoed it. "Peggy," I said, "we're not going to put this out. The drummer's killing the record."

She started crying, "That's the third arrangement I've written on this song, and you're turning it down."

"No, I'm not turning it down," I said. "We'll record it again next week. You'll still be in New York."

I told Gordon to tell the drummer to leave that cymbal out of his case. But she'd cried. That was the third arrangement. I think Billy May had written one and another great arranger. She said, "I'm crazy about this Gordon Jenkins arrangement."

"We'll do it," I said. We did it over the next week, and got it that time.

Bob Weinstock (Prestige)
Teddy Reig made great records, but the man was not a nice person. He pulled some shit on me right away. I was very successful right off the bat, and [DJ] Symphony Sid—Teddy's close friend—used to play my records by Stan Getz, Kai Winding, J. J. Johnson, [Lennie] Tristano and [Lee] Konitz, and Miles [Davis]. He respected me 'cause I made good jazz. I didn't

give Sid a nickel [i.e., pay him to play the records on radio]. That burned Teddy Reig's ass.[6]

So one day I'm going out of the Royal Roost, and a big black Cadillac drives up. Teddy Reig opens the door and says, "Get in, kid." I wasn't afraid of anybody. I'd boxed, played football as middle linebacker, and at the time I was a military policeman in the National Guard. Teddy gets me in the car and says, "You're fucking up the jazz business."

"What do you mean?"

"You're paying these guys scale. You're not doing extra sides free, like I am" [i.e., Weinstock was paying additional money when more than four tracks were recorded during a three-hour session].

I said, "Why should I, man? Scale's cheap enough. I do four sides for three hundred dollars. What more do you want? The guys are cooperating with me. They do it for scale. They like me. Why should I fuck them?"

"Yeah, but you're ruining the business."

"What business? Your business? Fuck you. Open the door and let me out."

"Don't talk to me like that," he said. "You see the two guys sitting up front?"

I said, "Fuck you, and fuck them. Just open the door, man. If you want to fuck with me, you may beat me now, but you three will be dead tomorrow." I knew the mafia game. My godfather was in Al Capone's gang in Chicago, and my father grew up with Legs Diamond and Dutch Schultz. All those Jewish gangsters were his schoolmates.

Teddy opens the door. "Listen," I said, "I'm just doing it the right way. From what I know, it's cheap enough. So I don't know why you've got to fuck around. These are good people."

After all that, we became friends when Teddy stopped recording and went to work for Basie.

6. I include this incident here because its complications reveal much about the jazz record business. Symphony Sid (Torin) was a jazz DJ who broadcast live from the Royal Roost, a nightclub that "brought jazz to Broadway." He was also the club's MC and part owner—with Teddy Reig, Ralph Watkins, and Monte Kay—of Roost Records (founded in 1949, the same year Weinstock founded Prestige). Watkins owned part of the Royal Roost. Reig produced all of the label's records. Weinstock told me that, when the Roost went bankrupt, Reig "moved across the street to Roulette [Records] and [the infamously mobbed-up] Mr. Morris Levy," who had acquired the Roost catalog. See Teddy Reig with Edward Berger, *Reminiscing in Tempo: The Life and Times of a Jazz Hustler* (Metuchen, N.J.: Scarecrow Press and the Institute of Jazz Studies, Rutgers University), 39–40, 45.

Bob Porter (Savoy Reissues)

Teddy was a character by all means. He was loud, opinionated, boister-
ous, and he weighed over four hundred pounds at his peak. His big thing,
which he will be remembered for more than anything else, is the great
series of Count Basie records on Roulette. He signed Basie to Roulette
[in 1957] and produced, what is for my money, the greatest era of Basie
recording—at least by the New Testament band. The Old Testament band,
that's John Hammond's territory.

LOUIS ARMSTRONG, *LOUIS ARMSTRONG PLAYS W. C. HANDY* (ORIGINAL RECORDING, 1954; REISSUE, 1997, COLUMBIA/LEGACY)
George Avakian

Armstrong was probably the nicest person of all
the people that I ever recorded. He was a sweet-
heart—a terrific person in every respect. I don't
mean just a nice guy. He was really a human being
who had enormous consideration for everybody
in the world. I can't say enough about the man.

We were always friends. He'd invite me to his
house, and we'd sit around and chat. I brought up
the idea of doing the album of W. C. Handy songs because there had never
been one, which is strange. See, albums weren't all that important at that
time. They began to get important after the LP took off, around 1951 or
1952. Louis loved the idea, and I talked to his manager, Joe Glaser, about
it. When there was a break in his contract with Decca, we started.

Milt Gabler was a terrific record producer, and he adored Armstrong.
He did a great mixture of productions, and one of the things that he
did very successfully was to have Louis cover other people's hits rather
quickly, like "Because of You," Tony Bennett. Louis's version of "Cold Cold
Heart" [1951], the Hank Williams song, was unexpected, but it was done
very well. Louis was probably the most successful cover artist of all time,
though we never thought of him that way.

My idea was to do packages, what they now call concept albums. The
first one was *Louis Armstrong Plays W.C. Handy*. Louis was in love with the
idea. The second one was built on Fats Waller songs. After that, I started
to concentrate on Armstrong as an international figure. That was all tied
in with Ed Murrow's *See It Now* programs.

How did Armstrong prepare for the Handy album?

He said, "I haven't played too many of those tunes. You've picked a couple that I've heard only vaguely. We'll have to work them up and do them on the road. Then, I'll let you know when we're ready. We'll book the studio when I'm in New York or Chicago."

That's the way it came about. I think it took maybe five or six months of on-and-off rehearsing on the road before Pops called and said, "I'm ready. We've got three or four days off in Chicago. Can you do it?" We did. The preparation involved learning the tunes that he'd never played before, like "Chantez-les Bas," which is a very obscure tune, though Artie Shaw had recorded it.

Louis trusted me completely. He asked me how I wanted the routines to go on some of those songs. "You decide," I told him.

He said, "No, no, no. I don't want us to fall into the pattern that we do with stage performances where everybody has a good idea of what he's going to do on the next chorus, and all that." So on a lot of the routines he left it up to me. I felt that was a pretty big responsibility. But you couldn't go wrong with Pops anyway.

Whenever an idea was a little bit unusual, I'd take a chance and try it anyway. Of course, it was fun doing things [with tape] like correcting situations where somebody didn't back up Louis's vocal with as much closeness to the mike as he should have. I had Louis play behind his own vocal. I even had him scat behind his trumpet.

When the term contract expired, the one we'd signed before the *Armstrong Plays W. C. Handy* album, I had a lot of plans that Louis and I had discussed. For example, I'd suggested that he do the King Oliver repertoire, and that he perform with Duke Ellington, who was under contract to us also. Those were naturals. But Joe Glaser said, "No more term contracts for Louis. He's going to record on individual-date contracts for whoever pays the most money."

I was kind of shocked, but I shouldn't have been. Joe was a very tough guy on the dollar aspect of the business. As a result, I talked it over with Jim Conkling, the president of Columbia. He said, "Don't go along with it. Joe should've had an appreciation for what you did for Louis." And that was quite something because Louis's income, like Duke's after "Diminuendo and Crescendo in Blue" was recorded at Newport, had jumped way up. Joe used to introduce me to people in his office and say, "Here's the man who did this and that for Duke and Louis when I was having trouble selling them, and look what happened!"

Louis was pretty unhappy about it [Glaser's decision], but he soldiered through. And I've often wondered, "Did I make the right decision?" That could have been a classic set of recordings, though to some extent Louis did do some of those compositions for Decca in retrospectives of his career [such as *Satchmo: A Musical Autobiography*].

Steve Berkowitz (Columbia/Legacy Reissues)

At Legacy I have a dozen or so producers who are experts, both musically and sonically, in specific genres. We do anything from finding the exact right tapes to digging up what I call the "sonic archeology" of how a record was made. In some cases, if we don't have masters, we figure out how to make new ones.

For instance, when I came here from Columbia, people told me, "We have to redo *Louis Armstrong Plays W. C. Handy*."

"Why is that?"

"Because when they first put it out on CD, they couldn't find the master tapes. So tracks one through eight are actually all alternate takes. They're not the actual takes that were on the historic record."

"Well, where are the tapes?"

"Nobody knows. They're gone—period."

"What do you mean they're gone?"

"They're just gone."

We had to go through an incredible effort to find original pressings, to retransfer and to remix things, even to have masters again.

Ed Michel (Impulse)

Avakian invented LP programming, as far as I am concerned. If there was a recording hall of fame for producers, George would have to go into it for the things he put together, the four LPs of Louis Armstrong and *The Bessie Smith Story*—really picking the cream and putting it out on LPs. They informed my conceptual sense of what a historical overview should be. They gave me one sense of the form that was possible. The other thing was realizing that long works—like *A Love Supreme* or single pieces the length of an LP—were possible and made a lot of sense. I'd grown up listening to a lot of classical music. I could deal with a piece of music that was an hour long, but that didn't have much relevance to the kind of music I was working with.

MILES DAVIS, *BAGS' GROOVE* AND *MILES DAVIS AND THE MODERN JAZZ GIANTS* (RECORDED DECEMBER 24, 1954; RELEASED 1957 AND 1959, ON 12-INCH LPS, PRESTIGE)
Bob Weinstock

It was Christmas when we recorded "Bags' Groove" and *Miles Davis and the Modern Jazz Giants*. Everybody was down. Miles said, "Man, I need money. It's Christmas. My kid …" Monk called me on the phone: "I need money. My kid …" Then I got a call from Bags [Milt Jackson], who always had money, and he said, "I need some bread."

"We'll work something out," I said. So I called Miles: "Listen, why don't we have an all-star session? I want to use you, Monk, and Bags." Bags and Monk played good together.

He said, "I don't know."

"Don't worry," I said. "It's going to be good, and if it's no good, we won't issue it. Everybody just plays — simple stuff."

When Monk laid out during Miles's solos, people claimed that Miles had said, he was going to beat Monk up if he played. No, he didn't. He wanted that effect, without the piano. Monk had no hard feelings. They loved each other. It's like baseball all-stars. They love each other because of their abilities.

BUCK CLAYTON, *THE HUCKLE-BUCK AND ROBBINS' NEST: A BUCK CLAYTON JAM SESSION* (1954, COLUMBIA)
George Avakian

I'll tell you a secret about hiding splices. On the very first Buck Clayton Jam Session, somebody — I think it was Urbie Green, a very good trombone player — failed to get two notes during a solo. One of these things where he and the instrument just choked-up together. There was no way I could splice that in. You just got this soft kind of sound for two notes, and then he continued blowing a great solo.

I couldn't possibly ask Urbie to come in and overdub it. I felt that was too embarrassing, and I mentioned it to Buck. He said, "I'll come in, and I'll blow the two right notes on the trumpet down in low register." And he did. I don't know what two notes they are, and Buck couldn't find them either. We talked about it the last time I saw him before he died. He asked, "George, did you ever find those two notes?"

BUCK CLAYTON, *THE COMPLETE CBS BUCK CLAYTON JAM SESSIONS* (ORIGINALLY ISSUED 1954–1956; COMPILATION, 1993, MOSAIC)
Michael Cuscuna (Mosaic Reissues)

Lots of times with Mosaic [Records]—when I'm dealing with that material—I try to undo splices. I put together a Buck Clayton CBS thing where George [Avakian] did a lot of splicing. I tried to find the original takes that were the source of his [spliced-together] take and put out both takes. At this point in time, when you've got bands of that magnitude, if there's a moderately boring or routine trombone solo in between solos by Ben Webster and Buck Clayton, you can kind of put up with it, because all of that material is so precious to us now. Because it's never going to happen again, our criteria have changed, from when they did the initial albums to when we do authoritative reissues.

On the Buck Clayton project I found tapes in three conditions. I found some where there were clean, untouched copies. And because Columbia would always do two reels—an A-reel and a B-reel—I found tapes where I had to reconstruct. Then, I found ones where all there was was a spliced master. Reconstruction requires more patience than anyone should ever have to endure. When you're compulsive and you want to get it right, you go through it. But it's absolutely maddening. Not only is it time-consuming detail work, but you're actually undoing something that someone did, and which you feel at this point they didn't have to do. There are lots of projects where you run into that kind of thing.

Perhaps the producers at that time felt that they were the audio equivalent of, say, auteurist filmmakers such as Alfred Hitchcock, Preston Sturges, and John Ford?

I wouldn't use that analogy. You can use it to describe a whole project. The Buck Clayton Jam Sessions were George Avakian's idea. In that since he was the director. But in the sense of splicing to make "the best possible product," you're actually being a film editor. I think they approached it in the same sense that a film editor will call for three shots of a scene from different camera angles and then put the whole thing together in a way that's best. Film editors have a lot more autonomy than a lot of directors will lead you to believe. I think that's what they were trying to do: make the best possible frozen moments that they could.

ERROLL GARNER, *CONCERT BY THE SEA* (1955, COLUMBIA/LEGACY)
George Avakian

One of the ways that I used to hide splices was this. At Columbia Records we had a big stairwell, seven stories high, at 799 Seventh Avenue. There would be a speaker with a microphone in front of it up at the top floor. We'd play something into that speaker and then rerecord it with the echo of that whole seven-story stairway. That is a pretty extreme echo, but you could use it for certain tricks.

If there was a splice that sounded like a splice, and it was suitable to have (usually it was on the beat of a bar), it was useful to insert a soft cymbal. Bob Prince [an engineer] would go in there with a cymbal and a padded stick; the cymbal would be suspended by fairly thick cord. He'd listen for the point that was being played to him, and then he'd hit the cymbal lightly. That would hide the splice.

I remember the one place it really was necessary was Erroll Garner's *Concert by the Sea,* which was done on a 7½-ips Wollensack, a small German machine that weighed a ton. It was done by an army guy, with special permission from Erroll's manager, who then listened to it and said, "Gee, this is great!"

He sent it to me, and I said, "This was the best Erroll Garner yet, but the sound is awful. I'll see what I can do with it." I cleaned it up. But there was one place where Erroll hit a strong chord—"POW"—on the downbeat, and the machine went dead for an instant. So you hear this silent gap.

I covered it by this technique of echo plus the echoed cymbal stroke, and to this day, I don't know where it is. It worked perfectly. I can't find it.

Did producers at independent labels share your aesthetic at Columbia?

It wasn't an aesthetic. It was controlled by business. Most of those companies didn't do any editing, as far as I ever heard about. That was because they were operating on a shoestring. You can hear this on many releases. There were egregious errors they allowed on the tapes. It's expensive to tie up a studio for editing, especially if you get caught in a bad situation, where you can't quite do what you want to do, but you can work it out if you can take the time.

Some [labels] weren't all that interested in the quality of the product. They were in it to make some money. You can't knock them too hard for that, but I must say that—I don't want to name names—but I might as well say Herman Lubinsky at Savoy Records. It was notorious for exploiting musicians. Very often, musicians didn't get paid. Certainly, they didn't get paid composer royalties. That was a sad situation. Everybody in the business hated Lubinsky. The guys needed exposure; they would record with him for years until they could get away. Let's forget people like that.

DAVE BRUBECK QUARTET, *BRUBECK TIME* (1955, COLUMBIA)
George Avakian

At the beginning, when we were given a chance to use Ampexes on an experimental basis, we were still cutting on discs. We were told, "You cannot cut the tape because you don't know what will happen. There'll be clicks, or it will fall apart or something." I was credited with being the first person who cut. There was a bit of a flap when the writers found out about it.

One prominent writer, who is now very well known in another field, a wonderful guy I don't want to embarrass, called me one day. "Hey George," he said, "I hear that the new Brubeck album you put out has splices in it. How come?"

I said, "The playing wasn't always perfect, and in order to make it come out better, I did certain inserts from other tapes."

"George, how can you do that? You're messing with an artist's creation"—and so forth.

Finally, I said, "Look, I'll give you Dave's number. Why don't you call him and ask him what he thinks about it?"

Later the phone rings, and the guy is on the phone. I said, "Well, did you have a nice talk with Dave?"

He said, "Yeah, I sure did."

"What did Dave say?"

He said, "George saved my fucking ass."

Through good trial and error, I developed things. For example, Dave sat to the right; the rest of the piano was to the left. The piano was reversed with Erroll Garner so that he faced the opposite wall. Over the course of the first two or maybe three sessions, that's the way it worked out best because of their different sounds. With Erroll, the bass and drums were subordinated; with Dave, the piano was part of the rhythm section. Dave and the bass and the drums had equal voices.

DUKE ELLINGTON, *ELLINGTON AT NEWPORT* (1956, COLUMBIA/LEGACY)
George Avakian

Newport '56 was the first time anybody recorded on location at any kind of musical festival. I asked Duke Ellington to do a special composition that we could call the "Newport Jazz Festival Suite." He did, but the biggest surprise was when Duke told the guys, "Look we've all worked very hard for this, and George has knocked himself out, but don't worry about the performance. Billy Strayhorn and George have set up a studio for tomorrow morning, and we're going to go back to New York and make patches." (Which I did successfully, very few patches, but I wanted everything to be as perfect as possible on that composition.)

Then Duke said, "After we do this, let's just relax and have a good time. Let's play something that we haven't played for a long time."

He called for "Diminuendo and Crescendo in Blue." The guys kind of looked at each other. They were saying, "Yeah, I remember." "Well, I don't." Paul Gonsalves was one of the ones who said, "I don't remember that one."

"It's just a blues," Duke said. "We change keys, I bring you in, and you blow until I take you out. We change keys again, and that's it."

Actually, Gonsalves had played it maybe three times, but the surprise element of forgetting the tension of making the first recording ever at an outdoor festival resulted in a tremendous performance.

There was a girl who broke out dancing in the boxes up front. On the album, we couldn't use a photograph that showed her face. Our lawyer said, "We'll get sued."

I disagreed, "Listen, she would love it." I was busy. I didn't have time to run out and say, "Who are you?" and get her to sign a release.

I saw her the following year, and she said, "Why didn't you use a better picture of me where they could see my face?" She was very pretty. I explained, and she said, "Oh, that would have been all right."

"I know that," I said, "but you don't know lawyers." She had platinum blond hair. She was very small, about five-foot-two or three, and slim. Kind of an interesting figure. I found out later that she had a padded bra. Don't ask me how. She deliberately left the top buttons of her black dress unbuttoned while she danced. She was a character.

SHELLY MANNE AND HIS FRIENDS,
MY FAIR LADY (1956, CONTEMPORARY)
John Koenig (Contemporary)

Shelly Manne & his Friends' modern jazz performances of songs from MY FAIR LADY

When my father was working with [filmmaker William] Wyler and looking for sources of material, he'd go to Broadway shows. Being a New York kid, he was familiar with that world. My mother's parents were Hollywood people. They wrote the screenplay to George Cukor and Katherine Hepburn's *Little Women* in 1933, and won an Oscar for it. My grandfather directed the Marx Brothers' *Animal Crackers*. All the Marx Brothers movies—or at least the early ones—were based on their shows, which were on Broadway.

My father brought that literary orientation to the enterprise of producing records. One of the things he came to be known for was doing jazz versus Broadway shows with Shelly [Manne] and André Previn. It certainly yielded some very good records.

Am I correct, Contemporary happened because of the Hollywood blacklist? Your father refused to name names for HUAC [the House Un-American Activities Committee].

Contemporary originated as a home for contemporary classical composers, with whom my father had become close while cultivating composers in the course of his activities as a film producer. But Contemporary came after Good Time Jazz, which was how he got started. In the very early fifties, Howard Rumsey, the leader of the Lighthouse All-Stars, approached my father.

My father was already a modern jazz enthusiast—indeed, he was enthusiastic about the avant-garde in all arenas of the arts, an interest that was perhaps leavened by his being a part of the famous literary circle of European expatriate intellectuals presided over by Salka Viertel, a circle that included Bertolt Brecht, Arnold Schoenberg, Thomas Mann, Lion Feuchtwanger, Christopher Isherwood, and many others. Interestingly, my father became inserted into that crowd because in his early days in Hollywood, he had rented a guest house on the Old Coast Road in Malibu from Mr. and Mrs. Hanns Eisler. Eisler was a German composer who tried to make the best of things when he came to America by composing film scores. The Eislers, who were childless, took a liking to my father, who was then in his early twenties. The Eislers were members of Salka's circle

43

and brought my father to the salon. He clicked with Salka and remained a close friend until the end of her life—at least until she left the States to live with her son, Peter, and Peter's wife, Deborah Kerr, in Klosters, Switzerland, which I believe was in the late sixties or early seventies. Eisler later became known—and in this country, reviled—as the composer of the East German national anthem. When the Iron Curtain fell, one certainly could have imagined that he would be consigned to oblivion. However, it happens that one of Europe's most prestigious music conservatories, the Hochschule für Musik Hanns Eisler Berlin, was named after him and it is, today, turning out top musicians who are making careers on the world's most important stages.

At any rate, Howard and John Levine were running the Lighthouse and decided to record the All-Stars. But it quickly became apparent to them that they didn't have the resources or the time to run a record company and a "saloon," as Howard put it to me. So my father took the first Lighthouse album (then a 10-inch LP) and put it on the Contemporary label, thereby relegating the contemporary classical projects to the "Contemporary Composers Series." But he'd started GTJ more or less as a lark (remembering that he'd been captivated by the idea of making records from his early days tagging along on John Hammond's sessions), and he was doing very well in the film business up until the time of the blacklist. He worked in film until *Roman Holiday* wrapped in 1953.

The remainder of his life was basically colored by the blacklist. One reason I think he was so hands-on at Contemporary was that it was the one area of his life over which he had control. It was his refuge from the world. His star was rising in Hollywood at the time the blacklist hit. Olivia de Havilland wanted him to direct her next picture, from having worked with him on *The Heiress*. All of that came to an end.

It's sadly ironic that the person who got my father into Hollywood was Bud Schulberg, because Bud was one of the people who testified later, admitted he'd been wrong, and named names. My father had the attitude that, no matter what, you don't name names. He was loyal to his friends.

My father's family was made up of Republican politicians and judges in New York. His father was a judge. His uncle, Sam Koenig, was the secretary of state of New York and the political boss. Fiorello La Guardia was a close friend of my grandfather's. He was always at the house. My father grew up in the atmosphere and was taught by his father that, if you do what's legal and what's right, you can never get in trouble. He was disabused of that belief. It was like getting his legs pulled out from under him.

I saw the FBI file. Wyler had said that my father was indispensable and that he needed to be working. He couldn't do this picture—which was *Roman Holiday* [1953]—without him. Plus, it was said that he had two small children, my sister and me. That I guess allowed him to work on *Roman Holiday*, although because of the blacklist he didn't receive a credit. I have photographs of my father—lots of them—on the set with Audrey Hepburn, Gregory Peck, Wyler, and Eddie Albert. He was right there in the middle of it—not just a supernumerary. He told me how he'd worked with Wyler and the writers on the script. He and Wyler took the *Queen Mary* from New York to Europe to prepare. They had some writers with them. I find the script, which won Dalton Trumbo a posthumous Oscar, an interesting political footnote. I liked Dalton. I met him. He's certainly an important figure, but that was not a great script. The picture's tremendous amount of charm had very little to do with what he did. It was about Audrey Hepburn. You can't not look at her when she's on the screen, which is virtually every scene. Anyway, Wyler was supportive to the extent that he was able. He'd never traveled as far left as my father did, either.

LENNIE TRISTANO, *LENNIE TRISTANO* (1956, ATLANTIC)
Tom Dowd (Atlantic Engineer)

The role of jazz producer is entirely different from perhaps any other field of recording. I don't seriously believe that anything has changed or will ever change because, when you're dealing with jazz musicians, you're dealing with skilled players who are masters of their instruments and who are masters of the art of scales and various levels of playing.

The most important function for anybody who tries to contribute to or encourage jazz artists and jazz performances is not to paint the picture but rather to capture it. It's like being a sports photographer, instead of a portrait painter. The artist is the impressionist, the artist is the creator, and you are just a damn witness. The minute you start getting in his face—"Why don't you do this or that"—it's not a good marriage.

In those days, because Ampex had not yet invented or manufactured an adequate, professional two-track tape recorder, I was using a Magnacorder, which had heads spaced 1⅞ inches apart for the left and right channels. I recorded a lot of the jazz things for Atlantic on that instrument while taping a mono version at the same time.

When we finished the *Tristano* sessions, I could not give Lennie the original tapes because they were stereo and, if you played them [on a monophonic machine], you'd hear two tracks a second and a half apart. You'd go out of your mind. I reduced everything to mono and gave Lennie a 7½-ips copy. God knows what he did with those tapes. That's not a criticism, but he used them or did homework on them and then added to them, cut and edited them. He did whatever he damn well pleased. That's fine; that was his privilege.

VARIOUS, *THE RIVERSIDE HISTORY OF CLASSIC JAZZ* (1956, RIVERSIDE)
Orrin Keepnews

I started producing in the early fifties, and tape was firmly with us by then. In terms of professional longevity, I'm older than stereo, but I am younger than tape. I'd been an English major at Columbia, though that's slightly inaccurate. When I was at Columbia, the Journalism School was a graduate school. That's where I firmly felt I was going; so I was officially a prejournalism student. I was sure that I was going to be a newspaperman when I grew up, but I apparently never grew up. Before I got through with my senior year, World War II beckoned.

I have a very real reason for thinking of John Hammond as a mentor. We started Riverside [in 1953] as a reissue label, with the rights to reissue stuff from the Chicago-based Paramount label of the twenties. (When I use plural pronouns, I'm referring to my partner, Bill Grauer, and myself. We started Riverside jointly.) The Paramount material had no metal parts in existence; they had all been destroyed years before. Our source for material became John Hammond. He lent us a vast collection of mint-condition Paramount shellac records. He just flat-out said, "Here they are. Take what you want. Borrow them and tape them." He lent us a substantial amount of records: Blind Lemon Jefferson, Ma Rainey, and other scarce Paramount recordings—Jelly Roll Morton and King Oliver. They were the basis for Riverside's reissue program, for getting the label underway. Hammond gave us this great push to get started.

The fifties were a heyday for the formation of independent labels. Of course, they didn't start at the same time, but the most noticeable thing about that phenomenon—and I can think of a half-dozen examples—was that they were the result of fans turning professional. This is what Blue Note was. It's what Prestige was. It's what Riverside was. In California, it's what Contemporary and Pacific Jazz were. The self-professionalizing of a bunch of enthusiasts. I used to say, if you own the company, there's nobody to tell you that you're not qualified to be a producer. That's how a lot of us started out. Nobody could tell us not to. It was our operation. In the same way, I managed to lose a perfectly good hobby by turning it into a business.

ORCHESTRA CONDUCTED BY GUNTHER SCHULLER AND GEORGE RUSSELL, *MODERN JAZZ CONCERT* (1957, COLUMBIA)
George Avakian

The very first recording Bill Evans ever did was with Gunther Schuller, who was conducting a large orchestra with compositions written by such people as George Russell. The orchestra was rehearsing, in pieces, "All about Rosie," a George Russell composition. I was sitting in the control room, getting the balance. Gunther hadn't done the piece all the way through. He said [to me], "George, let's try a take and see how it goes—now that you've got a balance."

"Okay," I said. I knew there was a piano solo, which I hadn't yet heard. So we went into the composition, and the solo came up. It knocked me practically off my chair! "Wow, who is this? This gangly guy, wearing studious glasses, that I've never seen before?" At the end of the take, I said to Gunther, "Gee, I think this is an okay take, as is."

"Yeah, you're right," he said. "Let's go on to the next one." There were no more piano solos, but I immediately went through withholding slips to check out this guy's name and address. I chatted with him briefly and told him, "That was really wonderful. If you're working around town, let me know. I'd love to come hear you." In the back of my mind I'm thinking, "I should sign this guy, although I have Erroll Garner."

That's how Bill and I became friends. About three weeks later, I decided, "Well, I haven't heard this guy play yet because he didn't get any jobs, but I should talk to him about the possibility of recording."

I called him up, and he said, "Oh, I just signed with Riverside Records, but maybe it won't last. I'd be very happy to talk to you about recording." Of course, it never happened. He was always under contract to somebody.

Had you considered Riverside as competition before that?

Yes, by then Riverside was definitely one of the best independent labels. In fact, the guys who started it were close friends of mine. They were Columbia University students who had just graduated: Orrin Keepnews and Bill Grauer. They started a magazine called the *Record Changer*, and eventually they began producing records. They used to work at a little basement place at 125 La Salle Street, right near the old Julliard School on Claremont Avenue. My wife and I were living on Riverside Drive about two blocks away. I'd see them pretty often.

MILES DAVIS, *MILES AHEAD* (1957, COLUMBIA)
Ed Michel (Impulse)

I find it fascinating that the same artist will make very, very different kinds of records for different producers. The records Charlie Parker made for Norman Granz [at Verve] are not much like the records that he made for Dial [with Ross Russell] or the records he made for Savoy [with Teddy Reig]. That's true of most artists as they move from place to place.

The differences have a lot to do with what the record company is in a position to do for the artist's career, rather than where he is in his career. For Miles, the move to Columbia had a profound effect on where he was going to work and how often he was going to work. It changed the entire equation.

George Avakian

When I signed Miles Davis [in 1955], there were fifteen months left on his Prestige contract. My brother [Aram] pushed me into it. I went to his lawyer and said, "Can you work out a deal with Prestige whereby we can record Miles and then not release tracks until the Prestige contract expires?" The reason I decided to do this was that my brother and I had heard Miles play at the first Newport Jazz Festival. He was a walk-on. He played two numbers with an all-star group and stole the show. It was fantastic. "Go ahead," my brother said, "make that kind of a deal." I did, and as it worked out, I ended up producing Miles's first sessions with John Coltrane and the group, although they weren't released until a year and four months later.

In my conception of the first album with Miles, it had to be the quintet. I needed to record something and have it ready in the can, in order to release it as soon as the Prestige contract expired. The album had to be called, I felt, 'Round Midnight. That was the composition that brought down the house at Newport. The publisher kind of messed things up by saying, "You can't call it that. The song's title is actually ''Round about Midnight.'" That album is the only time, I think, that the title ever appeared as 'Round about Midnight, except for the song's first recording, made by Thelonious on piano with the Cootie Williams Orchestra on a Vocalion single.

I knew I needed to do something else for the second album that was different. I had the title of the album ready in my mind. It was *Miles Ahead*. The concept would be Miles before the public, ahead of everybody else. He's moving ahead—forward motion. He's going to be a star.

The concept of the Gil Evans Orchestra came about this way. I've mentioned the recording I did with Gunther [Schuller] conducting the orchestra with Bill Evans on piano. I'd done another recording with Gunther conducting. The *Miles Ahead* album is a direct outgrowth of that. I'd recorded with the Brass Ensemble of the Jazz and Classical Music Society [*Music for Brass*, 1957]. Gunther conducted on one side and [Dimitri] Mitropoulos conducted Gunther's composition on the other: a debut which I get a big kick out of. Gunther talks about it as "George Avakian's two-for-one, cheapie debut—me as the conductor; me as a composer." It's a very good LP, quite wonderful. Two of the album's compositions, not by Gunther, were by J. J. Johnson and John Lewis. They called for trumpet solos. In planning the session, I said to Gunther, "I think I could use Miles. He'd be great for this idea." Miles was all for it, and he's on that recording with a twenty-piece orchestra. I pioneered in that kind of orchestral jazz.

Now we come to the time when I had to plan Miles's beginning career on Columbia. I said to Miles, "You've got to do something different. Let's go to the [*Birth of the Cool*] concept of a nine-piece orchestra, but expand it. We don't want to go back to the old nonet."

He said, "I like that fine." As I said, he'd already recorded with Gunther and was very impressed. In fact, he had even come to the recording session on which Mitropoulos conducted Gunther's composition "Symphony for Brass and Percussion." I introduced him to Mitropoulos, and Miles, ever the thinker, tugged on my sleeve and said, "Hey, do you think he'd let me play with his orchestra?," meaning the New York Philharmonic.

I answered, "Well, you never know, Miles." He was always planning—not in a bad way. He was a very, very brilliant guy: had brains to spare.

I said to him, "What about the type of sound that we had in that session with Gunther? Who would you like to do it with? There are two choices that come to mind immediately. One is Gunther; the other is Gil."

"I'd like to do it with Gil," he said, "because he's my old friend." Incidentally, Gunther had played in the Miles Davis Nonet. He played French horn.

So there we were. The concept was going to be a larger orchestra with Gil conducting. I knew that if the three of us talked it over in the office, the phone was going to ring. I suggested that we have lunch. We planned the whole thing over lunch, on two consecutive days at Lindy's. On the second day, we were seated next to a table with Henny Youngman, Milton Berle, and God knows who, cracking each other up with jokes, looking at us as though there's something weird. "Who are these two strange-looking white guys with this bizarre young kid?"

Do you know the story about the girl on the cover? I'd already put Miles on the first cover, 'Round about Midnight, a photograph my brother took. I was tempted to do the same on the second one. I wanted to establish his face. The conception of the *Miles Ahead* cover was arrived at by Neil Fujita, the art director. "This is the title," I told him. "I don't know what we're going to do on the cover."

He said, "I have an idea." The next day he comes in with this stock photograph that he'd gotten from a photographer somewhere.

When Miles saw it, he asked, "George, how can you put that white bitch on the cover? Get her off there. Put a black girl on there. Put Frances [Taylor]." She was his girlfriend. She was a dancer in *West Side Story*, a wonderful girl. Boy, did he abuse her. Talk about O. J. Simpson beating up on Nicole.

I said to Miles, "We'll change the cover." In the back of my mind, I'm thinking, "Gee, we can't put a black girl on a sailboat. I hate to lose the concept of the cover." Then I said, "Look, what we should do is have you on the cover again because we really want to establish you as a rising force on Columbia Records. Pick out any photograph of yours that you want." He picked another of Aram's pictures. That was done after I left Columbia. The fifty thousand–odd covers that we had already manufactured lasted that long.

The reason Miles agreed to let the [original] cover stay on until the supply was exhausted was very simple. It was Miles thinking ahead, thinking of his career. I said, "Miles, if we kill the cover, it'll take many weeks to create a new cover and manufacture it. We had these covers made in advance. They were easy to make, and it was economical to make them. All we have to do is put pressings into them and ship within forty-eight hours, maybe twenty-four, as the orders come in. You don't want to lose weeks and weeks of an album that is beginning to sell very well."

"No. Keep the fuckers, but then change it," he said. That's what we did.

When Miles Ahead *was first reissued on CD [1991], there were loud complaints. I know you were many years retired, but what was the problem? Teo Macero [Davis's long-time producer at Columbia] produced the reissue, right?*

Part of the problem was Columbia didn't describe how that first reissue on CD was really done. Teo was asked to make an electronically stereoed, rechanneled version.

At the [original] recording sessions a new two-track Ampex had been placed in our studio. We were asked to use it experimentally and see what we thought of what they called "binaural recording" [i.e., stereo]. We did set up a first session with Miles and Gil so that there was a stereo split. We listened to a little bit of tape and decided, "We'll push the buttons and let it run throughout the sessions." So there did exist an almost complete two-track tape of the sessions, but it wasn't entirely complete.

Teo found some of those tapes, and then he found that they'd been heavily edited—which nobody was that aware of. Except me. I was very aware on account of, sometimes, the splices didn't match well in tempo. Gil Evans was a bug for perfection of notes and blend. He'd say to me, "That isn't important. The fact that the playing is smoother on the insert that we put in is more important."

I could have argued with him and probably won. But it would have added hours and hours to the process, so I didn't. The cost factor was pretty serious. Nobody had ever done a project like this before. Remember, I was doing it with a guy [Miles Davis] who was still considered a junkie, and although I was pretty sure he was clean, he wasn't a star then.

I had a method—which [composer] Bob Prince called the Herr Doktor Avakian Schnipprocess—by which I would change the speed of a performance by cutting out snippets of tape and sometimes inserting them with an echo to hide the insertions. It wouldn't work with the blend that Gil got in his arrangements. It worked only with simple arrangements or improvisations. I'll describe the process to you briefly. What I would do, first, is try to speed up the slower section of the tape at the splice point. I would do it by marking beats, usually on the string bass. Then, the first snippet away from the splice point would be as wide as I dared to make it, depending on the tempo. So that the next beat, I would take out a little less and a little less and a little less. That meant that I might have as many as a dozen or more splices in a long stretch of tape. Then I'd play it and hope that I'd had managed to speed up the tape enough so that it matched at the splice point.

Believe me, I had to go over the tape again and again—recopy and then cut the copy. I didn't have more than two tape machines in the studio; it was quite a process. If it didn't work, even then at the splice point, I didn't dare go deeper into it. I would open up the tape at the other end of the splice and put in blank splicing tape with talcum powder on the back, so the tape wouldn't stick on the heads, and then cover that with a touch of echo. It worked beautifully. But I couldn't do that with a subtle blend of nineteen instruments. There, we were stuck.

Preparing the reissue, Teo also had another problem. He didn't know what splices Gil and I had made. There was no written record. Once you did it, that was it. He couldn't go back to the cut-up A-reel—the reels were marked A and B, and the stereo reel was marked C—because the A-reel had been so cut up that it was thrown away. Teo could tell only by listening to what we *might* have used, but that was terribly difficult. There were so many takes that had been used. Worst of all, Gil never wanted to record a take until he had everything perfect. As a result, I ended up not telling him that I was taping. I knew good performances were going to waste.

In the editing process, we had to listen to various cues other than take-one or take-two and so forth to know where we were. By the time you lifted material out of that, you don't want to write down what you did. It was impossible.

So Teo decided he would just reedit the whole thing as though he were editing a brand new session. He used as much as he could of the two-track tape, and where he couldn't do that, he either used another take from the two-track, or he rechanneled a section of the monaural master. That's why the sound wasn't all that great. For example, one performance includes a section on which Miles doesn't play at all, because it was part of a rehearsal. I must admit—and I never said this to Teo—but I think he was so busy trying to edit the album with no score, because the scores didn't exist, that he never realized he'd left out a section where Miles was supposed to play. Or if he did realize it, maybe later, he decided, "It sounds all right." Which it does, if you don't know that Miles had originally played on that part. The problem began with Columbia not explaining what Teo had done. [In 1997, Sony Legacy straightened out kinks and reissued a definitive version of the album.]

SONNY ROLLINS, *SAXOPHONE COLOSSUS* (1957, PRESTIGE)
Bob Weinstock

With "Bags' Groove"—the Miles, Monk, and Milt Jackson session—and "Walkin'"—Miles, J. J. Johnson, Lucky Thompson, and Horace Silver—and with *Colossus*, we'd gotten into the LP era. Tommy Flanagan, Doug

Watkins, and Max Roach: Sonny came in with the group he wanted to record. We agreed. But once he was there [in Rudy Van Gelder's studio], it was like a ball game. The team's either hot or cold. And that's the way I played it, like middle of a Stanley Cup, seventh game, with Mario Lemieux playing against Wayne Gretsky.

I'd sit out in the studio. I'd be out there with the musicians. I left Van Gelder alone all the time. I never tried to tell him anything about recording. The man was a genius. I'll tell you how I met him.

I knew his work, because I'd always buy Blue Note records. I kept seeing "Van Gelder recording" on the record credits. I lived in Teaneck, New Jersey, and it was 1954. One day I was walking down the main street and noticed a sign: Optometrist Dr. Rudolph Van Gelder. I went in and asked to see him. He came out, and I asked, "Are you the Rudy Van Gelder who's recording Blue Note? I'm Bob Weinstock."

He said, "Come in. I know all about Prestige."

"Well, I've been listening to your stuff for six or eight months, maybe a year." I talked to him and asked, "How do you do it? It sounds different—better."

"I have my techniques," he said. "I don't discuss it. It's there on the records. If you hear it and you like it, fine."

I asked him, "Are you under contract to Blue Note? Can I do something with you?"

"I can record anybody," he said. "Call me. We'll set up a session."

So I got Miles to record with him first. We went in there, and Rudy took over. I didn't say a word. I listened to the playback, and it was great. You could hear the drums, the bass. It sort of sounded like an echo, but it wasn't a deliberate echo chamber. He just added dimension to the recording.

So back to Saxophone Colossus.

You get to "Blue Seven," which to me is a classic, I heard it building and building. When I saw Sonny Rollins was playing his ass off, I'd give him a high sign. Other times, I'd show him the stop watch and throw it on the couch. That meant, "Play, man. Ignore the clock."

I did that to Lucky Thompson. He played twice as much as Miles, I think, on Miles's "Walkin'" session. He nodded, closed his eyes, and kept playing and playing. To me, we were in a game. Spontaneity ordered it.

I've had bands, like the great Gil Evans, a monster arranger, one of the best in the history of jazz. He came in and did a session [*Gil Evans and Ten*, 1957]. Lee Konitz was there. Good people.

I took him aside. "Gil, nothing's happening. I don't know why, man."

He said, "I know."

"What can we do to make it swing and cook?"

"Let me forget the charts," he said, "and play like we were just playing."

But it still had the Gil Evans stamp. It was free and swinging. We eliminated the collar that was around the music. That was my style. My underlying thing was it had to be happy. It had to cook and swing. It had to be funky, too, little by little even with some of the modernists. I always tried to mix a variety of players from different schools. They liked it, and they inspired each other.

So even though you were recording musicians who played in post-Parker styles, your own style of production resembled that of Norman Granz.

That's a good observation. Because I produced Miles and Rollins, Trane, Monk, and Milt Jackson, people thought I was a real modernist. What they didn't understand was that I also loved the Norman Granz stuff.

Granz knew two things: swing and play pretty. He made such good records. He was a hero. One of the first things that really got me excited when I was in high school was his Jazz at the Philharmonic. Then, let's talk about Alfred Lion. The man was a genius. He went from New Orleans jazz up to the latest modern things: Cecil Taylor and Ornette Coleman. He was my real mentor, but the thing is, I didn't copy Alfred. Blue Note was bebop-oriented and Prestige was funky-oriented. There was overlap. Alfred had funk with Jimmy Smith and [Stanley] Turrentine. But I had Turrentine first when he was with Shirley [Scott].

While I'm talking about old people in the business, Ross Russell, who recorded Bird on Dial, he shaped my philosophies of life. But he got fed up [with the record business]. "Now that I don't have Bird, there's nobody to record," he said.

"But you've got Wardell Gray, and you recorded Dexter [Gordon]. You can keep going on. You make good records. You know what you're doing."

"No, if it's not Bird, it's no good." He said, "You take Wardell Gray. Get James Moody." He'd tell me what to do, give me lessons.

SONNY ROLLINS, *A NIGHT AT THE VILLAGE VANGUARD* (1957, BLUE NOTE)
Sonny Rollins (Saxophone)

I still feel at odds [with recording]. I really do. And it's strange, because when I look back on my early career, when I first began playing and making records in the late forties, it didn't bother me so much. Of course, I was pretty young at the time, but still I wasn't critical, perhaps because I was usually on somebody else's date. But somewhere along the way I began to become very concerned about leaving a really good recorded legacy, and I was very concerned about all of the notes coming out right. That has persisted up to the present time. I'm not very comfortable in the recording studio.

I don't care how many ideas you have. Even if you have some brilliant jazz ideas, it's going to be difficult to get them across unless you have (A) a distinctive sound or (B) a loud sound. These are musts. You must have either a powerful sound or a sound that's distinctive enough, which can grow out of ideas. A loud sound is something that you have to work on, but it's very important. As a player coming up, I ran into a lot of circumstances where you had to develop a loud sound. There were always guys who had big sounds in those days because a lot of times you had to play without microphones.

These things were impressed upon me coming up in the various sorts of rhythm-and-blues environments where I took the occasional gig. Not every great had a big sound, but most of them did. If they didn't have a big sound like Gene Ammons, then they had a very distinctive sound. You had to have one of the two to really make it.

CHARLES MINGUS, *THE CLOWN* (1957, ATLANTIC)
Tom Dowd (Atlantic Engineer)

Nesuhi [Ertegun] had this empathy for the traditions. He was a magnificent jazz historian, and he used to teach jazz and humanities at UCLA.[7] He knew American music and the traditions of American music better than most Americans will ever learn. He did it by listening, by living with people, by sharing their experiences. He was a great humanitarian. He

---

7. From John Koenig: "My father recommended Nesuhi to Lawrence Morton, then chair of UCLA's music department, for that job. Lawrence had originally asked my father to do it, but because of commitments and the blacklist, he couldn't."

CHARLES
MINGUS
THE
CLOWN

tried to capture musicians doing what it was they were doing, put them at ease doing it, and encourage them to continue. Those were Nesuhi's strengths.

He and Ahmet were educated to have the opportunity, if they chose, to become diplomats. They were both multilingual. Nesuhi spoke Turkish, Italian, German, English, and French. He could wear different musical hats, attitude-wise. He could also wear different hats when dealing with people from different societies.

Sue Mingus (Columbia)

Charles and Nesuhi [Ertegun] were very close. That friendship was seminal to the music and to the relationship he enjoyed at Atlantic. It was a very warm and friendly climate. Charles loved Nesuhi, and that love was reciprocal. In Charles's opinion and certainly in mine, Nesuhi was one of the finest people in the record industry. He was very understanding of Charles's artistic needs, and respected them completely. Not everybody can write and perform and record exactly what they want—even less and less these days. Charles had an open road. Nesuhi completely respected his artistic needs and sensibilities and allowed him to do what he wanted to do. That was really fundamentally important.

Joel Dorn (Atlantic)

Nesuhi recognized Mingus for what he was before anybody did. There were people who knew Mingus as a composer. There were people who knew Mingus as a bass player. There were people who knew Mingus as this larger-than-life character. But Nesuhi really got it. He understood that Charles Mingus was a major American musical figure. So he didn't approach him as a jazz bass player. He approached him for what he was, a composer/bass player/bandleader: a one-of-a-kind, singular musical personality.

Don't forget, at that time, Nesuhi had Ornette, Mingus, Coltrane, and Ray Charles all under contract. And Herbie Mann, the Modern Jazz Quartet, Hank Crawford, David Newman, Chris Connor, and Jimmy Giuffre. That was no minor league collection of people. When you have Mingus, Trane, and Ornette, all under contract, all at the same time, somebody's paying attention.

It certainly wasn't money that attracted those jazz artists to Atlantic. Everybody was, basically, giving the same deals, though every once in a while Columbia and RCA—Capitol, to a degree—would offer more money. It was Nesuhi. First of all, he had impeccable taste, not only in music. For example, at the same time Nesuhi had Coltrane under contract, he was collecting René Magritte, and he had a rare-book collection. He wasn't your typical A & R guy. He had vision—rare, even in those days. Not only did he see artists for what they were when he signed them, he understood the long-term implications. He didn't sign Mingus in order to get a hit. He signed him so that he could capture an important artist's work at a pivotal time in his career.

Second, Nesuhi was very unobtrusive as a producer. Notice the records he made with Coltrane, Mingus, Ornette, and the MJQ. They weren't *Mingus Goes Broadway, Christmas with John Coltrane,* or *Ornette Plays the Hits.* He documented what they wanted to do. He was an egoless producer. He used to tell me all the time—because I was not an egoless producer— so he'd tell me all the time: "I'm very fortunate." And it wasn't said in that self-effacing, bullshit way. "I was able to sign the people that I wanted to sign when I wanted to sign them. They did their great work for us."

He was always artist-oriented, as opposed to someone who says, "I'm going to get him. Now, I'm going to show you what I can do. I'm going to make a hit with so-and-so." He signed artists for the right reasons. And it's not like he had nothing to do with their work. He had a lot to do with it. He made sure that the sound was right, the atmosphere was right. They got to do what they wanted. He was a great sounding board. But he wasn't one of these obtrusive producers who always had an idea for somebody.

He signed talent, and he let the talent develop. And if such-and-such a record wasn't a hit, sometimes you let people do stuff. Whereas, the more commercially oriented producers always had an idea. But he was a real documentarian in that respect. Very few people were.

Nat Hentoff was also an artist-producer in that sense. He was a writer, but he was sympathetic. The guys knew that Nat knew their music. When they did something with him, it was because he was the right guy. They knew he was with them in a spiritual sense.

Tom Dowd (Atlantic Engineer)

Mingus was the worrier. He was overpowering and demonstrative, but he always wanted spontaneity. When we were doing *Pithecanthropus Erectus* [1956], I had devised a means of taping a microphone onto the tailpiece of Mingus's bass so he could rotate and turn around. Keeping him still while he was trying to look at this or that guy, give them a head motion, was tough. I couldn't keep him on microphone; so I managed to fasten the microphone to the instrument. He could roam around, rotate, or do whatever he wanted.

We were doing this one selection. It might have been "Haitian Fight Song" or something like that [on *The Clown*]. It was something dynamic. Mingus is playing. He looks over and gets the piano player's eye. And he gets the drummer's eye, but he can't get the horn players' attention. He keeps motioning to them.

Finally, he picked up the bass while he was playing, and he did a pegleg across the room, up to where the trombone player stood. It's Jimmy Knepper. He played something, and Mingus pulled the horn away and punched him in the nose and went back to playing. He's like, "I was trying to tell you not to play there, dummy." It was that kind of expression. Knepper was so deeply entranced in what he was doing. All of a sudden, he's got a fist in his face. That was Mingus.

Ed Michel (Impulse)
Nesuhi came with an art sensibility, but he also, I mean the Ertegun brothers, first and foremost, sold records and knew a lot about that. Artists respond to the encouragement you give them or the lack of encouragement.

John Koenig (Contemporary)
To me, growing up, Nesuhi was like an uncle. He was the guy about whom my parents said, "If you ever need an adult and we're not around, call Nesuhi." I memorized his phone number.

As a kid, I'd met Ahmet, but we didn't become close until later. He was always full of fun. He was a very dynamic character, and one of the most charismatic people I've ever known. When he'd come to Los Angeles, if he were here for two weeks, we'd have dinner with him twelve of those fourteen nights. It was like that for years. He'd announce to the assembled notables at the table, and they were usually people of some note, "John's father was Nesuhi's boss." It was true, but he said it, I guess, to puff me up or something.

Nesuhi and Ahmet were interested in American things. Their father had been one of Atatürk's closest advisors. After the Turkish republic was founded in 1923, he became the Turkish ambassador to England, Switzerland, France, and then to the United States, though I'm not sure it was in that order.

Nesuhi was five years older than his brother, and he took Ahmet to his first jazz concert. They were both interested in jazz, cowboys and Indians, and gangsters, which is what they understood America to be about. Ne-suhi took Ahmet to a show—Nesuhi was fifteen, Ahmet was ten—at the London Palladium. It was Duke Ellington and Cab Calloway. He was im-mediately captivated.

When they moved to the United States, they moved to Washington, D.C., which is a different kind of place. They were attracted to the black musi-cal culture there, and I guess because they were Turkish, Ahmet didn't feel like an alien in that world the way a native-born white person might have felt in the thirties. He went to prep schools. He was an intellectual. I don't know if people know that about him. He went to graduate school at Georgetown in philosophy. I don't know if he finished his master's de-gree. I think the war and the death of his father may have had something to do with that.

SONNY ROLLINS, *WAY OUT WEST* (1957, CONTEMPORARY)
John Koenig (Contemporary Reissues)

After the company went over to Fantasy [in 1984], they issued the catalog in not very good editions because, number one, my father didn't add reverb at the recording stage. That was always done in mastering. He had an EMT [reverb] plate, a mono plate. Number two, [engineer] Roy [DuNann] had devised a noise-reduction system, which was very simple. He referenced the tape machine so that it would record 6 dB hot at 10 kHz, and then when you played it back you referenced the machine down 6 dB at 10. That brought down the tape hiss. It was an early, broad-brush Dolby system, but less complicated. If you hear a record made off of a good set of lacquers, either that my father, Roy, Bernie [Grundman], or I cut at Contemporary, they are pretty spec-tacular sounding.

I tried to explain all of this to the engineering people at Fantasy when the catalog went over. Contemporary had beautiful, pristine, brilliantly mastered metal parts on the part of the catalog that was active at the time of sale, and they trashed all of them and started over again. That was a big mistake, but they weren't going to listen to me. One of my problems in life is that I've always been viewed as Les Koenig's son. I explained to them how our mastering notes worked. Every time we cut a lacquer, we wrote a new note, a new page that said what we'd done and if we'd changed any-thing from the prior version. These were detailed moves that you had to do because these were live [meaning not multitracked] sessions. Things had to be helped or brought down: some for purely audio reasons; some to get the material onto the disc.

I thought Ralph Kaffel was a very good steward of the Contemporary catalog, but I said to him, "This mastering is problematic."

"Talk to George Horn," he said.

I told George Horn this is what you should be doing and why. I said, "Refer to the mastering notes." For example, Sonny Rollins's *Way out West*, with one or other of its sides, we probably did ten or twelve separate lacquers over time because the plant would blow the parts, and they would need a new lacquer. Each time we did one, we started new. [Lathe] cutter technology had improved over the years, so the high end was freer on the later versions—something unbeknown to collectors, who always want the original issue. I suppose I understand that on one level, but they didn't sound as good as the later ones.

George said to me, "We want to honor what the producer said."

I said, "With whom do you think you're speaking?" It was like talking to a wall.

In addition to the sound of Contemporary recordings, your father seemed to care a great deal about how albums looked.

Yes, he superintended it closely. But when he encountered [photographer] Bill Claxton, for example, he'd rely on Bill's eye. At the same time he formed a close association with Bob Guidi and, later, with George Kershaw at Tri-Arts, an arthouse company. They did layout work.

It was a difficult thing for me when my father died. I had been playing [cello] in the Swedish Radio Symphony in Stockholm. He died suddenly at age fifty-nine, which is younger than I am now. Rightly or wrongly, I felt that, if we were going to stay Contemporary, we needed to be a little bit more with the times. If I was recording someone who hadn't had a record before—for example, George Cables—no one knew him as a leader. I felt like the audience needed to identify with the person. I always wanted to have a good portrait of someone who was new, so that the public could identify with the artist. While that was often the practice with the fifties and sixties Contemporaries, a lot of them were fanciful. A lot had cartoons and illustrations. As a kid, I didn't know West Coast from New York jazz. It was all music to me. It all came to me on records, and I listened to it in my house. I wasn't as aware of the cultural significance of the Contemporary covers, particularly those from the fifties. But I think it was something my father was conscious of and did on purpose.

He was very detail-oriented. Whether it was Nat Hentoff, Leonard

Feather, or any of the other illustrious people who wrote liner notes for Contemporary albums, they were always scrupulously edited.

Most likely it comes from the Hollywood model, but, very early, he "ran credits" on albums.

I think you're right. He provided all of the details about the songs: composers and publishers and so on. Also technical data, which I think Nesuhi saw and emulated on Atlantic's jazz records. Although Atlantic records looked good, Tommy Dowd didn't make as good a studio as we had with Roy DuNann. Also, Bernie Grundman—he's a preeminent disc-mastering guy (we used to say mastering)—he got his start at Contemporary. My father trained him to cut lacquers on the same lathe he trained me. It's interesting. That lathe was the very lathe used to record the sound for what's generally regarded as the first talkie, *The Jazz Singer*. Audio quality was one of the most important things to my father. Contemporary was known for it.

Sonny Rollins (Saxophone)

The one [the cover] on *Way out West*—it happened a long time ago. I'm pretty sure that it was my idea: the hat and the gun belt and all that stuff.

It was very striking, very unusual. It was a big kick at the time. But I thought it went well with playing unusual songs for a jazz album. I thought that the whole thing was really right.

It's incredibly funny, ironic. It anticipates one of the best jokes in Blazing Saddles. *I look at it, laugh, and then think, "This isn't funny. It's true. There were plenty of black cowboys." Plus jazz is metaphorically associated with myths of the West: the musician as outlaw hero; the music as a movement or push outward. The cover says that. It works on many, many different levels.*

That's right. I've never thought of it in those words, but that's quite true. When I was a boy, I had seen these all-black films. There was a fellow who used to sing with Duke Ellington's Band, Herb Jeffries. He was in an all-black western. I remember that. I've forgotten whether it was *Rhythm on the Range* or *Bronze Buckaroo*, but that made an impression on me. And of course, as we all know, there were black cowboys. All of these things were in my mind.

William Claxton (Photographer)

I told him to keep his Brooks Brothers suit and skinny black tie. I knew the desert pretty well, so I knew exactly where to get the right kind of

Joshua trees and cactus in the background. I went to a prop house and rented a steer's head—a skeleton—because I couldn't depend on finding one out there. And we put a holster on him.

I picked him up. He was a terrific guy to be with, very nice, and we just drove out to the high desert, near Mojave. I had shot pictures there before. I put the skull out in the sand, and he put one foot up on it. He had this long, thin body. He looked great. He just posed beautifully. And he had great fun doing it. We laughed a lot.[8]

THELONIOUS MONK SEPTET, *MONK'S MUSIC* (1957, RIVERSIDE)
Orrin Keepnews

I've found—and this perhaps has a good deal to do with my early training at the hands of Thelonious Monk—that I've always tended to present ideas: concept ideas or who-to-play-with ideas or repertoire ideas. I've always made it abundantly clear that I am making suggestions. I don't care to say, "Hey, this is the way it has to be," and lay down a bunch of rules. I find that the idea—if it's properly understood by the artist—the idea of making suggestions is extremely valid. A variety of things can happen. Ideas can be accepted or, hopefully, when they are rejected, it's not just a matter of somebody saying, "No." It's a matter of being spurred on to come up with a substitute or variation.

For example, a lastingly important thing about the album *Monk's Music* is the combination of Coltrane and Coleman Hawkins on the same record.

8. Aware that he photographed Mel Brooks and Carl Reiner for the cover of their first comedy LP, *2000 Years with Carl Reiner and Mel Brooks* (1961), I asked Claxton (January 21, 1990) if, to his knowledge, Mel Brooks had seen the cover to *Way out West*. I reminded him that it anticipated one of the best jokes in *Blazing Saddles* (1974). The film's audience thinks it's hearing typical movie music when, all of a sudden, Sheriff Bart (Cleavon Little) spots the Count Basie Orchestra—in the middle of the desert! They're playing "April in Paris." Claxton told me, yes, he'd shown Brooks the album-cover photo at the Brooks/Reiner photo shoot, but he'd never connected his photo with Brooks's movie. In a later interview (not with me, and I can't remember with whom), Claxton said that Brooks had subsequently confirmed he was conscious of the connection. See http://www.jazz.com/jazz-blog/2008/4/9/revisiting-jazz-classics (accessed May 11, 2015).

Now, I didn't suggest that, but I made some instrumentation and personnel suggestions to Monk which caused him—in saying, "No, I don't want to do that" or "I've already done something too much like that"—to say, "How about if instead I do ...?" Thereupon came that magnificent idea.

In general, if I go back to the notion of being a combination of facilitator—what I call a catalytic agent—and concept maker, a lot of methodology depends on the nature of the artist/producer relationship. There are some people with whom I've felt the freedom to make suggestions and come up with concepts, though that's actually not cut-and-dried either. For instance, Thelonious was certainly one of the most self-aware musicians I've ever worked with, but with him, I felt encouraged to make suggestions. After I got to know him and understand working with him, I never for a minute thought that I could possibly succeed in imposing on him. I didn't have to worry about making suggestions. He was never going to let me get out of line, and so that was fine. That freed him on my part. I was more cautious with the artist I felt was in danger of letting me walk over him, because I didn't want to do that.

CHET BAKER, *CHET BAKER SINGS* (1957, WORLD PACIFIC)
Ed Michel (Impulse)

One of the first things I did, when I was a baby editor, was practice on tapes from *Chet Baker Sings* [produced by Richard Bock, with whom Michel started working in the late fifties]. I put together a glorious fifteen-minute tape of "Look for the silver ... oh shit. Look for the ... shit, silver lining ... shit. Goddamn it, shit. Look for the ... shit." It went on and on and on. I can't find it anymore. It breaks my heart. I loved to play that tape for people. Chet required an inordinate amount of editing, especially when he sang, because he wasn't a very good singer.

He was my first junkie. I have no good memories of him at all. Whereas, by the time I knew Art [Pepper] fairly well, I was used to that shit. I didn't know that anybody could be as irresponsible as Chet was. His mystique is really lost on me. He was a dodo surfer who could play really good trumpet. He was a killer trumpet player for a minute and, apparently, got back to it again. But I was so burned that I can't listen to much Chet Baker anymore.

On the other hand, I did have a chance to hear Chet playing with Bird, or it was actually Bird playing with Chet's quartet [1952]. Chet was holding up his end just fine, and that's coming from a guy who didn't like him very much. He was okay. He could play.

George Avakian (Columbia)

Musicians are fabulous in terms of what their ears can do. I'll give you a great example. You know Chet Baker, of course. When I was developing the pop album catalog on the basis of a lot of good jazz recordings, I did everything in addition to the international department. But I loved the jazz stuff most of all.

The Phillips Company had just taken over Columbia's European catalog, and they wanted to do a special promotion in France on new releases by Chet Baker, Benny Goodman, and Harry James. They asked if I could get those artists to read something in French, which they could then use as broadcast promotion. They planned to dub in a French voice asking questions; they gave me the questions.

My first reaction was, "Well look, this is impossible. None of these guys speak French." For some reason, that never seemed to cross their minds. They simply said, "Can you do this?"

I was about to refuse when I mentioned it to my brother, Aram. He was a great photographer and filmmaker; in fact, he was the man behind the first film ever made at a music festival, *Jazz on a Summer's Day* [Newport, 1958]. He's credited only as film editor, because the guy who produced it—put up the money—was a real s.o.b. He told Aram, "You don't get any credit except film editor because that is what your contract says."

So anyway, my brother says, "Look, George, it's no problem. I'll be Harry James. You'll be Benny Goodman, because you speak French with an Armenian accent, and it comes out sounding like a Jewish accent. And Chet Baker will be Chet Baker."

I said, "That's fine." My brother spoke French fluently. "But Chet doesn't know a word of French!"

"That doesn't matter," Aram said. "He's got the ear. Call him in, and I'll write out what he has to say, phonetically. You watch. He'll rehearse and do it very well."

Well, I didn't believe it. Chet came in, and he listened to Aram and me do our parts. He studied his script, went out to the table in the studio, and started out. It was good. I could understand him very well.

"Let's make a tape," I said, thinking I'm really going to be splicing for hours and hours. Instead, we had to make, I believe, two splices. That man listened to the way Aram pronounced his script. Then he listened to us make our part, and studying his own phonetic script, actually spoke French for the entire script. It was almost unbelievable. The script ran about three pages! Unfortunately, the company was in such a rush to take this over to Paris that I gave the tape to a guy who took the plane that night. I didn't make a copy, because we did it in a small studio with a one-tape machine. I wish I'd made it with a two-tape machine. They wanted to rush, rush, rush, right away.

LAMBERT, HENDRICKS, AND ROSS, *SING A SONG OF BASIE* (1957, ABC-PARAMOUNT)
Creed Taylor

When I was growing up buying and listening to records on Blue Note and Prestige, there were sometimes great moments and sometimes long periods of waning interest: bass solos too long, unnecessary drum solos, and an improper use of space. Miles, you recall, always talked about space. When I got out of school—I went to Duke University—I thought the first place I was going to hit was New York City and Birdland and, somehow, I didn't know how, jump into recording jazz: make some records I'd like to listen to. If I liked what was coming out, I felt other people would also.

I started at Bethlehem Records, and after I'd been with them two years, I called Sam Clark, the head of ABC-Paramount, and told him I'd like to come over and make some jazz records. They'd just formed the record company. It was as simple as that; they hadn't done anything. I moved there in 1956. Down the hall from me was Don Costa, who was doing Paul Anka, Steve and Eydie, and Ray Charles. Actually, I borrowed Ray Charles from Don Costa when I started Impulse at ABC in 1960.

So your career began with magnetic tape already in studios. How did you learn to work with that medium?

I'd say it was intuitive. I walked into tape. I never dealt with anything else. Tape was 15 ips [inches per second] and single-track. Actually, I produced *Sing a Song of Basie* with something like thirty overdubs on one track—an Ampex machine with ¼-inch tape—complete with all the hiss I could possibly accumulate.

It's very simple to explain. Probably, if you talk to Jon [Hendricks], he'd have a different story. If Dave were still around, he'd have a different story.

But really what happened was Dave Lambert was somewhat of a vocal contractor. He made a living in the studio with either jingle singers, or doing his scat thing with jazz bands.

He brought in a group of singers, and we tried to get them to swing, and they did not swing by any stretch of the imagination. I talked to Annie [Ross], Jon, and Dave. I said, "We've got this tape here. You guys have the concept. You know how to phrase like a trombone section, and Annie knows how to phrase like the trumpet section. She can do the shakes that the Basie trumpet section did, and all that kind of stuff." Jon was the tenor soloist, or whatever instrument happened to be doing the solo that he'd scat.

Then it started coming together. We laid down the basic rhythm track with Basie's rhythm section at that time, and started adding vocals: Annie's lead trumpet, then she would do the second trumpet, third trumpet, and fourth trumpet. We just built it, and with no regard of any kind to hiss in the audio, because we were creating something that made sense. The other concept, using studio singers, they might as well have been poor man's Swingle Singers or something. It did not work. With Dave, Jon, and Annie, it developed by itself and sheer determination on our parts.

JOHN COLTRANE, *COLTRANE* (1957, PRESTIGE)
Esmond Edwards

Bob Weinstock was my mentor. Prior to working for him, I had no experience. I wanted to be a jazz photographer. As a kid, I lived in a block adjacent to Arthur Taylor's, and I knew he was a drummer. One day I said, "Hey A. T., I'd like to see a jazz session and take pictures." It was the *Lights Out* session with Jackie McLean on Prestige. I drove over to Rudy's studio [Rudy Van Gelder]. I took some pictures and showed them to Bob. He liked them and chose one to use on the cover.

He and I were both the same age. We were both about twenty-eight, twenty-nine. I used to go by Bob's office as I was making my rounds, showing my portfolio and trying to get photography gigs. We talked jazz, and one day he said, "Why don't you come and work here part-time?"

I said, "Okay." I'd work in the morning and go around to agencies in the afternoon. I sent out catalogs for Bob and whatnot. It just expanded and became full-time. I started going to all the sessions and taking pictures. One day he said, "Look, you go to the session." That was a Coltrane date. So that was my very first as a producer—the session that became the album titled *Coltrane*.

I started designing the record covers in addition to doing the pictures. I had a kind of one-man show going there: producing, shooting pictures, and designing jackets. That's how it got started. Later, Bob became a full-time executive, and we started getting other people. Elliott Mazer came in, Don Schlitten started doing some things, and Ozzie Cadena was always around doing various things.

At the time did you know of any other African Americans producing jazz?

Very few. I believe I was probably the first given any kind of official standing. When I left Prestige [1961], I was vice president. Around the same time, Quincy [Jones] became a vice president at Mercury. Of course, that was a big difference in pay scale. There were people running their own labels, like Tom Wilson and, of course, Charlie Mingus.

Do you think the artists, most of them African American, responded to you differently for being black?

Not to any great degree. They were, maybe, proud to see me there, but I think I still represented the label, the establishment, and they always had some resentment toward Prestige. They felt they were being ripped-off. They weren't being paid enough, and to some extent they were being ripped-off. Being Bob's representative, I think their response to me was mixed. They were kind of glad to see a black guy there, but the black guy was working for the president. I was like a trustee of a chain gang.

JOHN COLTRANE, "RUSSIAN LULLABY" (1958), *SOULTRANE* (PRESTIGE)
Bob Weinstock

We had a basic framework, and we'd discuss who we were going to use. I didn't try and shove people down their throats, and they didn't try and shove 'em down my throat. Same with the material. I'd have suggestions. They'd have suggestions. My knowledge of songs was tremendous.

I'd say, "Hey Trane, do you know 'Russian Lullaby'?"

"Sure, man."

Boom. "Russian Lullaby," just like that. He could teach it to everybody on the session. It was all very loose. I hated charts. I hated arrangements. That's where me and Alfred [Lion] differed. Alfred would have rehearsals.

I never had a rehearsal. I didn't believe in it. I believed jazz had to swing and be loose. It had to be mutual. You couldn't tell those giants—and they were greats—what to do.

Esmond Edwards (Prestige)

With Prestige we worked on a limited budget. Things were, more or less, done in the studio, no rehearsal as a rule. It was a matter of getting compatible musicians together and, to some extent, giving them a direction in advance. A lot of times things were kind of ad hoc. You get four or five guys in the studio, and they're scratching their heads, "What are we going to do now?"

I used to go to sessions as a photographer and watch how Bob functioned. I'd say, "Okay, let's try such and such a tune. Let's try a standard. Let's do a blues." Blues were kind of a stock-in-trade. "Let's do," what Bob would call, "a funky ballad." That's the way things more or less went down.

We had a kind of formula. Bob would call for his blues ballad, "I Sold My Heart to the Junkman," that kind of thing. He'd say, "You've got to have the funky blues and some standards—a standard ballad and an up-tempo standard." If you look at a lot of those albums, unless they were predominately originals by Mal [Waldron], Eric [Dolphy], or somebody like that, they're kind of jam session dates. A lot of Gene Ammons's dates were pretty much in that formula.

If there was a group that was more organized, they would come in with their material rehearsed. It was then a matter of seeing that the sound went on the tape properly and that you didn't go overtime—stuff like that. In those early days, though, overtime wasn't much of a problem. The union wasn't very active, and the musicians weren't that militant about watching things like that.

Did you regard Coltrane leaving Prestige as inevitable?

Even though Blue Note, Prestige, Riverside, and a couple other small labels were the dominant ones, they got the artists when they were young, available, and didn't have a reputation. The majors would not touch an artist without a reputation. The routine was Prestige or Blue Note would get the guy off the train or plane, record him, and stick with him until he developed a voice and a name. Then Atlantic, Columbia, and RCA would come in and dangle big bucks. The little labels couldn't compete.

I remember Sonny Rollins. I never had the pleasure of working with Sonny, but during a time when he was free and we were trying to get him back, he came out to Jersey to talk to me. He told me that RCA had offered him, I think it was, fifty thousand dollars. We're talking '61! I said, "What? Sonny, that's incredible. Take it."

There was no way Prestige could come up with that kind of money or make it back if they did come up with it. I doubt if RCA made it back. We just couldn't compete with those kinds of figures. They could write it off with Elvis Presley profits. That was the business we were in. It was jazz. The major labels could make those kinds of deals and take those kinds of chances. With CDs maybe they made back their money on reissues, but at that time it just didn't compute.

Bob Weinstock

We were a farm team. Norman Granz [Clef and Verve] was pretty decent. He utilized the people in his Jazz at the Philharmonic. But to me Nesuhi Ertegun—I don't know if his brother Ahmet had anything to do with it— Nesuhi was a fucking snake in the grass. I detested the whole Atlantic bullshit. Losing an artist wasn't the problem. Sometimes, I had an artist and Blue Note would take him. I'd take a Blue Note. That's fair in war. But if you look at the Atlantic catalog, I think they had one artist—Tony Fruscella—you can say was an unknown or a lesser known. The rest they took from everybody else. Bob Thiele at Impulse wasn't as bad, but he was pretty bad, too. I used to press my records at Columbia, at CBS, in their custom pressing division. They knew how well Miles was selling for me, and they knew how much to offer to get him away from me.

Orrin Keepnews (Riverside)

You want to know my biggest frustration? It's that, if I hadn't been so goddamned noble, I could have produced the first album John Coltrane did after he left Prestige. It was generally assumed at that point—because of our closeness with John and his closeness with Thelonious—that when he got through with Prestige, he would sign with Riverside.

John and I had a conversation which basically revolved around the fact that he knew exactly how much money Monk was getting per album from us. John said that he had certain goals. He knew how much money he wanted to make from his recordings as a leader, and he didn't think it was appropriate for him to ask for more than Monk was getting. Therefore, to reach his total goal, he was going to have to sign a contract with us calling for four albums a year!

Like a noble schmuck, I said, "John, I can't ask you to do anything like that! For you to commit yourself to go into the studio and be solidly creative four times a year is a burden. I don't think it's appropriate or fair. Let's think of some other way to let you reach your goals." Somehow or other, we didn't get back together again. The next thing that happened was Atlantic gave him a Lincoln Continental as a signing bonus, and I never got to record John Coltrane as a leader.

EDDIE "LOCKJAW" DAVIS, *THE EDDIE "LOCKJAW" DAVIS COOKBOOK* (1958, PRESTIGE)
Bob Weinstock (Prestige)

One day I said to him, "Esmond, we're doing a session with Eddie 'Lockjaw' Davis"—*The Cookbook*—"with Shirley Scott on organ."

"Oh yeah, I know Lockjaw," he said. "I used to see him a lot in town."

I said, "It's good that you know him. Why don't you run the session? I'll be there." So he did, and it came out good. I showed him how to take ordinary material and make a hit. I said, "Hear this blues? It's kind of funky."

"Yeah, that's right." He knew what I was talking about.

"Well, I'm going to make this 'Blues in the Kitchen' the feature of the whole album. I'll show you how." I went out. I said, "Lock, let's see. We're running about five minutes a tune. Why don't you play 'In the Kitchen' for about eight minutes? Stretch out and let Shirley stretch out. Be real funky."

"Okay, I got it," he said.

You had to learn what to feature in each album, though you couldn't always figure in advance. You don't know what the musicians are going to do, but once you figured it out, you'd go for it.

Esmond Edwards

I did a lot of editing. As a matter of fact, I learned to edit by watching Rudy [Van Gelder]. He was so funny. When he would edit a tape, he'd hunch over the editing block so you couldn't see what he was doing, and he wouldn't answer any questions about it. How much could he hide? He wasn't editing with earphones, because he certainly needed input from me if we were taking out a solo or a couple of measures. I had to be able to hear it to be able to tell him what needed to be done.

Eventually, we bought our own Ampex two-track machine, which I kept in my office in Jersey, and instead of spending the money on him editing, I started doing all the editing in my office myself. I learned to do it and became quite proficient at it. It stood me in good stead in later years when I went to Cadet/Argo in Chicago and started working with Ramsey Lewis.

ORNETTE COLEMAN, *SOMETHING ELSE!!!!* (1958, CONTEMPORARY)
John Koenig (Contemporary)

Contemporary began [in 1951] because my father decided he wanted to have a forum for what were called contemporary composers. He'd worked with them on movies. Aaron Copland was one of the composers he worked with on Wyler's *The Heiress*. There were others. He became friends with Ernst Toch, who'd been an influential Austrian composer in the first half of the twentieth century. I think that, perhaps, this interest in new things led my father to be receptive to Ornette Coleman and to record him for the first time, when Ornette was getting thrown off bandstands and beaten up because of people's objections to what he was trying to do. To his credit, my father was receptive to that. Nesuhi certainly was, too. Ornette made a little splash with his two Contemporary titles, and then he made a splash at the Lenox Summer Festival, which John Lewis founded. And so Nesuhi signed Ornette to Atlantic and made those fabulous records.

BILLIE HOLIDAY, *LADY IN SATIN* (1958, COLUMBIA)
George Avakian (Columbia)

I finally signed Billie to Columbia, but my new assistant, Irv Townsend, wanted to produce her. I said, "Okay, go ahead and do it. I'll do another one with her later." I should have told him, "Look Irv, I want to do it. I have some ideas on how to record her." I wanted to record Billie again with a small group. Irv wanted to do her with strings, which he did.

Frankly, I don't think the results did her justice. For one thing, her voice was kind of shot in those days. It would have been much better with a small rough-and-tumble group like her old Vocalions and the Teddy Wilson Brunswicks. So that was a bad second-guess situation.

I wanted to encourage Irv. He was a close personal friend. In fact, I brought him into Columbia. There was an opening in the advertising and publicity department for a person to write copy—including publicity material. The department was so small that there was one person running it with an assistant. Irv came in and then became head of the department. He was a very good musician, played clarinet like Benny Goodman. He wanted to produce. "Start doing a couple of things," I said, "and maybe we can get you into the department." I had the endless problem of no budget for more help. I found somebody else who could do his job, and he, more or less, slid into the pop album department on the sly.

DUKE ELLINGTON AND HIS ORCHESTRA, *ANATOMY OF A MURDER: FROM THE SOUND TRACK OF THE MOTION PICTURE* (1959, COLUMBIA)
Teo Macero

[Irving] Townsend did the original tracks in Hollywood. When I got them [in New York], I put them all together, made little vignettes. I took some of the things and moved them around—fixed them up, because there were a lot of short cues. Then the last cue—I think it ended on a high C—I remember putting it in, repeating it seven times. I thought Duke would probably kill me. But he came in to hear the tape, and he heard the ending. He turned to me and said, "Teo, I should have done that in the picture."

I learned production from experience, from putting on concerts when I was very young. We had a big band in high school. I started to write some arrangements at that time. We gave a few concerts and played for all the school dances. After that, I went into the service. When I came out, I went to Juilliard, and I started working with Mingus [at Debut Records].

SHELLY MANNE AND HIS MEN, *AT THE BLACK HAWK*, VOLS. 1–4 (1959, CONTEMPORARY)
John Koenig (Contemporary)

We owned three Ampex 350-2 machines: two stereo machines and a mono machine, our microphones, and a very simple, passive console. The passive console was essentially eight or ten pots.

My father sent Howard [Holzer] up [to San Francisco] with his station wagon full of gear. Those microphones had long cables. They would set up in some available room with power amplifiers and preamps. At Contemporary, the signal came in passively to the console and went out as a left-and-right stereo mix. I don't quite know how they did the monos simultaneously. We always recorded two stereo machines simultaneously. The record electronics of the Ampexes essentially served as mike pres [microphone preamplifiers]. That's where we got our level from.

It's been said of Shelly, and I believe it, that he's the first drummer who knew what he would sound like over the speakers. There wasn't close miking, really, but Shelly didn't play loud. He had beautiful wooden drums with calfskin heads and the most wonderful sounding cymbals ever. There would be a mike sort of aimed at the snare and the rack tom; maybe there would be one for the floor tom. There might be one for the kick and one for the high hat.

CHARLES MINGUS, *AH UM* (1959, COLUMBIA)
Nat Hentoff (Candid)

Mingus and Teo worked together in a number of live performances, and they got along very well.[9] Teo looked like a suburban businessman. He had a very equitable temperament, and he was almost the antithesis of what you might conceive of as "hip" in his language, but the musicians

9. Macero spoke to me specifically about neither *Ah Um* nor *Kind of Blue* (for which he did postproduction). He told me next to nothing about producing Dave Brubeck's *Time Out*. But he once chided me for pairing an image of the Brubeck album with Avakian's name in an article I'd written (and for thus creating a false impression). He was rightly quick to point out my implied misattribution. While it's possible that Macero's lack of anecdotes about these landmark albums indicates weariness with traveling well-worn paths, it's unlikely. Macero enjoyed recalling past triumphs. Much more probably, these recordings were what more than one producer called "free rides." The musicians showed up prepared, and Macero's biggest job was to keep the stopwatch. Notice, for instance, how much Avakian says about *Miles Ahead* and how little he says about *'Round about Midnight*. The quintet album—Davis's first for Columbia—required little production, and Avakian says as much. On a related note, Keepnews points out that Monk came to the studio ready to record, and Macero says little about producing Monk.

Note further that *Explorations* (1953)—Macero's first recording as composer, saxophonist, and bandleader—had appeared on Debut, the record label created by Mingus and Max Roach. At that time Macero was part of the Jazz Composers Workshop, a co-op (and Mingus's album by the same name). Macero and Mingus shared an interest in modern classical music and in jazz/classical crossovers, what was called Third Stream music.

trusted him, partly because he was a musician. He got along well with Mingus, and he got along well with Miles Davis.

Teo Macero

I knew what kind of sound I wanted to get. When I got in the control booth, I knew what a saxophone sounded like because I was a composer by that time, writing a lot of symphonic music and all kinds of different things. It wasn't difficult.

George [Avakian] was my boss. He brought me to the label. He came to one of my concerts down in the Village. After the concert, he said, "Would you like to work at CBS?"

"Yeah," I said. "How much does it pay?"

"Ninety dollars a week."

"When do I start?" I was making only forty-two hundred a year teaching school: blind and retarded kids.

He said, "Come down tomorrow or the next day for an interview, and I'm sure we can put you in there in two weeks." That's what I did. George was responsible for my going there, and he was responsible for *What's New* [1956], my record for Columbia.[10] We did a lot of weird things on it—overdubs, slowing down the tapes. In those days we didn't have the technology of today. So we improvised, used all kinds of things.

I was a music editor; that was one of my jobs. I used to have to paste sixteenth notes into a violin concerto by so and so. I used to do it with pianists. Pasting was my bag. If they gave me a score and they gave me an engineer, I'd say to the engineer, "We cut here. Go back, and check take one. See if we can get that same note on there and put it here on take two." We'd go back to take one, cut it out, and zap it in.

I edited music for about a year, and I did very well. I made a lot of money. I was making about eighteen, twenty thousand bucks a year. That was because I worked overtime.

All of a sudden, Mitch Miller said, "Would you like to join the staff downstairs as a staff producer?"

I asked, "How much does it pay, Mitch?"

"Seven thousand five hundred."

"I'll take the job." Within about three or four months, I was making

10. See *What's New: New Jazz from Teo Macero and Bob Prince* (Columbia, 1956). Mitch Miller was head of A&R at Columbia Records.

more than twenty grand. In those days, that was a lot of money. I had an expense account and an office—all kinds of secretarial help. I produced classical music, big-orchestra pop music, singers, banjo music. It wasn't just jazz. And I still arranged and played dates on the side.

We were really far ahead of our time in terms of how to splice things, how to balance them up. We used to put on the echo right then and there [while recording, rather than while mastering]. In '57, we were still doing monoaurals. When you went into the studio as a producer, you really had to come out with a finished record. You had no way of remixing it. That was it. You had to know how much echo to put on it. You had to listen to the balance, and so forth. Those were techniques that I picked up rather quickly. I just used my ears. If they told me, "This is wrong," I'd fix it.

The producer had a lot of roles when I was working. They took care of the artist's needs and wants. They made sure his career was being taken care of in terms of promotion and the record clubs. They made sure that he made the right kind of records. They were always looking out for his interests.

It wasn't just making records. We were really into it. We did everything. We did promotion. We went on the road. We did whatever we needed to get them in the record club—made all kinds of deals, even internally, with the company. I used to have to take all these people out to lunch, wine and dine them, and say, "Look, I'm making this record. I'll make something else for you—a special track or two—if you put this record in the club."

MILES DAVIS, *KIND OF BLUE* (1959, COLUMBIA)
Michael Cuscuna (Mosaic)

I think Teo was very right for Miles. As a musician himself, Teo knew Miles as a musician, and of all the people who came into Columbia to learn editing and producing, Teo was the most jazz-educated. He was the logical guy to take over producing Miles.[11] [Which he did, fully, with *Sketches of Spain*; on *Kind of Blue* Macero did postproduction.]

As a staff producer you were assigned to people. Cal Lampley was doing Miles after Avakian; then Irving Townsend; then as Teo became a

11. When Irving Townsend left New York for Columbia's West Coast division, he turned over production of *Kind of Blue* to Macero, who subsequently produced all of Davis's albums until the early eighties.

full-fledged producer and Irving moved to L.A., it fell to Teo to do Miles. Teo did all of Andre Kostelanetz and various other people on the roster. Generally, you got assigned someone and, unless you ended up hating each other after the third album, you stayed with the same people. That's pretty much the way staff producing worked.

Teo Macero (Columbia)

The producers were really *el supremo*. They governed the companies. Whatever we said was law. The legal department, all the business-affairs people, and the promotion people took their cues from us. Today, we take our cues from them. That shake-up was about the time that Clive Davis came into the picture. The lawyers took over. The business people took over—the accountants. You had to convince them that something was a great idea, but how were they going to understand an idea if they had to imagine it? We had to make a record before they could even understand what the hell was going on. But if you had an idea, like what we wanted to do with *Sketches of Spain*, they wouldn't have known what the hell we were talking about.

It's very hard for creative people to put up with that mindset. It's like hitting your head against a stone wall. "Jesus, what the hell am I doing? I'm trying to make a great thing here, and they don't understand the music. They don't see it at the same level that I see it. They've had different kinds of training."

When I was at CBS, all of the producers were musicians; the president of the company was a musician. You could go to him, "Mr. Lieberson, I have an idea," for Miles, Thelonious Monk, or Charlie Mingus.

He'd ask, "You believe in the artist and the project?"

"Yeah."

"Then do it. If you have any problems, check with me. We'll help out any way that we can." The producers all used to help each other out. If you had a particular problem in the studio, you always got some help. They'd jump in. It was wonderful. Producers were really musicians, and they helped each other.

I always encouraged my artists to be experimental, to do different things. Today, it's not that way. You've got to worry about the salespeople. They tell you what to do: what's hip, what's happening in the market, what's going to sell. And they're full of bullshit. They don't know.

When you had a sonic concept in mind, say, about using echo, did you tell Miles, "We're going to try this"?

I wouldn't bother him. If I wanted to try something, I did it. I wouldn't ask artists. I didn't want them to feel inhibited and to start saying, "Maybe this is wrong." I thought they should be free to do what they had to do. I used to do it [what I wanted] on my own and say, "How do you like that?"

We used to do all kinds of experimental things in the studios that nobody was doing. That's why the monaural records—even when you hear them today—sound so goddamn good. They were mixed properly, right then and there. You had to work at it. You couldn't say, "Take one," sit back and hope for a great sound. I worked on the sound so that when they finished the record date or they finished a tune, they could hear the way it was possibly going to be on the record. The way it is nowadays, when you finish a date, it doesn't sound like what's going to be on the record. You change all kinds of things around. I tried to give them a sense of what the record was going to be like when it came out.

Bob Belden (Columbia/Legacy Reissues)

As demonstrated aptly on *Kind of Blue*, when Miles said play this for however long you want, jazz musicians tend to play eight-bar phrases. They tend to circle around Tin Pan Alley forms and structures. Modal playing was difficult for those people who were involved in Tin Pan Alley structures because they couldn't think of what to do except play a harmonic cliché over D minor. Now Miles Davis himself was progressive. In college he was a B student at Julliard his first semester. Second semester he dropped out. He studied. He and La Monte Young used to get high before ear training because they could hear the pitches better.

So Miles was totally up on twentieth-century classical music. So was Teo, who'd worked with [Edgard] Varèse and [Serge] Koussevitzky. He was trained at Julliard. He was one of the rarest individuals in the record company, a bona fide classical music composer who was an A & R guy.

With *Kind of Blue*, Miles developed a linear approach to playing—a scalar approach. He had made a limited sound to where, if you listen to the way he played, it's very chromatic. He played against the scale. It's like ebbing up and above a little line.

It's not like bebop, which is very Bach, very contoured, but in such a way that nobody plays up slowly. They play up, and they play down. They play up, and they play down. Or they honk. But Miles figured out a way to play where he soloed above stuff.

Dave Holland (Bassist on *Bitches Brew*)

Miles was often known for what you might call a minimalism in the music. I've often thought that *Kind of Blue* was probably one of the first minimalist records. In terms of the material its basic structure was very simple, but then because of that, it opened up a lot of possibilities.

DAVE BRUBECK QUARTET, *TIME OUT* (1959, COLUMBIA)
Teo Macero

People ask, "How'd you put the microphone? What kind of microphones did you use?" It has nothing to do with it! I don't give a damn. I don't even want to know. I used to tell the engineers, "I don't know about that stuff." But I'd listen to it and say, "That's it. That's the way we're going to go." I had an idea for this and a sound for that, a positioning for this and that. I learned from the engineers who did dates. I wasn't stupid. I'd pick up on things they were doing and how they'd mike it.

I went from there and used my own judgment. I got to the studio much earlier than anybody else, and I'd work with the engineers. I'd say, "I really want to get a tight sound on the bass drum and the high hat. Can we put another mike right near the high hat so I can hear that 'cha, cha' on the snare drum?" I did that back with Brubeck. If you listen to his records, the drums sound superb.

Do you regard your role in making a record as analogous to that of an architect in designing a building? You weren't an engineer, but you knew something about it?

I knew a great deal because I'd studied it. When I was at Juilliard, they had what they called an Acoustics Department, and I used to work in the Recording Department making masters to earn an extra fifty cents an hour. So I had a lot of experience, and I was playing and listening. I'd say, "I don't know if this should be done. Maybe we should bring this up a little more. Fix this and, maybe, EQ [adjust the audio-signal frequency of] that a little bit. Put some high end on it. It's a little dull." Over the years, I learned my craft.

CECIL TAYLOR QUARTET, *LOOKING AHEAD!* (1959, CONTEMPORARY)
Nat Hentoff

There was a marvelous guy on the West Coast named Les Koenig, who had Contemporary Records. He'd been a movie producer, and he was blacklisted. He loved jazz. I forget how we knew each other.

But by the way, the thing he did as a producer—which I should have

done and I missed a good chance—when musicians went into a Contemporary record session out in Los Angeles, from the time they walked into that studio, the tapes were running, whether they were playing or not. Over time, he picked up some very interesting sounds and, sometimes, conversation. The first record I did for him, if it wasn't Cecil, it was two of the great ragtime pianists, Lucky Roberts and Willie "the Lion" [Smith]. Each had a side; each was solo. In the time it took to set up, maybe forty minutes or so, they started swapping stories about the old ticklers, the ragtime players all along the East Coast, and I sat there like an idiot, not recording it. That stuff was lost forever. Koenig, I'm sure, would've had it.

I'd known Cecil since he was about nineteen, and I wasn't much older. We met in Boston. We used to hang out at the same record store. He was at the New England Conservatory, and we went to a couple of concerts together. We were friends. Maybe that was the reason Les asked me to record Cecil. I don't know.

Of course, nobody was going to tell Cecil what to do. The album I did for Contemporary, I guess you could call it a ballad album. It strikes me as some of the most durable stuff that Cecil would do. Soon after that, he got his own vision of what his music should be, and I find it exhausting. I can listen to it for a while and, probably, when it's live, I can listen to it longer because he does other things. I don't know that I'd record him again.

NANCY HARROW, *WILD WOMEN DON'T HAVE THE BLUES* (1960, CANDID)
Nat Hentoff

I did an album with a singer named Nancy Harrow. At the time, the standard engineering practice was to put the singer in a baffle, sort of like an enclosure within the studio. "We aren't going to do that," I said. "The musicians can't hear her the way she is with that damn thing, and she can't hear them." It worked out fine. The musicians just had to think twice. They were used to that kind of system, and I always thought it didn't work out well.

Did that idea come from your work on The Sound of Jazz *[CBS's 1957 television show]?*

No, it was common sense. But I'll tell you what did influence me before I ever did anything in the studio. I don't know how I wound up there, but there was a London FFRR [full frequency range recording] recording [session] with, I think, Ernest Ansermet. This was a big orchestra. There was one mike hanging from the ceiling, and it worked out beautifully!

I've always been opposed to miking everybody, and they were starting to do that at the time.

MAX ROACH, *WE INSIST! FREEDOM NOW SUITE* (1960, CANDID)
Nat Hentoff

I asked them what they wanted to do. I'd seen Max and Abbey [Lincoln], at a place called the Village Gate, do the "Freedom Now Suite." I said to Max, "Obviously, somebody has asked you to record this?"

He said, "No."

It was Max's concept.

Did he pick out the album cover?

He was involved in it. I was certainly very much aware that the whole thing had to be exactly the way Max and Abbey and Coleman Hawkins—who was interested in it, too—wanted. As I recall, I said to Max, "I think we can get an AP photo of kids at a lunch counter." I'm pretty sure we showed it to them.

I do remember we both thought it was a great triumph when we found out that South Africa had banned the album. It was very exciting to see what happened. Coleman Hawkins, I don't think he had ever seen the music as finally developed in the studio, but he majestically rode through all that stuff, and Abbey had the hardest job of any singer I've ever seen. I mean how do you make a scream into music? But she did it.

JOHN COLTRANE, *GIANT STEPS* (1960, ATLANTIC)
Tom Dowd (Atlantic Engineer)

There were two or three musicians who would get to the studio early. John would always be there a good hour before the session. He knew what two or three songs he was going to do. Much in the tradition of a classical musician in a rehearsal room before a concert, he would stand in a corner, run scales and change reeds and mouthpieces, warming up and forming his idea for the day.

He'd record, and you'd say, "That was wonderful."

"No, let me try one more." Then that would be it. There was one particular obbligato or something that he played that didn't ... or he wanted to try it the other way one time, that kind of a thing. He was never an overpowering, demonstrative type person. He was never negative.

What microphone setup did you use with Elvin Jones?

Three, maybe four microphones. I didn't have that many to play with, but Elvin understood that. He'd play to the microphones. After we made one or two passes, to which he'd listened, he'd say, "Move this one over there. I'll do this," or "I'll do that." Elvin didn't employ a monster, 33-inch bass drum. He had a small bass drum, and because of his speed and the double-flex pedal he was using, he was a little light. I needed a mike somewhere down around the bass drum. If afforded the opportunity, I placed two mikes overhead and one between the high hat and the snare drum. That covered the whole kit. If I couldn't afford that, then he'd play accordingly.

On the other hand, [Ed] Blackwell [Ornette Coleman's drummer] was a much heavier drummer. I never had to put anything below waist-high on him. Everything came up. If I put a microphone or two about waist-high in front of him, and then two more over the back of his shoulder, about six, seven feet up in the air, I caught everything he did.

This goes back to a whole pile of drummers—some jazz, some rock 'n' roll—who abhorred more than one or two microphones. They wanted to play their kit, not have you play it.

ORNETTE COLEMAN QUARTET, *THIS IS OUR MUSIC* (1960, ATLANTIC)
Tom Dowd (Atlantic Engineer)

I seldom used the same microphone for Ornette that I used for John [Coltrane]. Once or twice I used a condenser microphone on Ornette, but for the most part I used cardioid microphones because they had a better empathy for capturing the sounds he was generating. It's like wearing dark with blue sunglasses or amber sunglasses. I just thought the one particular microphone had a better warmth for capturing Ornette's playing as opposed to one I used for John on the soprano, which was an entirely different air column. The soprano is a different radiating type instrument from the plastic sax. Even though John did sometimes bite down and want a harder sound, for the most part he was a softer player, whereas Ornette was a snappy, biting player. The same microphone wouldn't be ideal for both. That was my concept on it.

Like John, Ornette would be at the studio before the date was to start, and he'd say, "I want to play this for you, or this is what we're trying to do today." Or he and Don Cherry would be standing there practicing how to make expressions together because the two instruments, the pocket trumpet and the plastic sax, were so dynamically different that you couldn't notate or anything like that. You'd have to play it and then say, "I want it to go like *wooow!*"

"Oh, you mean like *wooow?*" That's how the dialogue would be established. There are some things you can't write and you hear.

When it's not the way you want it, you say, "I didn't mean that. I meant this," or "Can you do it this way?" That's dialogue. That's something you'd try and understand. Now, you might listen to their endeavor and say, "Hey, it's better when you do it the other way."

They might look at you and say, "You mean like this?"

You'd say, "Yeah."

"Oh, okay. We'll try it."

You might save time or have something that's tighter or more concerted if you made those kinds of suggestions. When we recorded, we knew what songs we were getting into, and it was just a matter of getting that quick sensation, that rush when something went by that you'd say, "Damn, if only so-and-so had been more.... Let's try one more."

Somebody would look and say, "Why?"

"Well, man, maybe we can get a better one." You don't want to say, "So-and-so screwed up." You don't do anything as obnoxious as that. You just say, "Maybe when we get to this part or that part, we should try and do such and such, and it will be better."

If somebody said, "What do you mean?" You'd say, "Come in [the recording booth] and listen to it." You'd play it, and then let them say, "Hey, you shouldn't have gone on that chord, or you played the wrong *bomp doo doont.*" You take the curse off. But you're also gaining their respect by letting them know you are sensitive that something went wrong.

WES MONTGOMERY, *THE INCREDIBLE JAZZ GUITAR OF WES MONTGOMERY* (1960, RIVERSIDE)
Orrin Keepnews

Nat Adderley's *Work Song* and *The Incredible Jazz Guitar of Wes Montgomery* were done in the same week, but that was primarily because of

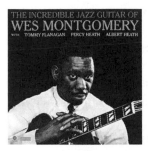

a piece of logistics. It was a matter of economic necessity with the shoestring record company which Riverside was at that point.

Wes was still living at home in Indianapolis. I had no problem with bringing him into New York to record, but I was forced to be very practical and say, "I'm not going to bring you in just for one thing." Nat Adderley had this idea of doing an album involving himself, Wes, and Sam Jones on cello, as the front line.

We simply constructed the idea of doing both of those albums during the course of Wes's single trip to New York. In order to make things more interesting or less hard on the musicians, I conceived the idea of alternate sessions. I planned to do each of those albums in two days of work. In those days, rehearsal was an unheard-of luxury. Basically, Nat's album was scheduled for Monday and Wednesday, and Wes's was scheduled for Tuesday and Thursday. It was partly economics and, then, partly convenience and logistics. That was many years ago. It's now something, interestingly, legendary. Then, it was something practical.

ERIC DOLPHY QUINTET, *OUTWARD BOUND* (1960, NEW JAZZ)
Esmond Edwards

Each artist was different: Eric Dolphy, a case in point. You didn't need to do much with Eric except tell him that he had a session on a certain date. He was a nice, easy-going, very dedicated guy. He didn't want anything to stand in the way of his music. He wasn't much interested in anything else. That was his life.

In some situations it may have been improper to impose restrictions or philosophies on what he was doing. Some artists are so unique in their abilities that they just do what they do. If you want to record them, you record them. You take them as they are. If not, you leave them alone.

How did you meet him?

I'm not sure. My recollection is that somebody came to me and said, "Hey, you've got to hear this cat." I remember going to a rehearsal room on Broadway, one of those studios, and I guess whatever group he was playing with was rehearsing. I listened and said, "Wow!" I approached him about signing. That's my memory of it. I wish I were like Orrin Keepnews and could say, "Yeah it was June 25, and he was wearing a polka-dot shirt."

Did you plan the Outward Bound *session with Dolphy?*

No. I said, "This guy is a killer."

"Eric we've got a date on such and such a day." He came with his music and the sidemen he wanted, and that was it. When we put him with the Latin Jazz Quartet, that was probably Bob Weinstock's idea. Eric would come in and play. Whether it was the Latin Jazz Quartet or the New York Philharmonic, he did his thing.

When you signed him were you aware that he was a triple threat on alto sax, bass clarinet, and flute?

No, as a matter of fact, when he pulled out his bass clarinet, Rudy Van Gelder and I did a double take. It was phenomenal. That's some of my favorite playing of his, on the bass clarinet. I love that sound.

The only problem I had was between Eric and Rudy Van Gelder. Rudy is a great engineer and a real martinet in the studio. You couldn't smoke in the control room because the tars and nicotine would clog up his switches. You couldn't ask him any questions about what kind of equipment he used. They were custom-built, and he didn't want anyone to know what kind of speakers he was using, stuff like that. Which was okay.

But in the studio he had rather strict parameters as to how he wanted to set up his microphones. Here's Eric doubling on an alto [saxophone] and a flute on a tune, and Rudy wanted to mike the alto primarily. When Eric was to play his flute solo, he had to almost bend double to be close to where the mike was set up for the alto. He protested vehemently. Rudy was adamant. He didn't want to move the mike. It was quite a crisis. I think Rudy prevailed. Of course, he knows what he's like. I don't want to sound like I'm putting him down. Rudy was an excellent engineer. He set the tone, no pun intended, for jazz recording.

You served as intermediary between engineer and artist.

That's always one of the producer's functions. When you're in the control room, you're looking out for the artist, and it's your responsibility to see that the artist's sound is captured on the tape as truly as possible, or if you are not trying for a true sound, then you want some kind of distortion of what would be a "true" sound to get that. But it's one of the producer's functions to see that the sound gets on the tape as desired.

Did Dolphy listen to playbacks with you, or did you and Van Gelder handle that task?

Artists always have to listen. Again with Rudy, see, if an engineer today acted like Rudy, he'd be out of business. Rudy was the arbiter, or he wanted to be the arbiter of the sound, and he was very dogmatic about that. Engineers today, if you say you want the saxophone to sound like a fart, they won't tell you, "No, that's no good. You can't do that. It's messing up the sound." Which Rudy would do. Today, engineers are more sycophantic: "If that's what you want, I'll give it to you." No, the artists always come and listen to the playbacks. That's not something the producer and the engineer arbitrarily set up. Now, if they're not around at the mixing time ... Of course, we had no mixing back then, so that wasn't a problem. We recorded directly to the two-track, and that was it. Today, you can fiddle around with the sound and what the guy hears at the original session might have no relevance to what comes out on the record. A lot of times it's possible they would and should be in the studio when the final mix is made.

When I started, we were recording mono and doing a two-track backup in case stereo ever caught on. When stereo looked like it was going to make it, we had to go back and reedit all the stereo tapes that were in the vault and have them released as stereo LPs.

PEE WEE RUSSELL, *SWINGIN' WITH PEE WEE* (1960, SWINGVILLE)
Bob Weinstock

He was the greatest. He could play with anybody, but people didn't realize that. We were the first ones, on the Swingville label, to take Pee Wee, put him with Buck Clayton, and let him play swing. Bud Freeman was another one like Pee Wee, a great player. We put him with Shorty Baker. That's what we would do on Swingville. We mixed people, put modern rhythm sections— Osie Johnson, George Duvivier, Ray Bryant, and Tommy Flanagan—with older-style players.

COLEMAN HAWKINS, *AT EASE WITH COLEMAN HAWKINS* (1960, MOODSVILLE)
Esmond Edwards

Coleman Hawkins was one of my real heroes as a kid, because of "Body and Soul" [1939]. At our little teenage parties we used to dance to jazz records: Basie and Duke and so forth. When I got to record him, it was like, "Wow! This is really an experience." But you could tell Coleman about a session six months in advance, and he would not do anything toward preparing for it.

I'd always been a big fan of popular songs, Arlen, Porter, Gershwin,

At Ease with Coleman Hawkins

all those guys—twenties and thirties. I did a lot of listening to the radio. We didn't have a phonograph in my home until I was in high school, but there was so much music on the radio back then: WNEW in New York, *Make-Believe Ballroom*; there were like two, three jazz shows on every night, WBON, Symphony Sid; there was jazz all over the radio, Willie Bryant, Willie and Ray. So I had a vast knowledge of songs.

I'd say, "Hey, I'd really love to hear Bean doing such and such a song." If I had a session to prepare for him, I'd call the various publishers, get the sheet music, and take my little briefcase of music to the date and propose them to him. "How about this one, Hawk? You want to try that?" I'd have his bottle of scotch there. No, he was a vodka man.

He'd look it over; run it down. "Yeah, it's all right." He didn't give a shit one way or the other. It was just music. He owned the tune after getting a reasonable familiarity with it. And that's just the way it worked. He didn't care. Given the music, he could play it.

Surprisingly, a lot of the tunes which I considered well-known standards, he wasn't that familiar with, but the guy, you could stick the music in front of him. He'd run it down once. And it was like he wrote it the second performance.

What Colman Hawkins titles did you produce?

I think I did everything on Prestige: *Hawk Eyes*, *Hawk Flies*, the *Ballad Album*, the *Moodsville* albums. He did two.

You learned with each individual or group how best to approach the session. A guy like Jack McDuff, he generally had an organized group. They'd come in with material already rehearsed.

Sometimes, you'd give the artist a direction. "Okay, Hawk, we're going to do an album of ballads." But like I said, I'd have to come in with all the tunes. He would not have given any thought at all to the session, prior to coming in.

The things that Mal Waldron was involved in, he always had some of the tunes that he'd written, either for the occasion or in his repertoire. Moving forward to when I worked with Keith Jarrett on *Byablue*, *Bop-Be*, and *Shades* [at Impulse], we did three albums. All you needed to do with Keith was to run the stopwatch. He was totally prepared. He had his trio. He was very professional, very organized. He knew what he wanted to do, and I completely respected his talents and ability. My function basically was, "Hey, that was five minutes and forty seconds."

A lot of times I was a combination of traffic cop, psychologist, and pro-
ducer/director, trying to keep things moving—waking a guy up when he
was on the nod so he could start his solo. Everything. It depends.

You worked with some famous junkies. Was there a problem with guys
coming to sessions strung out? For example, did you know that Coltrane
was hooked?

I did not. Coltrane was a very cool guy: very contained, very quiet. He
didn't involve himself in a lot of the ribald and frantic behavior that some
of the other guys did, guys like Donald Byrd, Jackie McLean, Doug Watkins, Paul Chambers, and Arthur Taylor. There was always this heavy
playing the dozens, put-downs, and so forth. Coltrane held himself aloof
from most of that, and he was not, at least obviously, on the nod. It was
many years later that I heard he'd been involved in drugs. Whether he was
at the time we were working together, I don't know.

Gene Ammons, he was our typical junkie. He'd sit there with a lit cigarette in his mouth, nodding, the ashes burning up his tie, and you'd swear
he was in a trance. When it was time for him to play, he came out of it
and blew his butt off. Then he went back to dozing again. You had to be
prepared for him not to show up. But Gene had a sound. I still love his
playing, and I never felt short-changed by him. In his worst moments he
played a lot more saxophone than a lot of guys being touted today.

Red Garland was famous for showing up an hour, two hours, three
hours late for a session. He was so self-effacing and gracious—that great
big kewpie grin of his. "Oh man, my grandmother died"—again.

You just said, "Okay, Red, fine." But the wonderful thing about Red was,
even though he'd come three hours late, in an hour and a half or two hours
he had recorded the album. He's the only guy I've ever seen late for a
New Year's Eve gig! He was playing at Count Basie's on Seventh Avenue
in Harlem. Big night—biggest of the year. Midnight, no Red Garland. He
shows up about twelve thirty, smiling, casual, with some bullshit story
about the subway train being messed up. You could never get mad at the
guy. He had that kind of personality.

Mal Waldron really surprised me. He might have gotten involved when
he started working for Billie Holiday. Mal was a very intellectual, straight-
arrow guy, very serious, a consummate musician. In Chicago, after I'd left
Prestige, I saw Art Blakey, who was working out there, and Mal was playing with him. The man was utterly fucked up. I mean he was so sick he
could hardly stay on the bandstand. That was one of the saddest experiences I've ever had because I had so much respect for Mal. I thought that
he was smart enough and together enough not to fall prey to that kind of

thing. That was one of the saddest nights of my life when I saw him like that. But he pulled out of it, cooled down.

Jackie McLean was very strung out. He'd come by the office, yelling and screaming at Bob that he was about to be put out. "I've got to have money for the rent."

Bob would give him some money, and the next day Dolly would come by: "How come you didn't give Jackie any money?" Thirty years later, they're still married and doing very well. Some of them were strong and managed to survive. I have to give them respect. They had some mental and physical constitutions.

TEDDY EDWARDS AND HOWARD McGHEE,
TOGETHER AGAIN!!!! (1961, CONTEMPORARY)
John Koenig (Contemporary)

 I remember going to sessions as a child. My father would talk to me about his vision of getting a good performance out of people. Probably the single most important thing I got from him in that area was to make the performers feel comfortable. It was always his practice to make it feel like it was—I won't say a party, because it was work—but casual and not high stress.

There was a great record on Contemporary by Teddy Edwards and Howard McGhee, *Together Again!!!!*, which included Phineas Newborn, Ed Thigpen, and Ray Brown. Wonderful, wonderful players, and they were all listening to each other and not playing so loud that they needed to have headphones. That aspect of production—comfort and relation to each other—is important. Part of that is not being hungry, not needing a cigarette, all of that stuff, and part of it is being able to relate to one another in the studio, both visually and sonically.

I'm guessing that the method was to close-mike the musicians and get a clean ...

That's not true. They didn't mike that closely, but they had [Austrian AKGs] C-12s and [Neumann] U47s and very high-quality, high-end dynamic, condenser-tube mikes. On many sessions you would see the piano have two microphones directly over the hammers. We virtually never had the piano mikes inside the lid. We would position the tenor sax or trumpet a few feet away from the microphone. We picked up a lot of the room, and it was a very large room. People refer to it as a warehouse, which it was, but it was also a recording studio. It had one wall entirely of hardwood, and then there were louvers at the top of it that had acoustical tiles on one side and wood on the other so you could adjust the sound of the room to most benefit what was being played and, also, to increase or decrease the cubic feet of air. Actually, I never liked the sound of that room, because I was used to playing on concert-hall stages which were all wood, and I was playing a wooden instrument. That was my own personal bias, but as time passed I came to realize that a lot of detail in Contemporary's studio was created by the concrete floor that we had.

The benefit of having that kind of setup, where people aren't playing too loud, is that you get a lot of complex phase information coming from other instruments on all the microphones. I think that's what created the ambience that you got at Contemporary. Very little was added.

STAN GETZ, *FOCUS* (1961, VERVE)
Creed Taylor

Stan Getz's *Focus* was recorded in Webster Hall. That's on Eleventh Street in the Village. It's now a nightclub. I did a lot of Stan's stuff there. It had very similar characteristics to Rudy's temple.

The album was thought through. That was Eddie Sauter, the composer and the arranger. That one I did not tamper with at all. It walked into the studio as a work of art. It was one of those things—like who's going to change a Stravinsky lick in the middle of *The Rite of Spring*? Then Stan, the genius that he was, just walked in and played that stuff, one time down. Everything was live. No overdubbing at all.

RAY CHARLES, *RAY CHARLES AND BETTY CARTER* (1961, ABC)
Sid Feller

There were a couple of mikes over the violins, a mike over the violas, a mike over the cellos. And if there was brass, there would be one for the trumpets and an overall, although some engineers liked to have a mike for each instrument in the brass section. In other words, first, second, third, and fourth, there would be four mikes.

They had those great big panels [in the studio]. Without telling the guy, "You have to play louder on third," we could make him play louder in the booth. In other words, we controlled the balance in the booth.

In some studios they had only one mike for everybody. There, you had to stop the take and say, "I'm not getting enough of the third trumpet. Could you move in a little closer?" We had to adjust the person, not the mike, because the mike was in the middle of the floor. You could move a chair in a little bit, or you could let him lift his horn higher or play a little louder to match the other players

Later, with multitrack machines, which wouldn't happen until Ray had a studio in California, he became interested in the studio work himself. He learned all about mixing and setting up the recording studio. He had a twenty-four-track machine and began to stay in the booth and do the engineering himself. We would make the records [the instrumental tracks] outside without him. Then he would add his voice later.

One time, he laughed at me like crazy. I was in New York, and I wanted to change one chord. I called him in California, got him on the phone, and asked, "Do you mind if, instead of writing a G7 chord, I lead up to it with the D minor seventh, then to the G7?"

He laughed so loud. He said, "You didn't have to do that! You could change it. I wouldn't know it."

But that shows the extent to which I went. I wanted to make sure he wouldn't be surprised when we got on the date. That was very important. If it was something between Ray and me in the studio, the way he should sing or what I was hearing inside the booth, I would go outside [into the studio] to the piano and talk to him. I remember a time I thought something should be changed. His first reaction was, "No, I like it the way it is."

"Okay," I said, and I went back in the booth.

But the man had a brain that was moving all the time. The next take, he played it as before, but the next time he changed it just a little bit toward what I was suggesting. That didn't work, and he went back to his way. This went on for fifteen or twenty minutes of takes—stopping and going. Then, all of a sudden, he went to the way I'd suggested. It became part of the creation, and that's the way he recorded it. I'm trying to prove that he wasn't a stubborn man in the sense of it's my way or no way. He was smart enough to figure it out as a musician. I'm a musician. So if something worked, he would buy it, depending on how he wanted to sing the song. And then there was nothing left to discuss.

GIL EVANS ORCHESTRA, *OUT OF THE COOL* (1961, IMPULSE)
Creed Taylor

I thought that the audience for jazz was, generally, of a higher level of intelligence with more access to money to purchase albums. That audi-

ence I perceived as being more aesthetically oriented: "What does my record come in? Does it look good on the coffee table? Are the notes informative?"

By the way, I was going to call the label Pulse! That didn't clear with the copyright or trademark office. So I came up with Impulse. It fit the idea of improvisation. I wanted to set apart the label from all the other genres of records which were on ABC-Paramount, the parent of Impulse. That was Lloyd Price, Danny and the Juniors, Frankie Avalon, Eydie Gormé, and Paul Anka. I was trying to put something together that would really distinguish it from the other packages.

Also, we didn't release anything until I had four packages together [in 1961]. They were Oliver Nelson, *Blues and the Abstract Truth*; Ray Charles, *Genius + Soul = Jazz*, the Basie Orchestra with Quincy's arrangements; and Gil Evans, *Out of the Cool*, which, if you recall the cover, had a photograph of Gil seated on a stool. He's holding a manuscript. It was set up to have the look, the class, of Madison Avenue, to give him an entrée. Instead of the shadowy, artistic type of photograph that depicted jazz musicians as, at that time, moody or whatever. "Oh, he's a pretty good-looking guy. He's intelligent-looking. I thought jazz was down-in-the-basement and seedy." The other package was Kai Winding and J. J. Johnson, *The Great Kai and J. J.*, the two trombone players. All four albums went out together. They made an impact at wholesale, which was then called the Independent Distributer Family, which has sort of departed the scene now.

The gatefold sleeve was a unique physical concept for LP packaging at that time. Maybe classical records had been done that way, but generally, even aside from the graphics, it made the packages stand out. Also sheet lamination gave it that glossy look that you couldn't get from spray lacquer.

Orrin Keepnews (Riverside and Milestone)
Creed Taylor is about the only case I know of where a jazz producer specifically went after the creation of broad-selling products, sometimes succeeding amazingly well artistically as well as commercially.

Creed Taylor
No matter what anybody said about how Gil worked, *Out of the Cool* took forever. It took three days without anything happening, because Gil worked much the same way Duke Ellington worked. He didn't write down

arrangements, or if he did, he came in with an arrangement, threw it away, and then came up with a figure for the section in the middle of the take. He'd go over and whisper in the trumpet player's ear and give him the lick. Then, the trumpet player would give it to the next guy and so forth. Then he'd go over to his trombone players and give them something. I saw him write notes on the back of a matchbook cover, or write notes on a piece of manuscript and then hold it up and pass it around to the whole band. He was very spontaneous, especially with "La Nevada," but when it started happening, it sure did happen.

The budgets on those projects meant that the albums could have been done only for a major label.

We weren't doing typical Prestige or Blue Note types of recordings, where you either had Horace Silver come in totally rehearsed or you had giant jazz players, with no guidance, sit down and record.

Did you work as George Avakian had with Miles Ahead: *record and then edit?*

There were edits, and we did record rehearsals. Unfortunately, who-ever wound up with the tapes, when the age of the CD came, included bonus tracks that were meant to be out-takes. That was the worst thing that could have happened to many of those classic recordings.

OLIVER NELSON, *THE BLUES AND THE ABSTRACT TRUTH* (1961, IMPULSE)
Creed Taylor

In meetings with Oliver before the date, I had quite a bit of input. We knew what players we had. Bill Evans and Freddie Hubbard at that time were flawless, magic. Eric Dolphy! On the date, Oliver was so orderly and everything he did was so well structured that I didn't have to do any-thing except, maybe, occasionally say that a dif-ferent solo should follow or the solo shouldn't be that long or it should be longer—that kind of thing. I didn't effectively get into any rearranging of elements on that date.

Dolphy reaches a new level on that album. As a fan, I try to account for the difference between his work at Prestige and at Impulse.

I account for it from a philosophical point of view. [Bob] Weinstock, Norman Granz, Orrin Keepnews, and you mentioned John Hammond, I believe they had such a high, almost hands-off regard for the freedom of jazz that if the producer put himself into restructuring what was going on, then they believed it would lose its spontaneity. That's why they're on one side of the fence, and I am on the other.

Certainly, Norman Granz was a one-of-a-kind, historic concert producer. With concerts, it's a whole different story. You've got the visual part of the crowd, and the shared excitement. That didn't carry into the production of records.

RAY CHARLES, *GENIUS + SOUL = JAZZ* (1961, IMPULSE)
Creed Taylor

I borrowed Ray Charles from Don Costa to do the Impulse recording. Ray was signed to ABC. So, anyway, I was able to get him. Quincy had also been recording for me at ABC.

Ray nailed it. He walked in on time, sat down, and played the Hammond B3. I didn't have to get involved with that recording too much, except to change some of the lengths of the solos and to ask Clark Terry to play a certain little thing with his plunger. The arrangements were all Quincy's.

Actually, I asked Ray to say something. We got a hit out of the song called "One Mint Julep." "Ray," I asked, "on the break, why don't you say, 'Just a little bit of soda'?" So that's how he happened to say, "Just a little bit of soul, now." I didn't tell him to say "soul."

You were a trumpet player. Did you sit down with arrangers and go over the charts, or did you subcontract the job?

Quincy and I talked about the arrangements. He was very slow; he took forever. He'd show up a day late, but of course what he showed up with was great stuff. I could ask him to change anything, and he very quickly did it. Like "Killer Joe." We worked on that song a lot: kept stretching it out and out, that unison, female riff behind the soloist. "Cool Joe"—that kind of stuff. Quincy and I had very good feelings about each other. We agreed on just about everything, until he went to Hollywood. And then everything changed.

JOHN COLTRANE, *AFRICA/BRASS* (1961, IMPULSE)
Creed Taylor

I just started talking to him one night down at the Vanguard. I asked him if he'd like to come record at ABC because I'd just started this label

called Impulse. He knew about it. He'd heard *Out of the Cool*, Gil Evans, and he certainly loved [Oliver Nelson's] *Blues and the Abstract Truth*. I guess that was sort of the attraction for him.

After recording his material, did Coltrane and you listen together to the various takes?

It was actually during, because he'd take breaks. He'd come into the control room and listen. Coltrane was not a verbal person at all. He would kind of nod and smile or whatever. "It's okay." He wasn't picky. After I went over to Verve, we were still in the middle of editing some of the *Africa/Brass* session. He came over to Verve. I put him in a listening room, and he heard everything. The album was pretty much decided already, and he agreed. He liked it.

LOUIS ARMSTRONG AND DUKE ELLINGTON, *TOGETHER FOR THE FIRST TIME* (1961, ROULETTE)
Bob Thiele

The association with Ellington goes back to the development of a friendship in the early forties. I was really a fan, even though I was doing recordings. We hit it off, became good friends. Armstrong is almost the same type of situation, but I wasn't as close to Louis as I was to Duke. We certainly knew each other. I love a picture that Louis gave me. It says, "To Bob, a really swinging cat." Those older musicians, they knew when a guy was serious and dedicated, really interested in the music. That's how a lot of these friendships developed.

I wanted to record the two of them together. I wanted Louis to do just Ellington songs. The original plan that I had was possibly to use a couple of Duke's musicians and a couple of Louis's musicians. Duke was the guy who said, "Let's use Louis's band, and I'll play piano. Let me be his sideman." Duke and I selected the material. We went over all of his songs, and we came up with the songs that finally appeared on the album.

CHARLES MINGUS, *CHARLES MINGUS PRESENTS CHARLES MINGUS* (1961, CANDID)
Nat Hentoff

Norman Granz was my model. He had utter trust in the people he wanted to record. He never told them what to do, at least as far as I can remember.

Even to the point where, if Charlie Parker wanted strings—and people did want them in those days; Billie Holliday wanted them—Granz against his own better judgment would do it. Some of the musicians used to complain that he'd be sitting in the control booth reading a newspaper during the sessions. But that's when I think the session wasn't, from his point of view, so hot.

Once I decided that I wanted a particular leader, then the leader decided what sidemen he or she wanted. When possible—and I think it was always possible in our cases—the leader would choose someone to edit the final tape so that the final cut was the musician's, not mine.

In a sense I was a supervisor/producer or whatever. I don't like the kind of A & R people I used to see who would, over the PA system, say something hurtful or just nasty, thereby putting everybody down. If I had anything to say to anybody, I would come into the studio and say it to the leader. I would never interfere with the sidemen because that's the leader's job.

My main job was not much of a job at all, just to keep the atmosphere congenial when things got stuck. If there was too much paper on the date, I would do what I think is the standard thing to do. I would say, "Why don't you play the blues for a while?" That usually would manage to calm everything down, and often we would use the blues cut because it was so relaxed after all that tension. But by and large I did not interfere much at all. I made sure there were plenty of sandwiches and beer and stuff like that, which I think is an important function for the A & R man. The main thing was knowing whom I wanted. I wouldn't dare tell Mingus or Max Roach or Booker Little or any of the people I asked to make recordings, I wouldn't tell them what to do. I would just try to smooth things out if there were any hassles, and there were very few.

Charles Mingus Presents Charles Mingus *is a famous case of smoothing things out. Did you suggest that the band dim the studio lights and pretend they were playing a club?*

Mingus did. This is a group—[Mingus, Ted Curson (trumpet), Eric Dolphy (alto sax and bass clarinet), and Dannie Richmond (drums)]—that had been working for a long time. They were about ready to disband, and Mingus wanted an aura or an atmosphere very much like the club. I think it was the Showboat that they had been working in. It was a fairly small club, and when we came into the studio, he said to the engineer or whoever was around, it wasn't quite darkness, but it was pretty close to it. I don't know why, he just thought it was a good idea, and it certainly worked out very well.

It also helps, at least it helped me, to have an engineer who knew something about music but, more to the point, would not become the dominant force in the proceedings, like Rudy Van Gelder used to do. I mean Van Gelder is very good, but he really was a tyrant. I used a guy named Bob d'Orleans who was very hip but laid back. Again, the whole thing is atmosphere. There oughtn't to be anything to get anybody's back up. The only thing should be the music, and if you have either an A & R man or an engineer who wants to run the damn thing, then you've got a mess.

Years ago, [*New Yorker* writer] Whitney Balliett used to say, "It's not a good idea," and drama critics have said this, too, "to know the musicians because then it gets all involved with the reviews and stuff." He finally decided, especially in jazz, you really have to know the musicians.

Mingus had been a friend of mine since I was in Boston doing radio. You just talk to musicians as people. I never had any personality problems with any musician, actually. For one thing, I guess it was clear to them (a) obviously, I'd asked them to record, and that meant (b) that I liked what they did and, more to the point, that I knew something, not as a musician but as a fan or a listener. I knew something about what they did and why they were distinctive. The same with writers or painters or anybody else. If people have some idea of what you're all about, then you are not likely to have any kind of temperamental problems with them.

JOHN COLTRANE, *LIVE AT THE VILLAGE VANGUARD* (1962, IMPULSE)
Bob Thiele

The jazz recording was really letting guys play and sort of moving them along, using my own judgment as to when I felt we finally had the proper take—that there was no need to go further. What a lot of people don't realize is that most of the recordings I've made through the years have been pop records. They were made strictly with me in complete control, directing balances, the songs, the arrangers, the artists themselves. But in the jazz field my style has always been to let the guys play and let them know when I feel they have it right.

My role was to guide musicians with respect to the music they were playing. Many musicians have this terrible tendency to keep recording the same song over and over again because they're never satisfied. The finished project was, I think, a reflection of what I was satisfied about, what I liked. And that was it. The same thing even applied with pop records. I wasn't thinking about the audience out there—the masses out there. I was making records that I could take home and enjoy. Most of the records that I've made throughout my whole career were made for me.

At Impulse were you assigned to produce Coltrane?

Assigned isn't really the right word. I was asked really, and I was pushing it, too. When they [ABC-Paramount] made a deal with Creed Taylor to start a jazz label, which was Impulse, I was already working for the ABC pop label, recording people like Frankie Laine and Della Reese. But once Creed departed, I said, "Hey, let me take a shot at it. I'd love to continue the Impulse label."

They said, "Go ahead. It's your baby." My first Coltrane involvement was *Live at the Village Vanguard*. That's when I first met him, at the actual recording. I probably made more jazz records for Impulse than before that time or afterwards.

Most of your Impulse recordings were done at Van Gelder's studio. Did your relationship with him begin at that time?

It actually did. A few of them were made away from Rudy. I did some recording on the Coast, and I did some recording here in New York. I don't want to be derogatory, but he was always locked in to what he felt was the proper placement for musicians in his—there's no question about it—extremely unique studio, but I always felt there was a sameness with a lot of his recordings.

MILES DAVIS, *MILES DAVIS AT CARNEGIE HALL* (1962, COLUMBIA)
Teo Macero

The day of that recording [May 19, 1961], Miles canceled the recording as we were shipping equipment out the door over to Carnegie Hall. I said, "Miles, you've got to be fucking crazy." That's how I talked to him. "This is insane. But if that's your wish, that's your wish." I went over there anyway, talked to the stagehands and the boss backstage. I asked, "You got any kind of recording machine?" I wanted to record it just to give to the son-of-a-bitch.

"Yeah, I've got a little Webcor here," he said. "I have four pots."

I sat in the corner, put on the tape, and recorded the concert. It was monaural. There was distortion because we didn't have any limiters. It was straight from the mike onto the tape machine.

After the concert, I took the tape and threw it at Miles backstage. I said, "Fuck you! This could have been great. The sound could have been wonderful. But you fucked it up."

He called me at two o'clock in the morning; wanted to put it out right away. Miles didn't give a shit about fidelity. He was concerned about the performance, and the performance was unique.

STAN GETZ AND CHARLIE BYRD, *JAZZ SAMBA* (1962, VERVE)
Creed Taylor

Jazz Samba, it took three hours to record that in a black church in Washington, D.C. Stan and I took the shuttle down one day about noon. We got to the church at one o'clock, and we caught the five-thirty shuttle back to New York after we finished recording.

We did it on a two-track, 7½-inch portable Ampex. There was a kind of small auditorium in the church, and they set up in the pulpit. I sat outside with the guy who brought the portable Ampex by and monitored it with a headset.

My main concern going back [to New York] was Keter Betts, the bass player. I told Stan, "I hope we can EQ this thing. I think we've got some boomy bass."

And did I think it was going to be a hit? No. I didn't realize what we had. I really didn't. Afterwards, I started listening to the songs "Desafinado," [Portuguese for] "slightly out of tune." I thought it was curiously attractive, but I didn't know it was going to do what it did.

Bossa nova was a new genre, which nobody knew or could identify with. It was even difficult for some people to pronounce. So it was *Jazz Samba*. I thought the best thing to do was to depict the music with an abstract painting. Somebody brought this artist [Olga Albizu] by, and the image looked perfect. It didn't make any particular statement about what a jazz samba was, because there was no jazz samba until *Jazz Samba*. There was no preexisting graphic image to go with it. It would have been a mistake to put Getz on that cover because he had such a solid association with the jazz community. I also had a problem with the management of the record company: "Jazz doesn't sell. Why are you going to call it *Jazz Samba*?"

"Because that's what it is. Nobody could figure out, what's a bossa nova? It didn't mean anything."

On *Getz/Gilberto* [1964], I'd already had the experience; the groundwork was laid with *Jazz Samba*. That did so well. It was like a pop album.

I knew we had it in the bag with [Antonio Carlos] Jobim actually performing on the *Getz/Gilberto* thing. Of course, the surprise was when Astrud [Gilberto] came in with her little voice to sing the lyric [to "The Girl from Ipanema"] with that accent. I knew the song was going to be an absolute smash. You would have to be deaf and totally out of it not to feel that.

Astrud was the only singer on that album. Her husband, João, was scheduled for the date, but the two were kind of holed up and wouldn't come out of the hotel. Monica Getz went over and got them to the studio. Antonio had said that Astrud was actually not a great singer but that she could sing in English. And we had the English lyric at that point. So she came over with João and it happened.

BILL EVANS TRIO, *MOON BEAMS* (1962, RIVERSIDE)
Orrin Keepnews

By the time he had a couple of albums under his belt, Bill Evans was a man with a fully formed conception of who he was and where he was going. The second album I did with him, *Everybody Digs Bill Evans* [1958], which was done immediately after he finished working with Miles Davis, is probably the most aggressive Bill Evans album there ever was. He was still influenced by those three tough horns that he was working with at that point [i.e., Davis, Coltrane, and Adderley]. But beyond that album, straight up to the end of my time working with him, there weren't stylistic differences. There are conceptual differences.

He was one of those celebrated lack-of-confidence people, and I felt very simply that my role as Bill Evans's producer was to be a combination of cheerleader and psychiatrist and facilitator and catalyst. I wasn't trying to throw ideas at him necessarily.

The only time I ever imposed a concept on him it was a pretty easy concept. I wanted to have an all-ballads Bill Evans album. It didn't take a very bright guy to figure out that that was a good idea. What did take a bright guy was figuring out that it would be a terrible idea to say, "Let's go into the studio and play eight straight ballads." So I planned two trio albums—[*Moon Beams* and *How My Heart Sings!*]—simultaneously. We interspersed the ballads with things a little bit more up-tempo so nobody would fall asleep on it. I made an important contribution to the recording of that album by the logistics that I worked out.[12]

GENE AMMONS, *BAD! BOSSA NOVA* (1962, PRESTIGE)
Bob Weinstock (Prestige)

A lot of guys who worked for me—Esmond, Ozzie Cadena, Don Schlitten, Cal Lampley, and Bob Porter—knew how I thought. They really helped enhance Prestige by leaving me free for research.

When Esmond left for Chess, I immediately called Ozzie. He asked, "Well, Bob, what are we going to do to start this off?"

I said, "Gene Ammons is coming into town, and we've got this bossa nova stuff with Getz going on. Why don't we do a Gene Ammons bossa nova album?" We cut *Bad! Bossa Nova,* and we did this thing, "Ca' Purange (Jungle Soul)," that turned out to be a hit.

Cal Lampley had worked with Miles Davis at Columbia, right?

Yeah, he was also a musician. He produced "Misty" with Groove Holmes, and that was a big hit [Prestige's top-selling single]. Schlitten was my buddy for many years. We used to go to clubs. Besides real modern jazz, he produced a lot of funky albums for me with Illinois [Jacquet] and Groove Holmes. Then Porter was my protégé. He came to me when he was a high-school kid. We met in Sam Goody's [a record store].

He said, "Man, I've got to work for you when I get out of school."

"Go to college first," I told him.

He went to Whittier College and then he came by. "I went to college like you said. I want to work for you."

"Not now. I've got other people working."

He said, "If you're not going to hire me, I'm joining the army." So he joined the army, and when he got out, he goes to the L.A. area and gets a job with Aetna Life. He's a brilliant guy: research, numbers, whatever.

Finally, I said to Schlitten, "Cal Lampley doesn't have it anymore. He's too white now." (Even though he's black, Lampley sort of tended to white.)[13]

---

12. By the way, the model featured on the cover of *Moon Beams* is Nico, later of Warhol's Factory and the Velvet Underground.

13. This parenthetical aside belongs to Weinstock. Following convention, my comments appear inside brackets.

Schlitten said, "I keep writing to this guy Porter, your friend, your protégé. He keeps saying, 'Whenever you want me, I'm ready.'"

Schlitten knew real jazz but could do funk. Vice versa. Porter was funk but could also do real jazz. I said to Schlitten, "Tell Porter we're ready."

Porter came like a bolt of lightning, and we produced a lot of new artists in the funk idiom and had a lot of great sellers. But then the industry went bad. I said, "I've got to get out."

Don Schlitten (Prestige)

Weinstock's talent was that he liked the music. But he didn't know what to do with it. So he left everybody alone. That worked.

Cadena I wouldn't put in the same category as most of those people. He had a job to do. If somebody said, "I want you to record Milt Jackson," he would go and tell Milt, "Be at Rudy's Saturday at one o'clock and bring Hank Jones"—whatever it was. Then he would try and have them record one of the songs that he wrote or he'd try to get a piece of the publishing and all that sort of stuff. These are things that I would never even contemplate doing. You create a psychological something or other that I didn't have to contend with because I was like one of the band, rather than somebody else.

JOHN COLTRANE AND JOHNNY HARTMAN (1963, IMPULSE)
Bob Thiele

Coltrane was getting a lot of bad critical comments about some of his records. A lot of the critics at *DownBeat* and magazines like that, a lot of those guys didn't know what he was doing or what he was playing. They didn't understand it.

I got with John, and I said, "Why don't we surprise everybody? Let's do some familiar ballads. What the hell, why don't we try a vocal record? There are plenty of great singers out there."

In 1971, Weinstock sold Prestige to Saul Zaentz of Fantasy Records, a company whose financial success could be attributed to the massive sales of its primary act— Creedence Clearwater Revival. In time Fantasy acquired the following jazz record labels: Debut (Charles and Celia Mingus), Prestige (Weinstock), Good Time/Contemporary (Lester and John Koenig), Riverside/Milestone (Orrin Keepnews), and Pablo (Norman Granz). Debut Records is a particularly interesting acquisition. It was a wedding gift. Charles Mingus gave it to his ex-wife Celia when she married Zaentz, though it should be said that Celia actually ran Debut in the first place, as well as providing the startup money to establish it.

"Let me think about it," he said.

I was really surprised. He called up one day and said, "I'd like to use Johnny Hartman."

That's how that came about. I wasn't going to say no. I knew Johnny. He was a hell of a singer. But it was John who wanted him. It was almost like putting a pop singer—say, like an Arthur Prysock or someone—with Coltrane.

CHARLES MINGUS, *THE BLACK SAINT AND THE SINNER LADY* (1963, IMPULSE)
Bob Thiele

I was initially more impressed with his arranging capabilities as opposed to his bass playing. Not that he wasn't one of the great bass players! But I was always amazed at how he could come up with arrangements. That was really my reason for wanting to record him.

He was a real character. Once, I went into the office at ABC Paramount. I have a tendency to get up very early. I was always in the office, certainly, no later than nine o'clock—and on the back of my chair was a note with a knife through it, stuck into the chair. It was addressed to me from Mingus, saying that he hadn't been paid for his last recording date. He wanted to be paid as soon as possible, or else. Which, of course, I had nothing to do with. I would merely do the necessary paperwork. That would go to the accounting department, and they would send out checks. It was scary at the time but funny now.

The sessions for *Black Saint* stretched out a bit. He had a lot of basic stuff written down, but a lot of his arranging was actually almost improvised on the session. There were things that weren't written down, yet they sound as though they were. He would actually put things together on the session, not everything, but a lot of it. So he was a different kind of creator, as opposed to Ellington—unless Ellington was doing some kind of head arrangement that he started to play on the piano and guys just joined in.

ERIC DOLPHY, *OUT TO LUNCH!* (1964, BLUE NOTE)
Michael Cuscuna (Blue Note Reissues)

In working with the Blue Note catalog, I put a long, long time going through the unissued material. There was such a lot of it. It ranged from abysmal

and flat, unhappening performances to some incredible stuff that you'd think, "God, I can't believe this is sitting here just wasting away!"

The most interesting thing is when I started to go through the outtakes of a lot of great Blue Note albums, there were very few alternate takes. And in the few cases that there were, if you listened to the alternate takes alone, without the master takes, you were listening to a major disaster. Only two or three out of the five tunes would have alternate takes and a few false starts. They'd sound horrible by comparison with the chosen takes. Get to the master tape, and it was a masterpiece. *Maiden Voyage* was that way. *Out to Lunch* was that way.

Part of it was Alfred Lion's insistence—at a time when it wasn't common as an approach to jazz recording—on planning meetings and on rehearsals. He'd get the musicians to a point of comfort with the material from a rhythmic standpoint and from an ensemble standpoint. That way they could play fresh solos and everything else was perfect. It's in the pocket; everyone's playing together.

The greatness of those records, of the first-take, and on such difficult material, substantiates that method of working. Some of those records are just so vital, alive, and perfect. And the way people were dealing with incredibly complex material in those days was just awesome. There was youthful enthusiasm and intellectual curiosity coupled with such great ability. Those are the things that Alfred, by encouraging people to rehearse and compose, those are the things that really helped foster and contribute to that era, especially during the sixties.

So you're telling me that, at Blue Note, there was very little cutting and splicing.

If Alfred heard a great trombone solo on one take, and it matched the tempo and could fit into another other take, where everyone else was great, he would do that occasionally. That was the extent of it. Of course, if there was a fuck-up at the end, which happens a lot, you'd do an insert. But that would be it.

At Blue Note, a standard evolved naturally over time that's very hard to live up to for two reasons. First of all, everything costs so much. From a budget point of view, it's very hard to do what they did without it costing a fortune. Secondly, the level of, not musicianship, but the level of creativity in music today is nowhere near what it was then by any stretch of the imagination.

At Prestige, Bob Weinstock had a totally different opinion. He thought jazz was like blues in jam-session form, and he absolutely claimed that's what he encouraged. I don't know how much [of his method] was not wanting to spend time and money, or how much of that was true [based on what he thought]. It's a legitimate thing that some people will say, that some people feel and believe.

Verve was the swing version of Prestige. There was not a lot of thought given to a Verve album. There could be ten horrible albums for every masterpiece. They could have the most inane, fluff liner notes, and they could have the ugliest covers. If you go back, you can look at some of them, and the album sequence is the order in which everything was recorded. That means no one was even thinking about resequencing anything. It was an assembly-line thing. (Norman Granz had good taste in musicians and so did Bob Weinstock, even though they were of different generations.) But like any assembly-line thing, you're going to stumble onto some great stuff. There wasn't a lot of thought and effort put into that. If you look through it, it was pretty crank-'em-out.

Tell me about packaging at Blue Note and the distinctive design work of Reid Miles.

I don't know how Reid and Alfred met, but I do know how they worked. Alfred, even back in the 78 days in all of Blue Note's ads, it was a Bauhaus, art deco style that he leaned towards. That manifest itself very heavily in the 10-inch LP era. Reid came in right at the beginning of the 12-inch LP. He never liked jazz, never had any affinity for it. His musical tastes were almost completely classical music. He said when Alfred got a project ready for him to design a cover, Alfred didn't really give him the music. He sat down with him and explained what the session meant, what it felt like, and the image he wanted to project on the cover. It was through that, that Reid came up with his designs. For somebody who didn't grasp the music, he sure was right on target. I guess Alfred was a good conveyer of intent.

What kind of language did he use?

The way Alfred tended to describe music was to name emotions that it evoked. Something was exciting. It was different, avant-garde, very out. It was soulful. Very funky. Of course, if it was funky, then you got pictures of guys in front of soul-food stands. Or you got models on the cover. Alfred was basically a very effervescent man when it came to describing the music he was involved in making. It would have been a little bit intellectual and a lot emotional: what it felt like. Reid got a picture of what it felt like, and that's why the covers in almost all cases really fit the music.

Any idea why Out to Lunch *did not use a photograph of Dolphy?*

That's a curious one, made during an era when there were a few things like that. Alfred thought that music was great, but at that point, it was probably the most way-out thing he had done: hence, the title *Out to Lunch*. I don't think those tunes had names at the session, but I don't know who titled them. It could've been anybody from Freddie Hubbard to Alfred Lion. All of Dolphy's compositions except "Hat and Beard" had titles at the session, but the idea to name the album *Out to Lunch* was probably Alfred's way of characterizing the music.

There are a few covers like that—more symbolic than photographic. I don't know what the reason was. Years ago, I might have said, "Well, maybe they didn't have any good photos from the session." But that one happened to have been a great session for photos. There are a lot of great photos of Eric Dolphy taken by Frank Wolff.[14]

Reid told me that Frank always used to bitch him, not for cropping so much, but for cutting people through the forehead, which seemed to be a favorite thing of Reid's. He told me that he always told Frank, "Well, the hair's uninteresting. It's the face. That's the thing. If I have to crop through the forehead and lose the hair for a design, then too bad. That's the way it is." That was basically his attitude.

THELONIOUS MONK, *LIVE AT THE IT CLUB* (1964, COLUMBIA)
Teo Macero

If it wasn't a concept project, we tried to make it a unique entity, a unique record. With other record companies, you used to just go in and blow. We never did that. We always took pains to try to get arrangements or something going. At CBS, we were far ahead. Maybe people don't think that the records that we made in the fifties and sixties are as good as those Blue Note made in the fifties and sixties, but, in fact, I think that they are. I think they're *better*, because they're well edited. There's not a lot of blowing and a lot of mistakes.

Being a musician myself, when I heard something bad, I had to cut it out. I couldn't stand to hear a bad solo. A guy plays eight bars or twelve bars that were bad, I'd just take it out. I used to do that all the time with Monk and Miles's stuff. We took out many solos. Some of them were pretty good, in fact. But because of the length of the record and because of the

14. Blue Note was run by Alfred Lion and Francis "Frank" Wolff, who had been childhood friends in Berlin.

fact that we were trying to sell Monk or Miles and not some guitar player or saxophone player, it became a way of doing business.

I took out all of the drum solos. Listen to my records. You don't hear any of that stuff—except maybe occasionally with Joe Morello and the Dave Brubeck Quartet [most famously on the Macero-produced "Take Five," 1959] and, once in a while, with Miles. By and large, they're very short solos. The bass solos are out, too. I used to think of the rhythm section as a rhythm section. If you're going to sell an artist, you've got to sell the artist and not the bass player and the drummer.

I listened to one of my things at CBS, and I told a guy day before yesterday, I was goddamn mad because, on a Monk record, they put on two tracks that were never before released. I said, "If they're going to do that, that's okay, but if the tracks are bad, take them out." It embarrasses the record, and it embarrasses the soloists, too: "This guy's a slob; he couldn't play that tune." The next time you do it, be careful! If you want some help call me up. I'll come in and splice the goddamn thing, but I don't think you should put some especially embarrassing solos on a record, on a Monk classic record. People say, "Oh, you should leave the mistakes in for historians." I say, "Forget it!"

I remember this one from the president [Goddard Lieberson]. He said, "When you're doing a Broadway show, you don't want to put the dialogue in between, because once you've heard the dialogue, that's it. You don't want to hear it again. Let's just make it music."

"You're right," I said. I learned that lesson from him. For many years, when I did jazz, if I wanted something out, I took it out. I don't want somebody to say, "Geez, I've got to listen to that solo now. Oh my God, it's another five minutes." . . . Sure, if you want to make a historical record, and put that on it, great. You leave it as such, but you don't tamper with the records that are out there, that have been classics all these many years and infuse them with bad tracks.

Tom Dowd (Atlantic Engineer)

I knew Teo from the School of Jazz up in Lenox. He had a brilliant edge because he is such a wonderful musician himself. He could communicate with the artist on levels that I could never reach because he was inside the instrument.

The old formula for making records—where we play down the theme one time, then you take one and I take one, then we go to the half, then we trade fours, then we trade eights, and then we go out on a half—sometimes, when you got past the two-minute mark, it felt like they'd been playing for fifteen minutes. It made you squirm. So I know what Teo is talking about. There were times when the energy and the intensity were so high that, after you got through those trade-offs and the drum and bass solos, the impact was lost. You didn't care if they ever got back to the outline. So you delete and go right to the outline. It's not a reflection on the facility of the players but on the concept of everybody getting a solo. This equity thing, which was comradery, was not always in the best interest of creating the most forceful record.

RAMSEY LEWIS TRIO, *THE IN CROWD* (1965, ARGO)
Esmond Edwards

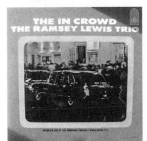

Ramsey was not the most precise pianist. [Editing tape,] I would take a note from bar twelve and move it up to bar two and stuff like that. Fortunately, [bassist] Eldee Young was like a machine in terms of keeping time, and I was able to do a lot of splicing without it being apparent.

When I went to Chicago, and [was] still dealing with Ramsey Lewis, we recorded "The 'In' Crowd" at the Bohemian Caverns in D.C. The performance was maybe nine to eleven minutes long. Those were the days when you had no chance of getting a record played if it was over three minutes long.

Fortunately, you could, however, get airplay on pop and R & B stations of an instrumental. They may play it a minute before the newsbreak or something like that. Radio wasn't nearly as tightly formatted as it is today.

I had to take this, let's say, nine-minute track and cut it down to two minutes and thirty-odd seconds. I did it, and it worked seamlessly. But I had to do all kinds of things, like maybe take the third chorus and put it up front. When he hit a clinker, find the same note somewhere else in the tune.

The tape looked like it had been through a buzz saw with all those splices in it, but it worked fine. I was able to do that myself.

So you left Prestige for Argo/Cadet [who's parent company was Chess Records]?

I went to Cadet and stayed in Chicago five years, '62 to'67. That's when we had—I think it's still unprecedented—three top-twenty jazz instrumentals in a row with Ramsey: "The 'In' Crowd," "Hang on Sloopy," and "Wade in the Water." They were all live sessions; all songs were extended. To get singles out of them, they were all heavily edited.

You produced all three?

Yes, I did. Chess did a best-of two years ago and never mentioned my name. Things like that really cut you. I didn't make a dime on any of those hits. I didn't have a royalty agreement. At the least, I'd like to see my name involved. To pluck my own strings, I think if I hadn't done the editing jobs I did, it wouldn't have happened. I didn't play a note or anything, but I made those records in the editing room. Regardless, while in Chicago, I produced Ramsey, Ahmad [Jamal], Baby Face Willette, Sam Lazar, Oliver Nelson, several Sonny Stitt albums, Al Grey, Bunky Green, Kenny Burrell, and Ray Bryant. The Soulful Strings was something that I put together against the wishes of the Chess brothers. "There were too many musicians involved." It turned out to be quite successful.

Jazz producers are routinely ignored.

They don't get nearly as much publicity as pop producers do, and I think deservedly so. The performer is the thing in jazz more than the producer. That's one reason I liked doing some pop things. I was able to have more input. I'm a frustrated artiste. Like when the disco thing came up, I said, "Wow, this is it!" Disco was strictly a producer's medium. It gave the producer a chance to try some ideas. With jazz, you sign an artist for what he does, and it's wrong to impose too much direction and repertoire. If you like him as a jazz artist, then you accept him as a jazz artist. I have no objection to trying to sneak in a kind of commercial track here and there, but only if the guy is amenable to it. You don't try to squeeze them into some mold that they don't belong in and which makes them uncomfortable.

JOHN COLTRANE, *A LOVE SUPREME* (1965, IMPULSE)
Bob Thiele

The budget at Impulse was certainly way above the norm for any company making jazz records, but I was always over budget with Coltrane. I was finally told, "You can't keep recording this guy. We'll never get these albums out." Thank God, I continued. Eventually, I recorded him at night, rather than announce, "Hey, today I'm going to be recording John Coltrane." I preferred to come into the office the next day and say, "Gee, we did a great album with John Coltrane last night!" Fait accompli. You never knew what the hell was going to happen in the record business. A guy could say, "Listen, you're fired." It was as simple as that.

A Love Supreme was all under John's control. He just told the guys what he wanted. As I recall, there was nothing written out. He would either sing it, or say it, or he'd tell them what to do. It was the same with *Ascension*, when he walked in with all those musicians. They played for thirty-two minutes. That was enough for an LP, and there were two takes. Everybody left the studio, and that was it. He blew my mind a bit, but I was excited.

Were the executives shocked that "outside" recordings were selling?

Yeah, they couldn't believe it really. The first time I recorded Pharoah Sanders—there was just a one-shot agreement we had with him—within about three or four months after the album came out, the president of the company called me and said, "You ought to sign this guy and make more records." We not only sold a lot of Impulse records in the United States; it was a worldwide thing. We were selling in Japan, France, and England—all over.

Was there something happening that made people open to that music or do you think that, given the chance, they'd be open to it now?

There's always some sort of a market, probably a small market today, where people are interested in new things, experimental music. But in those days, I can't really put my finger on it. I found out, while we were really at the height of making all those records, that it was basically [happening] at the college level. College people were really into it before anyone else was. We did a lot of research on it at the time. We found that you could go to a college campus and everyone knew who John Coltrane was. But that didn't apply to the masses of jazz fans. Most of the critics were against Coltrane anyway. They'd write about him, but it was detrimental.

I was involved with what people called the militant movement in the sixties. That's how I got to know Stanley Crouch and LeRoi Jones, who's now Amiri Baraka. We all became good friends. They assumed that Coltrane was some sort of a militant and that it was coming out in his music, which I don't think was the case. I don't think I ever heard him utter a word about the social conditions in the United States or the war in Vietnam. He just played music. He was a very soft-spoken guy. He really didn't have too much to say. I never heard him rave and rant.

3

LAYING DOWN TRACKS
Producing Multitrack Recordings,
1967–1990

....

EXEMPLARY RECORDING—MILES DAVIS, *ON THE CORNER*

Albums featuring Miles Davis's electric bands exemplify the era covered by this chapter. They demonstrate what a bandleader of genius, an ever-shifting cast of fearsomely talented improvisers, and one brilliant producer—Teo Macero—could create using multitrack tape. And that's why *In a Silent Way* (1969), *Bitches Brew* (1970), *Jack Johnson* (1971), *On the Corner* (1972), and "He Loved Him Madly" from *Get Up with It* (1974) are discussed at length in the following pages. They suggest that, while music continued to be made and recorded in studios, jazz albums could be constructed in postproduction—analogous to the way movies were shot on soundstages and assembled in editing rooms. This is the biggest change that multitracking brought to music making. As musician and record producer Bob Belden noted, once Davis began to conceptualize album tracks as assemblages of in-studio performances, he had no problem working out of continuity: something like, "Teo, put this thing we're going to do now before what we just did." Or as with *In a Silent Way*, Davis was content and trusting enough to play the music and leave the task of assembling the album to his producer. The tape loops and brutal, abrupt edits that characterized albums of this time can be assigned, at least partially, to Macero's modernist aesthetic (shared by Davis).

It's fascinating that the large audience for these albums heard, not studio games of cut-and-paste but tracks that resembled the turn-on-a-dime musical performances heard in concert—performances which actually imitated techniques devised in postproduction. Enabling the naiveté of this audience is an overarching goal of record production. That naiveté is what you, undoubtedly, are correct in believing. Jazz is a music of performance. It has developed as an art of composing in the moment. Records freeze those moments, fixing them in amber. It's no surprise, then, that for a century, jazz musicians have been suspicious of technologies for recording audio. To be forthright, Miles Davis's electric bands did not march single file into Columbia Studios, one musician at a time, and meticulously lay down his parts in tiny snippets, later to be stacked track on top of track. Despite the use of baffles, booths, and other means of isolating players' individual tracks, the various bands worked and recorded as units—each playing together in the studio. Obviously, they did not record the music onto acetate discs, as if it were 1940. But they could have. They were that good. The same could be said of free-jazz players of the era. How else could their bands record? When John Coltrane took his band into Rudy Van Gelder's studio and recorded *Ascension* (released in 1966), the album's producer, Bob Thiele, had very little to do, except hold on tight.[1] Editing was out of the question.

There's an important lesson here. As often as not, jazz production simply ignores many of the possibilities afforded by available technologies. Or better, jazz production almost always uses available technologies primarily to ensure that in-the-moment performances are recorded (and, later, reproduced) as perfectly as possible. Admittedly, exceptions to this practice increase as new technologies emerge, but they only prove the rule.

CANNONBALL ADDERLEY QUINTET, *MERCY, MERCY, MERCY! LIVE AT "THE CLUB"* (1966, CAPITOL)
Joe Zawinul (Keyboards)

After "Mercy, Mercy, Mercy" became a hit, we played a lot at the Fillmore West, Bill Graham's place, opening for big-time rock 'n' roll bands, which was unheard of for jazz bands to do.[2] We never played rock 'n' roll. We had the power. We could sustain a two-hour show and give the people all that energy, and yet there was a lot behind that energy—a lot of interesting music.

1. In my introduction to chapter 2, I declared that the jazz album was classical during the first half of the tape era (1950–65) and baroque during its second half (1966–90). In my opinion what distinguishes this latter period as baroque is, as Robert B. Ray puts it in an essay on film, its accelerated "emphasis on style, a propensity for digression, an aptitude for inconclusiveness, [and] a toleration of obliqueness" (Robert B. Ray, "The Bordwell Regime and the Stakes of Knowledge," in *How a Film Theory Got Lost and Other Mysteries in Cultural Studies* [Bloomington: Indiana University Press, 2001], 32–33). These "dispositions" of the baroque are manifest most evidently in the free jazz and jazz-rock fusion of the time, and they suggest why the later neoclassical jazz of Wynton Marsalis was regarded by some as a correction.

2. Zawinul composed "Mercy, Mercy, Mercy."

Miles Davis seemed to envy the audience you had with Cannonball Adderley.

Absolutely. Miles always had big audiences whenever or wherever he played, but he was particularly interested in getting the black crowd. That was a big concern. His band with Herbie [Hancock], Wayne [Shorter], and Tony Williams was phenomenal, but the audience was largely nonblack. When Weather Report came out and especially with Cannonball, we were 75 percent black.

LOUIS ARMSTRONG AND HIS ALL STARS, "CABARET," B/W "CANAL STREET BLUES" (RECORDED AUGUST 25, 1966; RELEASED 1967, CBS)
Bob Johnston

[Clive] Davis asked me, "What are you going to do next?"

"Louis Armstrong."

He asked, "What do you want to do that old man for?"

"You're too goddamn stupid to even talk to," I said.

"Well, you can't do it."

"I'm going to. I'll pay for it myself."

He said, "You can do two sides, but that's all you can do."

I did two sides with Louis Armstrong and cut "Cabaret." I used some people he hadn't seen for a long time. I told him I was going to be at the studio at ten o'clock. I came downstairs at eleven. I thought I'd fuck with him.

"What happened? You get in a wreck?"

"No," I said, "I was eating breakfast."

"You mean you made me wait an hour in this studio with those musicians [presumably, the string players] that won't talk to me? When I go up to them, they walk away." He said, "I'm going to get rid of you. Let's do this son-of-a-bitch and call it a day."

"Good enough."

"What do you want to do?" he asked me.

I said, "The banjo player is R. D. [Robert Dominick]. Why don't you call him and ask him to kick it off?"

"R. D., count it . . . R. D.?" R. D. and five people that Armstrong had not seen in fifteen or twenty years turned around. They were people that his wife helped me get. He walked over to me and gave me the dirtiest god-damn look.

I thought, "What is this?" I looked at him. "You're not going to kiss me." "Yes, I am," he said. He kissed me on both cheeks.

We went in and cut "Cabaret." We did it only one time. He was one of my favorites.[3]

WES MONTGOMERY, "GOIN' OUT OF MY HEAD" (1966), *GOIN' OUT OF MY HEAD* (VERVE)
Creed Taylor

I have to give Oliver Nelson an awful lot of credit for breaking the ice for me with Wes, musically, when he was able to put together this crazy thing. I had a 45 copy of "Going out of My Head" by Little Anthony and the Imperials. I gave it to Wes one night at the old Half Note down on Hudson Street. He took it home and listened to it, and he nearly flipped out. I had to talk to him: "It's not the treatment. We're not talking about the fact that it's done by a doo-wop group"—or whatever the idiom was called at that time—"that has nothing to do with it. This song's got great changes. It's a well-structured composition. Give [arranger] Oliver Nelson a shot at putting this thing together, something you can play on." That's how that came about.

Once Wes got into the studio and started playing, he was beaming from ear to ear. Then, that just carried forward to the A&M stuff that happened after Verve. There was no pressure on me. I thought we had the chance with good distribution to make Wes Montgomery popular. Period. I certainly couldn't care less what anybody else thought about it. My business was to make an appealing framework, a setting for the artist and not to say hands-off because he's jazz and that's pure art. Wes couldn't play anything that wasn't appealing anyway. He had to be put into orchestral contexts in order to get the programmer directors' attention at radio, to get him out to people who could not fathom the quartet context.

Was he at all embarrassed about having a hit?

---

3. Armstrong recorded "Cabaret" again, one year later, for ABC-Paramount, as the B-side of "What a Wonderful World," a song that did not chart until 1987, when it figured prominently in the movie *Good Morning, Vietnam*. Johnston had produced Bob Dylan's *Blonde on Blonde* earlier in the summer of 1966.

Wes didn't mince any words, and he never complained about anything, period. If he felt like he was being put in a compromising position, musically speaking, he would have said, "Creed, I'm only going to go so far. This is too far." At any point he could have said that. Or he could have radiated that feeling, and I would have picked up on it. But that wasn't the case. In John Levy, he had a great manager that fit Wes like a glove. I don't know if you know, but John was the original bass player with the George Shearing Quartet. He understood Wes, and he understood hardships of the road, and he understood how to negotiate with concert promoters. As a result, John took these widely appealing recordings and started getting Wes booked in major concert venues. Unfortunately, Wes passed away before he could really sit back and enjoy the fruits of his talent.[4]

ANTONIO CARLOS JOBIM, *WAVE* (1967, A&M)
Creed Taylor

I went with Herb Alpert and Jerry Moss [A&M] for about three years with the first CTI stuff. It was Wes Montgomery, *A Day in the Life*; Jobim, *Wave*; Nat Adderley, *You, Baby*, Herbie Mann, George Benson, and others. Out of that, it went straight into CTI [as an independent label]. We continued the packaging and utilizing Pete Turner, the father of 35-millimeter color photography. We got a lot of packaging awards, not just for the designs, but really for Pete Turner's photographs. When you bought a CTI album you could send away for a framed print. We sold a lot of them.

Did you give art directors ideas or, more or less, free rein?

I'd give them ideas and follow them through to the mechanical. At the time, it was called the mechanical: until we got finished with it. Here's an example. I was always very happy with Jobim's *Wave* album. It pictured the giraffe—Pete Turner's photograph. All four legs of the giraffe are suspended. He's running in midair. It looked like a wave to me, without putting a wave on the album cover. I always tried to do a one-eighty degree, something that was juxtaposed to the title itself, a visual metaphor.

4. *Goin' Out of My Head* was arranged and conducted by Oliver Nelson. It was Wes Montgomery's fifteenth album. It sold nearly 1 million copies, hit number seven on *Billboard*'s R&B chart, and won a Grammy Award.

DON ELLIS ORCHESTRA, *ELECTRIC BATH* (1967, COLUMBIA)
Bob Belden (Columbia/Legacy Reissues)

Remember the commercial that said, "Give it to Mikey. He'll eat anything"? I'm the guy that got to do fusion [produce it for reissue]. I figured, everybody was fighting over the legendary stuff. I'll do fusion. So I got all of it: electric Miles, Weather Report, Herbie, and a whole morass of stuff. There are hundreds of records to work on.

They wanted me to come up with important fusion titles. I said here was the first guy who came up with a jazz record that had the word "electric" in it. There are some cuts on it that were very much ahead of their time.

It has that swirling, psychedelic, George Russell sound.

But with the ego of Don Ellis. We're also doing Ellis's *"Live" at Monterey* [recorded in 1966]. It's fun because I was able to work on both of them and coordinate the vision. My thing is also big bands from the sixties. Anything I can do to get those things out, I do.

George Avakian (Columbia)

The performer who became a self-produced artist developed slowly but quite surely. When you got into multitrack recordings, which came along in the mid-1960s in a big way, very often the producer stood by while the performer went into the studio, spent many hours and miles and miles of tape playing the same eight bars over and over again, and feeling his way along.

I watched performers doing this, especially at Atlantic, when I was an independent producer after leaving RCA. I'd be recording or editing, and in the adjoining studio there would be a rock band going over the same thing endlessly, driving the engineer up the wall. It was maddening to keep hearing slight variations, while the performer expressed great doubt as to what was usable and what wasn't.

John Palladino (Capitol Engineer)

Rock groups stopped wanting to record at Capitol. They wanted to record at independent studios, and if you think about it a minute, you'll understand why. They wanted full control. They weren't going to walk into Capitol Tower and be exposed to all of the higher-ups there.

JOE HENDERSON SEXTET, *THE KICKER* (1967, MILESTONE)
Orrin Keepnews

Some of the most impressive improvisers I've dealt with were legendary self-doubters. People such as Sonny Rollins, Bill Evans, and Wes Montgomery fairly leap to mind. On the other hand, I don't think that Thelonious Monk, Miles Davis or, to take a more contemporary example, Joe Henderson, ever went in big for self-doubt. So I think that for some people self-doubt—their questioning, their questing, their looking for the better chorus that they know they can make—is an important part of their work. For other people it isn't.

I've always held that the first time somebody goes into the studio, he's the concept. You're presenting somebody who hasn't been presented before, so it's a nice idea to get in as many different aspects of his artistry as you possibly can. I do, however, think it is reasonably necessary—not always, but frequently so—that there be some connective thread, some reason why separate performances are together on the same disc. For the most part, there needs to be a concept. The exceptions to this come about when the artist is enjoying some period of vast popularity, and it becomes possible to issue the next album by so-and-so: sound the horn and attract crowds of people. What I'm saying is, sometimes the mere fact that it's the next album by John Doe is reason enough. If it isn't, you damn well better come up with some reason.

EDDIE HARRIS, "LISTEN HERE" (1967),
THE ELECTRIFYING EDDIE HARRIS (ATLANTIC)
Joel Dorn

I was hired by Nesuhi Ertegun. I'd been writing him since I was fourteen, trying to get a job at Atlantic Records—let him know that I was out in the water someplace. I always wanted to produce, but I wanted to produce at Atlantic. I wanted to do that spectrum of black music and the hippest white music that they did.

They'd had John Coltrane, Charles Mingus, Ornette Coleman, and the Modern Jazz Quartet. But they'd also had Ray Charles, who was the first great crossover artist, other than Nat Cole. Then, at the same time, they'd had the Drifters, the Coasters, Clyde McPhatter as a solo artist—Ruth Brown and Joe Turner. Later, Cream and Led Zeppelin. You talk about a fucking wet dream! I wanted to work at that place for that guy, doing that kind of music.

Great production happened at Atlantic Records. Leiber and Stoller, Ahmet [Ertegun], Nesuhi, Jerry [Wexler], and Tommy Dowd: all were classic fifties producers—into the sixties. In a certain sense, they became executive producers as they brought in new people like Arif Mardin and me.

The place was split up into fiefdoms. Nesuhi's was jazz, Ahmet's was pop, and Jerry's was R & B, although Ahmet was involved in R & B also. Ahmet was really the boss. Tommy worked with Jerry and Ahmet when they did their singular or coproductions, and he was the engineer for Nesuhi also, doing the jazz things. Tommy could do Ray Charles one day, Joe Turner the next, the Bobbettes the next, and then do John Coltrane. There was another engineer there, Phil Iehle. He was also one of the early engineers.

They had an early eight-track machine—which was revolutionary at the time. It was like, "Why do you need that? Two tracks is plenty. You put the strings and the rhythm here, and the voice there." It was an interesting place. Each of the main guys had an assistant. At first Arif worked for Jerry but later more for Ahmet. I was Nesuhi's guy. And Tommy was split between Ahmet and Jerry, although Jerry co-opted Arif and Tommy for a five-year period, when that whole Memphis thing was happening. We each had a realm.

Nesuhi pulled me in. He said—and I dug it at the time but not the way he really meant it—he said that he had kind of run the gamut of what he did. He wasn't in the clubs anymore. He didn't go to the Five Spot, the Half Note, the Vanguard, or the [Village] Gate every night, checking out the acts. He wasn't listening to jazz on the radio. He wasn't talking to managers. He was more involved in the record *business*. For eleven fucking years, I'd begged him to let me work for Atlantic. He brought me in, and he said, "My time is over, being on top of things. You're on top—so bring in the next generation."

I'm twenty-five years old, and my hero says, "Hey kid, do what the fuck you want. You passed the test!" So I brought Rahsaan, Yusef, Les McCann, Hubert Laws, and Joe Zawinul—all those kinds of people—and started working with them. When I signed people, I tended to sign artists I had a personal relationship with—more in jazz than anything. There was a family thing that happened. For example, we signed Les McCann, and I made a jazz hit record with him—a vocal called "With These Hands." He brought us Roberta Flack. And then, she was instrumental in bringing Donny Hathaway. That's the way that shit happened.

More than anything, I was interested in colors, not so much in the technical side of things. I tried to capture the music. I tried to get people who, what they did was what I wanted. If you had a rhythm section, you knew they played a certain way. That's what you wanted. If you wanted something else, you got a different rhythm section. So I used to capture what people did. I didn't tell them, "Play this. Now I want to loop this"— that kind of shit. I wasn't into that. I was more into the painting aspect of things, capturing what people did.

But I will give you a cutting-and-pasting story. The first week I worked at Atlantic, Nesuhi went to Europe. He left me a note. Eddie Harris was going to have some kind of dental work done. He wanted to come in and record twenty or thirty songs so he'd have albums in case there were problems with his teeth or his embouchure.

He did maybe twenty-one songs in two or three nights. Arif [Mardin] produced it. And there was a young engineer that had just started there named Bruce Tergeson. He was in the first generation of the engineers as artists.

My first job at Atlantic was to listen through all this Eddie Harris shit, pick out the best stuff, and make a record. One tune was like a twenty-seven-minute version of "Listen Here." I listened through all the stuff, and I was like, "Oh my God, there's tons of shit here!"

Bruce heard "Listen Here" and said, "This is a hit, if we make it shorter." So, more he than me, we edited it down to like seven minutes. Chopped it up. Took a chorus from here and a chorus from there. Whacked it up. It sold like a million singles and a million albums. It was a top-twenty record.

ROLAND KIRK, *THE INFLATED TEAR* (1967, ATLANTIC)
Joel Dorn

Rahsaan is my fucking credential. When I was in my golden period or whatever you call that shit, I made seventeen albums with Rahsaan. This is where I make enemies. Isn't that great! It's got nothing to do with the fact that I did them. I'm not saying, "Look at what I did." But when you listen to that run of music, isn't that some fucking whack?

Rahsaan did great work before Atlantic and after. We had a little run at Warner Brothers. But nothing was like the Atlantic run! In those days, if you worked at Atlantic as a producer, it took you a long time to get in there. But once you did—once they saw you were responsible—you could pretty much do whatever you wanted.

I kind of overdid it. I got too flamboyant. But with all that, they let me stay there a long time. Those situations don't exist anymore, where you're allowed to grab your paintbrush and do whatever you want to do.

To me, Rahsaan was right there with Hendrix and the Beatles, whoever was happening then. Tell me the other blind guy who played eleven things at once. He was the ultimate street poet, street musician—a repository of history. In that respect, he was a griot.

Rahsaan was really rough to deal with. But he and I were cool. Years later, his first wife told me, "You were just Rahsaan's little white boy. He needed somebody to get him in the door so he could do his shit." In the beginning, I was. I was such a junkie for him. I'd never seen anything like that in my life. But once he trusted me—which was about halfway through our work—he let me do whatever I wanted. But up until that point, I was standing there. I learned so much shit from him.

Sometimes in your life, you get into something in a disproportionate sense, and you become obsessed. There was a ten-year period where I ran directly into the wind and did whatever I wanted—whatever came across my mind—indulged myself beyond comprehension. But with all that, some stuff remains that's pretty good. I talk about Rahsaan, but at Atlantic I made hit records with Bette Midler, Roberta Flack, with Roberta and Donny Hathaway, Aaron Neville, and I had a bunch of other hits that didn't last. They were part of the times. They sold. And I was always making jazz records.

GARY BURTON, *THROB* (1969, ATLANTIC)
Joel Dorn

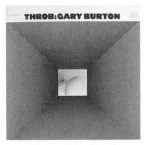

I made a record, called *Throb*, with Gary Burton that I think is a motherfucker, and it's like white-guy jazz, which ain't my shit. I did some nice work with him.

Our personalities were so different. He's really a polite guy—a patient guy. I must have really made him uncomfortable. I was always an ego-centered, hands-on guy. I was typical, I think. There was a whole run of these imperious producers, of which I was one. The tenor of the times was to let lunatics like me do what we wanted. I overdid it sometimes, but sometimes I really nailed some shit. Then it got grand. When I got fucked up behind Spector and the Beatles' records, it became very Wagnerian in my own way.

When I produced *Gary Burton & Keith Jarrett* [1971], talk about taking a free ride! They said they wanted to do it. I was producing Gary, and it was his project. So I got Gary Burton and Keith Jarrett. Everybody was like, "Wow, hip call!" That was one of the things that I caught.

But with Gary Burton, I put him in with Eric Gale, Chuck Rainey, and those guys. That's what we were doing: "Let's try this!" You can only make a certain number of incredible quartet records in your life, and at a certain point, you've done that, unless lightning strikes and you get a hit. So all of those projects, to me, looked like a canvas. Let's put Gary Burton here. Listen to those Burton records now. That stuff ain't going away.

JOHNNY "HAMMOND" SMITH, *SOUL TALK* (1969, PRESTIGE)
Bob Porter

Johnny "Hammond" Smith wanted to use Purdie [Bernard "Pretty" Purdie] on a date we called *Soul Talk*. It had two drum features from Purdie, which is unusual on an organ record. I found him to be the most energetic guy I've ever run across on a record date. He was into everything. He had this little sign he would bring in and put on a music stand. It said, "Pretty Purdie, the Little Old Hit Maker, Done It Again!" If you know the very first Purdie record on Prestige, that sign is on the cover.

I'm still in touch with Purdie. We talk to each other all of the time. He's older than I am, I think, but he's still out there playing. When they had that revival of *Hair* on Broadway, Purdie was an integral part of that show.

JAKI BYARD, *SOLO PIANO* (1969, PRESTIGE)
Don Schlitten

Jaki was nuts. If you left him alone and said, "Jaki, I want you to do a session. Do anything you want," then forget it, you'd be in a lot of trouble. There's an instance where you were working with somebody where you really had to be the captain. Otherwise, he went berserk.

I knew Jaki pretty good. I could allow him to go berserk just so far, which made him feel good. But

I couldn't allow him to go berserk all the way because that would be totally self-destructive. We did a lot of strange recordings at Prestige, but unfortunately none of them ever sold. Prestige was not too happy about all of that.

But I always had great respect for Jaki as a player. I thought, "The next thing we can do, that no one can complain about, is a piano album. Nobody could complain that it cost too much. Also, it would give vent to Jaki's insanity. He can go outside, and then he can come back inside again." By working closely with him—which included repertoire and some psychiatric care—we managed to do piano albums.

Once somebody sees you did a piano album and that it worked, then of course everybody wants to do piano albums. So that's how that came about. And before you knew it, Jaki was a pianist rather than a leader of a group. He did write some very interesting compositions, but there weren't too many people who could play them.

There are so many people who try to come in and out. I think the most successful person to do that was Chick Corea, but at his best he still sounds like second-rate Jaki Byard as far as I'm concerned.

I used to have a radio show, with a bunch of other people, on WBAI back in the sixties when I was working and producing for Prestige. One of the things that I came up with was the "book" concept: for example, the *Booker Ervin Song Book* [1964], the *Freedom Book* [1964], and *Blues Book* [1965]. The first one I did, I played it on my radio program. Roland [Kirk] always listened to my radio program. He liked my taste in music. So when I played this thing with Booker and Jaki, Richard Davis, and Allen Dawson, the phone rang, and there was Roland. He was totally knocked out by the whole idea. Some short time later, he got Jaki and Richard and did his own album: *Rip, Rig and Panic* [1965, produced by Jack Tracy].

HERBIE MANN, *MEMPHIS UNDERGROUND* (1969, ATLANTIC)
Tom Dowd

By then, I'd known Herbie Mann for thirty years. The first time I ever recorded him it was for Bethlehem Records when he was playing tenor sax. That's when I met him. Then he signed with Atlantic and did a couple things with Nesuhi [producing]. Herbie and I got tighter after *Comin' Home Baby!* [1962], his live album. By the late sixties, I was in and out of Memphis. Herbie and I talked about King Curtis, Duane [Allman], and all of those people. He asked, "What would it be like if I recorded down there?"

"You'd have a ball," I told him. "The guitar player [Reggie Young] and the bass player [Tommy Cogbill] are both really jazz sensitive. You'd like them both."

I don't know whether Herbie consulted Nesuhi, Ahmet, Jerry [Wexler], or Herb [Abramson], but they decided: "All right, Dowd. Take Herbie down to Memphis and see what you can do." I figured it would at least be interesting because it would give the two musicians that I mentioned a chance to do a little more jazz than what they were stuck doing in Memphis sessions, and the rest of the band [the studio players at American Sound Studio] was more than adequate.

Then Herbie came along and said, "I've got this upright bass player, Miroslav [Vitous], that I'm bringing along." Cogbill played a Fender. And he added, "I'm also bringing along [guitarist] Sonny Sharrock." I realized, "This is going to be pretty crazy."

We got in the studio and, after a day or so of jamming and running through one or two obvious songs, it was only a matter of how sophisticated Herbie wanted to be in dictating or requesting their participation in some of the things he wanted to do. By then, it probably didn't take more than a work week until we were up and gone.

That group of Memphis musicians was very traditional, which is not a reflection on them but a way to describe how that studio operated. In those days, there were nail-polish marks on the rotators. "This is where the bass is. If the needle gets to the red mark, it's too loud. Tell him to turn it down."

Gene Chrisman, Bobby Emmons, Bobby Wood, Tommy and Reggie all sat in the same place. It was like going to the same desk every day when you're working in an insurance-company office or a bank. They each had a place, and they had earphones. They'd sit there. One might look at the other and say, "You playing louder today?" There was that kind of communal thing among them.

They were very even-tempered and skilled. When we came in, my biggest concern was where will I put Herbie so that they can all see and hear him? When Herbie threw in Sonny and Miroslav, my first task was to get things going with Herbie. When it moved up to five pieces as we added ingredients, I made the adjustments necessary for what we were adding. But I wouldn't disturb the local guys because, if I did that, it destroyed whatever we were going for. I don't want to disrupt the tribe.

HUBERT LAWS, *CRYING SONG* (1969, CTI)
Creed Taylor

I'll tell you how I picked up Hubert Laws. I booked ... it was actually Elvis Presley's rhythm section in Memphis [substituting Mike Leech for Tommy Cogbill, it was the same session players as on *Memphis Underground*]. Stanley [Turrentine] was supposed to come down and do a date. Stanley's lawyer called the morning that the recording was supposed to begin and said, "Stanley's not coming under these circumstances." It was a contract dispute.

"Okay," I said, "we'll talk to you later." I gave Hubert a call; he came down to Memphis. We recorded for a whole day, and the record came out as *Crying Song*.

PHAROAH SANDERS, *JEWELS OF THOUGHT* (1970, IMPULSE)
Ed Michel

My first boss in the record business was Dick Bock at Pacific Jazz. I had been the house band at the Ash Grove. I'd play behind anybody who came in. One of the important things that I learned from him was, "Mix it so it sounds great. Mix it so it sounds good on the best system you can mix it on, but make sure it sounds okay on a cheap system. Play it back on a really cheesy playback system. If you can work it out so that you can play it back through a car radio, great."

That's the reality. Most people listen to pretty bad systems. If it sounds good on a good system, it's going to sound good on a pretty bad one. But if it sounds good on a pretty bad system, it doesn't mean it's going to sound good on a high-end system. You should have a sense of what the record is going to sound like on almost every system imaginable. You'll notice that, on almost all mixing situations, there are small monitors and real big monitors. Everybody will do a lot of listening on those small monitors. You've got to.

I took over at Impulse in 1969, when Bob Thiele exited. They needed a producer, and I came in cold. Coltrane was gone by that time. The first time I went into New York from L.A. [for Impulse], I recorded Pharoah, Archie Shepp [*For Losers*], Ahmad Jamal [*The Awakening*], and Albert Ayler [*Music Is the Healing Force of the Universe*]. [All four albums were released in 1970.] That's the way jazz recording works, especially if you're coming in from out of town. Any jazz date depends on the structure of the music to do the organizing.

I flew in to New York, talked to Pharoah on the phone, and set up the dates. There was very little preproduction on Impulse sessions. Pharoah had a traveling stock company of associates. As I recall, there were women cooking in one corner of the studio. Everybody was a percussionist in that band, in the same way that everybody in the Sun Ra band was a percussionist. Everybody had his own mike, but I didn't like boothing off people.

A twenty- or twenty-one minute side was about the maximum you could record in stereo and have a disc sound good. The sound quality disintegrated as the piece got longer and longer. Remember, too, LP sequencing was different than CD sequencing. You had to put things together so that they made sides that were long enough, but not too long. That said, I had to find a way to let Pharoah know when he was getting to eighteen, nineteen minutes. We worked out a strategy. I would flash the lights in the studio to signal him. Problem was, he frequently played with his eyes closed. When that happened, I had to turn down the level in the control room, sneak out through the door, and tap him on the shoulder.

How could you edit twenty-minute pieces of improvisation?

When people are playing free, there are no mistakes. I wasn't interested in editing that music. It wasn't like tunes with structure. I did a variety of takes. When one was right, I knew it.

AHMAD JAMAL TRIO, *THE AWAKENING* (1970, IMPULSE)
Ed Michel

Jamal absolutely knew what he wanted to record. He picked the repertoire. It was his working trio. They'd been playing together for a few years. We were recording during Ramadan. He was fasting during the day, until sunset. The only real condition was, he said, "At six fifteen, we've got to take a break. You've got to tell us precisely. We're all hungry."

I was warned that Jamal was extremely difficult and ate baby producers for breakfast, but actually he was wonderful. The studio we recorded in — Plaza Sound, where I'd done a lot of recording when I was with Riverside — had a beautiful piano. Mr. Jamal sat down at it, hit about three notes, and said, "Okay."

I said, "Let me run down one balance take just to make sure the sound is the way you want it to be." We did.

"Sounds right," he said. "Let's record."

The manager of Plaza Sound said, "There are these clients we have that do this children's television show, *Sesame Street*. It had just started. I had a five-year-old and a three-year-old so I already knew about *Sesame Street*. He said, "The music director is really crazy about Ahmad Jamal. Could he hang out in the studio?"

"Sure." And then I hung out with him.

He said, "We're looking for somebody to release recordings of the show. Would ABC be interested?"

I got very excited, because I knew what the show was like. But I went back and talked to the suits, who said, "Are you crazy? Children's records? They lose money."

As I recall, the Sesame Street album—[issued by Columbia]—went gold on the first day of its release.

ARCHIE SHEPP, *FOR LOSERS* (1970, IMPULSE)
Ed Michel

Part of the producer's job is to anticipate what the artist wants: be ready for things that are unlikely, but possible. With Archie you never knew what you were going to get. So you had to be ready for anything. I needed baby engineers to move around microphones. I tried to pick studios that were used to improvisational music, and to find engineers who weren't going to be thrown by the concept. But it was trial and error, like finding a good rhythm section. You keep moving pieces around.

Archie and I were like cats and dogs. One of us would walk in and say, "Good morning!" The other would say, "What do you mean by that, motherfucker?" It was a constant battle of nerves, but that was the way it worked. Having a lot of energy available means you're going to have a lot of friction. We were both anxious to get a good recording. As long as we didn't hit each other, it was okay.

ALBERT AYLER, *MUSIC IS THE HEALING FORCE OF THE UNIVERSE* (1970, IMPULSE)
Ed Michel

We recorded a couple of days, out of which we got three albums. Two were posthumously released. To put together the first album, I discussed it with Albert. He was pretty clear about what he wanted to do and what he wanted to say on things. Although he was not remarkably articulate,

he could make it clear to me. We used the choice takes. The other two albums were second choices. But I knew I had enough for three albums. We recorded a lot.

That was one example where I did some overdubbing. There's a place where Albert wanted a more intense and freer thing. He was playing bagpipes. We turned the tape over and used an open track to record bagpipes backwards. He was into experimenting with audio. He was the biggest surprise to me. I wasn't quite ready for everything, but he got me ready.

Were you shocked when he walked in the studio with bagpipes?

Yes. But people were fooling with bagpipes. At the end of his life, Trane had a set of bagpipes. Alice [Coltrane] told me that he used to play them a lot.

On Music Is the Healing Force, *Ayler's girlfriend gets writer credits.*

Maria [Parks] was pretty much a participant in what Albert did. She was managing a lot of things in his life. He was a very complicated set of issues, but he was surprisingly easy to work with.

I've read that Impulse pushed Ayler to become more commercial. Is that accurate?

Impulse didn't push any artist to do anything. I think Bob Thiele had wanted Albert to be more pop-oriented, which is one of the strangest contradictions I can imagine.

By the time you produced Ayler, he was heading toward a rock-blues thing.

He was using a guitar player out of [the rock band] Canned Heat. I think he was doing it because it was something that the band was capable of. Albert wanted to stretch in lots of directions. Like most musicians, he didn't have any objection to the idea of making a record that would get airplay, but he wasn't going to bend over backwards to do it either.

Nowadays, it's hard for me to believe that I first heard Ayler on the radio.

I knew there was a specialized audience listening to a certain kind of [free-form] radio. There was a core audience for the music, but I did have a sense that it was going to start from a point and expand out in time. I was making records that weren't going to sell very well for the first six months, a little better for the second six months, and ten years down the line they would be selling more like they should be. It happened for a while.

MILES DAVIS, *FILLES DE KILIMANJARO* (1969, COLUMBIA)
Dave Holland (Bass)

During that period we were in the studio a great deal. When Miles recorded, it wasn't like today. Very often, when you're doing a record, you plan a few days for it, and you go in and do the record. You know that it's a record that's going to be done in its entirety, and it's coming out at a certain time. But Miles, during this period, and I think often in his life, used the studio as another tool to document ideas that he had.

We were in the studio quite frequently when we were back in New York. We'd get a call that said, "We've got a session tomorrow. Be in the studio at eleven o'clock." And that's what we'd do. It wasn't necessarily with the idea that this week we're going to make a record. Some pieces were used on records, some were not used, and others were put aside, and perhaps used at another time. This was part of the way Miles recorded.

The first recording session I did with him was *Filles de Kilimanjaro*. I was shocked to find that we were recording right from the beginning. There was really no rehearsal. Miles just rolled the tape all the time. That was my first glimpse at the process Miles used when he was in the studio.

Bob Belden (Columbia/Legacy Reissues)

Kilimanjaro was probably the breakthrough in musical terms. There was always the myth that Clive [Davis] said to Miles make me a hit song or a hit record. You've got to prove to me where the hit track is on that record. *Kilimanjaro* wasn't intended to be a commercial record. It was really an artists-only record. They answered a lot of questions on that date. That record was in F. It's in one key. You hear what they can do with one note, one tonal center.

Mostly, what I found out [by producing material for reissue] was how strong an influence [drummer] Tony Williams and Tony Williams Life-time had on Miles at the time, and how competitive Miles was with his own sidemen.

It was a once-in-a-time kind of situation. They had this scene happening. They recorded it and put it out. Those guys were still back in the studio six or seven times before *Bitches Brew*. Once that record came out, Miles stopped recording in the studio. He got back into the studio in '72, '74, and '75, but for the most part that was it. So it wasn't just the beginning of a new era, it was the end of an era.

MILES DAVIS, *IN A SILENT WAY* (1969, COLUMBIA)
Teo Macero

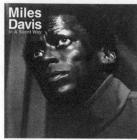

If you go back in the history of *In a Silent Way*, we had something like forty reels of tape that I had mixed: two huge piles. Miles and I went through that shit, and we cut it down to eight and a half minutes on each side. Miles threw out all of the garbage. I'm sure they're probably going to put all that stuff back in.

Miles left the studio. "That's it," he said—nine minutes on one side, eight and a half minutes on the other.

"Miles," I said, "we can't do that. Leave me alone for a little bit, and I'll see what the hell I can do." I built it up to make it eighteen minutes. If you listen to it very carefully—we were doing this with a razor blade, using any techniques we could muster, to bring that thing [up to LP length]. By itself—with the repeats—that's what really makes it a work of art.

Miles later on said, "Yeah, yeah, use that piece, that shit, up front."[5]

"Yeah, I hear that." It was well constructed. Miles approved everything. I rolled the tape every time we went to the studio from the beginning to end. That's why you got a lot of wonderful little vignettes here and there. There were a lot of things that we did with Miles, even in those days. I was recording Miles on two or three different tracks. He would wander around in the studio. Later on, we put three tracks on there of Miles. I don't recall the album, but we were doing that kind of thing. I could take what was coming direct and use that as the front, and then take another source and put a little reverb on that, and then take another one and do something else with it. We were doing a lot of experimental things in those days.

Bob Belden (Columbia/Legacy Reissues)

The music that came from that particular session—the actual date of *In a Silent Way*—was three or four eight-track reels. What Teo did was make an eight-track [copy], what they call a working master. We found out through research what actually went down. He compiled an eight-track master that was about forty-six minutes long from *In a Silent Way*, which had much of the material that made it onto the album master, and much material that didn't. (A lot of that I gave to [Bill] Laswell [for *Panthalassa*].)

---

5. Zawinul and Laswell clarify the meaning of this cryptic command. In short, Davis instructed Macero to omit the "head" or theme of Zawinul's tune and use its variation or exposition, which Macero then expanded through repetition.

Then Teo took that forty-six-minute master, and he made copies that he edited down to about thirty-something minutes. And that's it. There weren't forty reels of tape to go through.

Joe Zawinul (Keyboards, Composer)

Miles always liked my playing from way back when I worked with Dinah Washington. He used to tell me, "You think like nobody thinks." I didn't know what that meant, but that's what he said. I never actually was in his band. At the time I recorded with Miles, I was still in Cannonball's band, but I did a lot of sessions.

Miles not only said, "Bring some music" but "Bring those tunes." I used to go over to his house sometimes, go and play songs for him. He also said, "Nobody writes basslines like you." I did for a few of his tunes which were going around at that time. "Bitches Brew," I later put the basslines to it.

That particular song—which was "In a Silent Way"—he really liked, and I'd promised it to him to record. As a matter of fact, there was a fight between the Cannonball [Adderley] Band over that particular tune. I'd played it at a sound check one time—just noodling around on the piano—but I already had it all together. Nat Adderley came over and said, "Man, this is beautiful. It sounds like 'In a Silent Way.'" So Nat gave it that title. "We've got to record it," he said.

"Nat," I said, "I cannot do that. Cannon cannot do that. I promised Miles to do that." He got really upset. They said, "Man, you're in the band almost ten years, and you give this tune out to another band?"

I said, "Listen man, I promised and that's what it is."

Miles and I worked on that particular tune for a couple of evenings in his house. It was [sounds out the rhythm]. It had to be like that—straight rhythm.

So do you buy the theory that Tony played straight time because he was angry?

I don't know, man. I loved the way Tony played and all that, but he always had a little thing on his shoulder, I thought. Unnecessarily. He was a great musician, no question, and a great guy. But there were times when . . . I don't know anything about it on this particular project, but it could have been. Among the three keyboard players [Zawinul, Herbie Hancock, and Chick Corea], we didn't talk much about it, but there were words that I don't recall. I can't tell you if there was anything in the rhythm section, anything that wasn't happy.

Now, it really sounds good, but I was really disappointed in the beginning when I heard "In a Silent Way/It's about That Time." I thought it was boring: "In the studio we played and played in order to get two good sections and then he cuts them together? Bam. Over and out?" [On the album] there were no changes made to the melody. Nothing was re-arranged. It was just repeated too many times. It was stretched out and stretched out over and over again. Which is okay. I have nothing against that. But the total, original version of "In a Silent Way" is on my Atlantic record, *Zawinul* [produced by Joel Dorn]. [On Davis's version] he took off one whole part [the head]. Otherwise, on my version the only thing I did was, when I go up [sings], I played another chord. Miles kept it on the E. That's the only alteration; he changed one bass note.

What I really liked about those sessions was so many people without anybody stepping on another person's foot. That's a sign of greatness in a way. None of those guys were weak musicians. We were all into trying to kind of establish ourselves as something special. It's an accomplishment when you have people with such security, with such self-assurance, that you don't have to step on anybody, and it can come out as something with three ideas instead of one.

Dave Holland (Bass)

When I heard the record, I realized what had happened. There were other pieces recorded around this time, but it was surprising to me that Miles had used an extended piece for one side of the album. It was unusual, even today, for someone to use the entire side of an LP to do one tune.

Concerning the compositions, I knew that what was brought in by Joe [Zawinul] and what ended up on record were often dramatically different. The pieces were transformed and dissected in the studio. Often large sections of the tune would be discarded, and Miles might focus in on a four-bar section that he would use. There was certainly a great deal of remodeling of the compositions, which was, I know, a bit alarming to Joe [who had composed "In a Silent Way" and "It's about That Time"]. He'd find that the composition he'd written was suddenly being completely transformed by Miles's reworking of it. But this was one of the great touches that Miles had. He could take a composition and really make it his own in a conceptual way.

I also knew Miles talked to Tony [Williams] about the rhythm on "In a Silent Way." I remember him going over to the drums and discussing what he was thinking about for it and so on.

There were little figures that he'd written for the bass. He said to me, "Use this. Introduce it every now and then. Then, go back to this figure." But he'd sort of let you work out your own interpretation of what he was saying. When you landed on something that he liked, he'd say, "Yeah, that's it," or "Do it that way," or "That's the direction it's going in." Words to that effect, but he used very few words. That was one of the great things. He really did trust the musicians and expect them to reach their own creative conclusions, a lot of the time, about the material that he was presenting to them. He wanted their input on what he presented.

Bob Belden (Columbia/Legacy Reissues)

The beat, the groove, the rhythm, it's always there. It's never dull. That's why Teo could cut back and forth. If you listen to sessions prior to that one, Tony Williams was a monstrous drummer. But he showed up at the [*In a Silent Way*] session and saw Larry Young and John McLaughlin [in the studio] and freaked out. And that was the last time he ever played with Miles Davis. So there's this intense anger. It's this withholding the ultimate Tony Williams from your idol. And the album becomes a classic.

My honest opinion, Miles put it out the way he did just to fuck with Tony. I really think so. Teo assembled it in the way you heard it on that long reel. And Miles probably said, "We don't need this. We don't need that, and we don't need that." Then, Teo went back, made the cuts, and said, "We've got twenty-six, twenty-eight minutes of music." And I'm sure Miles said, "Well, make a record." Because he didn't care.[6]

MILES DAVIS, *THE COMPLETE "IN A SILENT WAY" SESSIONS* *(SEPTEMBER 1968–FEBRUARY 1969)* (2001, COLUMBIA/ LEGACY, CD; 2001, MOSAIC, VINYL)
Michael Cuscuna (Mosaic Reissues)

Producing a set like this involves, initially, research—going through every session tape done within this particular chunk of time. Then, without relying on LP masters, remixing everything: not to change the balance of the instruments, because most of it is three-, four-, or eight-track tape, but to remove that layer of extra tape hiss and the EQ and limiting that

---

6. In other words, Williams "freaked out" because he saw his own band, Lifetime, in the studio—anything but a veiled message that Davis intended to poach them or at least show that he could.

George Moore, Dave Brubeck's manager, confirmed (to me) that both Miles Davis and Dave Brubeck were issued a mid-sixties ultimatum by Columbia executive Clive Davis: go electric or go. Brubeck left the label that Avakian had signed him to in 1953. Deeply in debt, Miles stayed, plugged in, and signed a contract that required him to complete two albums every year. Subsequently, he issued one live album after another.

was added during the original mastering. So re-mastering is, basically, to get a better sound.

In the case of this particular set, because the *In a Silent Way* album was so highly postproduced, with edits and repeated sections and loops inserted, we actually included the LP master in the box set and also went back to the original multi-tracks and remixed the music as the musicians originally played it. That means there are really two very, very different versions of the material in this box set.

I don't think Teo was using any three-machine edits at that point. That begins on *Bitches Brew*, where there are a lot of edits that required you, in precomputer times, to use three machines to do a cross-fade, to transition from one tape to another. Most of the edits on *In a Silent Way*, I think, were hard edits. The ones you can't hear are, for the most part, lucky in the sense that the cymbal decay hid the edit where you go from one piece to another—that sort of thing. But the thing is, even with anything as elementary as an insert, when somebody fucks up on the ending of a tune, you always record like the last eight bars of the previous person's solo to get a suitable insert. That way there'll be an overlap of overtones, ringing cymbals, or room sound, so that you can get an edit that no one will hear. But this stuff was all a very new process for Miles and for Teo. Miles was sort of working it out in the studio and didn't really know how these sections were going to fit together, how it was going to work. So there are lots of times where it sounds like a bad edit, and it's really all Teo had to work with.

I'm not sure the label knew what they had with *In a Silent Way*. Side-long pieces were not anyone's idea of commercial. And this is just prior to *Live/Dead* coming out with a twenty-three minute "Dark Star." I think the album was basically Miles's own vision.

MILES DAVIS, *PANTHALASSA: THE MUSIC OF MILES DAVIS, 1969–1974* (ORIGINAL RECORDINGS, 1969–1974; REMIX TRANSLATION BY BILL LASWELL, 1998, SONY)
Bill Laswell

There are eight tracks, and there were eight musicians. Everybody has a track, including the drums. Surprisingly, there actually was a lot of separation. In most cases the music was well recorded. The only thing that's flawed on those recordings is, at points, you hear talking, which is actu-

ally on the original record, and there's a moment where something falls off the piano, like a bottle or something.

I'd think that in '69, nine out of ten or more people who bought records, that record included, would not have thought in terms of edits. They didn't think studio—tape machines. They just thought music. And so that album became their music. They didn't know how it was made—like we don't know how most things are made—but they certainly did not think studio manipulation, tape editing, and finding your result by way of using equipment as opposed to musical performance.

I didn't think that way either. I used to hear the live stuff, which had brutal edits on them. A thing is going in one key and then, all of a sudden, out of nowhere, it's a different rhythm, a different key. I always thought that's incredible how they do that. But what's even more bizarre is that Miles emulated studio edits with the live band. He would do it with hand signals, and they would actually jump from one idea to another on a cue, which was influenced, created, and made possible by referencing edits on the record.

In A Silent Way was unique in that it introduced an ambient approach at that time. It also introduced minimalism and repetition in terms of drums figures: rhythm and bass pulses. It's radical in that it brings those things out and the other instruments float in and out. When you hear the record, you don't hear the actual head that the band played. You hear the phrasing that was played around a head. The head does not exist on the record listeners heard. It does exist on the multitrack, but it didn't quite come together musically; so it was omitted from the recording. The result is the floating around and not the center: people playing in and out of focus. What you really get is, to me, the beginning of musical ambient recording.

The album that people heard was a huge influence on a lot of different hybrid musics, but it's not the sound experience that really happened in the studio, where there was a head that didn't work and Tony stubbornly decided not to play the drums [meaning, to do nothing except keep time on his high hat]. Those things went into creating an event which was captured on tape, and which was accidental, mistake-orientated, and mood-oriented. It does not necessarily adhere to composition and to doing your best. Another kind of energy determined the end result.

Some people are looking for what they believe is the absolute perfect

performance. Sometimes that judgment gets replaced by something that's totally irrelevant to the original concept—as like a mistake.

If you look at the way sampling, DJ culture, and hip-hop is done, the worst thing that can happen is someone has all the music prepared. The best thing that can happen is there's intuition and people feeding off ideas they're hearing for the first time, which means they're responding creatively, spontaneously, artistically, and naturally, without too much premeditated thought toward structure, composition, or even rules—especially rules.

Craig Street (Blue Note)

I can't imagine having to edit on tape anymore, but, that said, Teo's work as an editor is a major influence on how I approach music. Being a kid—hearing those edits and not knowing that they were edits; being ten and thinking, "That's how cymbals sound. They just stop." Having no understanding that someone physically cut the tape, that it was another piece of tape after the edit, even though it didn't sound that way to me, that was beautiful. It felt like music. It was there, and I believed the performance.

MILES DAVIS, *BITCHES BREW* (1970, COLUMBIA; REISSUE BOX, 2004, COLUMBIA/LEGACY)
Teo Macero

Now and then, Miles got his back up and created some problem. One time, that might have been *Bitches Brew*, we had a fucking battle in the studio. We didn't physically fight. He wanted me to fire my secretary. I said, "Fuck you. I'm not going to do that! She'll do anything for you, Miles. She'll give you the goddamn world. I'm not going to fire her. She's a great secretary, and she loves you."

"Fire that bitch!" He called up the president [Goddard Lieberson] and tried to get her fired. We went at it tooth-and-nail in the studio.

Then, I called up Mr. Lieberson and said, "I've got a problem."

He asked, "Is there anything I can do?"

"No," I said, "I think I can solve it." Miles started to pack up to leave the studio. I told him, "Goodbye." Then he made an about face, came back in, and took out his trumpet. We turned on the machines.

He said, "Come on out here, you white motherfucker."

"If I come out there, I'm going to fall all over you." But finally, I went out in the studio, and I stood shoulder to shoulder with the son of a bitch for the whole session. I pressed his shoulder against mine. That's how we made the record.

Sometimes the artists get crazy. I'd say, "Jesus Christ, what more can we do for you?" I got him a million-dollar contract.

When it's all said and done, though, Miles was very generous. He gave me a big fur coat one time for Christmas. He gave me a lot of gifts.

Bob Belden (Columbia/Legacy Reissues)

Let me say, Teo was offered the job of doing all this stuff [i.e., the reissues]. He was offered big bucks and a carte blanche. All Legacy wanted was for Cuscuna and me to work with him, to be kind of like his seconds: [do things like] "That's not the right title, Teo. It's this title. That's not John McLaughlin. That's Sonny Sharrock. Or that's not Chick; that's Herbie." Little stuff like that. He didn't want to have anything to do with us. Then, anything we did, he'd call one of us and scream—physically threaten us.

The irony of it was, we all liked the guy. He was a very charming, very intelligent guy, who, unfortunately, made his living as a second banana, but then wanted everybody to go, "He's the reason why this stuff happened." More than anything, what he was afraid of was that we'd find out what his whole function was. In some cases he was a major player. In other cases he was just there, along for the ride.

When the decision is made to create a box set around a particular era, a particular time frame, the producer's first role is to define the period you're dealing with. In the case of *Bitches Brew*, we had a choice because, about a year earlier, we had redone many of the LPs from that period on CD for Japan. That gave us a chance to look at all the master tapes. And the master tapes, because those records were so popular, were completely beat up. Actual sections of tape were missing because of oxidation; the magnetic particles disintegrated. You'd look up at the tape, and it would be clear for about a second. When we realized we had some pretty bogus masters, we decided we had to remix and recreate *Bitches Brew*. That's when it really got to be a producer's job.

We tried to adhere to the sound as close as we could: to get the balance and the perspective of the instruments that were on the original. Because of digital technology and the fact that we didn't go so deep into process-land, the sound was made clearer. The instruments are better defined.

The original *Bitches Brew* was released on LP [1970]. They started making copies of that LP master by 1972. For the most part, what the foreign entities were given was a second- or third-generation copy of the LP master. Then they recopied that copy and made all of their foreign masters from that, ending up with fourth- or fifth-generation copies. The CD that was out [when the reissue appeared]—the clamshell—was from a quad master, and it was a third- or fourth-generation dump. So albums had no high end or low end.

But what I found out [readying the recording for reissue] was how much of an influence Miles had on the sessions. He was directing the band to start and stop. He was even saying to Teo, "You can put this part and edit it onto this part." He was telling Teo what to do. For some reason, this record is just a little bit ... Miles has got a little more intensity—his focus on it.... *Bitches Brew* is not just about what album was issued. It was really the crystallization of this process he was developing as a composer and arranger.

At that time, because of a lot of the rock 'n' roll stuff going on, because Miles's new wife [Betty Mabry] was laying stuff on him, and because Columbia was suddenly a Nehru-jacket kind of company, I think Teo was able to say to Miles, "This is what's happening." Somebody was telling Miles what was really happening. Some people say it was Tony [Williams]. Some people say it was Betty Mabry. Since Miles was not around, I couldn't ask him. But apparently he got enough information.

I found out through Harvey Brooks that *Bitches Brew*, the character of that date was set by a Betty Mabry demo, one with [John] McLaughlin, Larry Young, Joe Zawinul, Mitch Mitchell, and Harvey Brooks. Betty was traveling with Miles. She was influencing him. She was hip. Keep in mind, it was 1968. She was way ahead of her time, and she was in over her head at the same time. From that crossover period—from soul and rock—Miles took the rhythm, and he took an element of the harmonic language which was kind of a triadic approach. By the time he got to *Bitches Brew* he had perverted that triadic approach, and it became this polychordal jungle.

Dave Holland (Bass)

Miles would take a tune that somebody brought in, and he might use only the bass line or only part of the bass line. I remember Wayne [Shorter] brought in the tune "Sanctuary," which had a lot of chord structure to it. And Miles basically reduced everything to a pedal tone that the bass played, a D pedal, underneath everything. And the melody floated over that. So that completely deconstructed the song. This was a technique I saw Miles do many times. There were a lot pieces that he reworked and did that to and just took a section of it.

Teo Macero

I did a concert—the Isle of Wight. It was 1970. Every major group in the world was there in England. I was in charge of recording all those artists: Jimi Hendrix; Emerson, Lake and Palmer; Ten Years After; the Who.

Before they went on, I'd go into this wagon where they were sitting. I used to wear a sweater—very conservative dresser—and everybody would say, "Hey, you don't belong in here, man. Leave us alone!"

They were smoking some joints, and I don't know what-the-hell else. I'd say, "Looka here, I'm a producer for CBS."

"We don't give a shit, man. Get the fuck out of here!"

"But look," I said, "I've got to record you in about twenty minutes. It would be nice if you'd give me some information so I don't make any mistakes."

The cat would say, "What do you do, man? Who are you?"

"Well, I work with Miles Davis."

He says, "You do? Did you produce that *Bitches Brew* record?"

"Yeah," I said. Every rock artist in the world knew that record! So I'd walk in the door: "I'm the producer of *Bitches Brew*."

They'd say, "Hey, come on in, man. Sit down and smoke a joint."

I'd say, "No, thanks. I got too much on my mind. We got three separate crews out there. We've been working twenty-four hours a day for six or seven days."[7]

YUSEF LATEEF, *THE DIVERSE YUSEF LATEEF* (1970, ATLANTIC)
Joel Dorn

I'd say to Yusef, "We're going to do an album of your impressions of Detroit when you were growing up." Or I'd say, "I want to use other rhythm players," or "I want background voices." With him, more than with anybody, I'd say,

---

7. True confession: One time, when I spoke with Teo Macero, I shared my enthusiasm for his creative editing on *A Tribute to Jack Johnson*, Miles Davis's recording released in 1971. Macero was among the first and best "producers" in the way that designation is now used inside hip-hop and much pop music. Beginning with Davis's "Circle in the Round" (1967), Macero stitched and sequenced tracks from snippets of raw materials recorded in the studio. He told me the story related above, but he recalled that musicians at the Isle of Wight Festival (August 1970) had admired him not for *Bitches Brew* (released in April 1970) but for *Jack Johnson* (released in February 1971). My friend Philip Mosley made me aware of the error in chronology. I have therefore substituted *Bitches Brew* for *Jack Johnson*, much like Macero would have "fixed" a fluffed note or a bad phrase in postproduction. My confession provides an occasion to emphasize one hazard of oral histories.

"Here's what we're going to do." And Yusef would return with material that fit the criteria.

The first one we called *The Diverse Yusef Lateef*, because we took an example of each thing that he'd been successful with on record prior to coming to Atlantic. I was a jazz disk jockey for six, seven years in Philly. I was into breaking records. I had a top-forty jazz show, with a dose of good taste here and there. I knew which older cuts of Yusef's had worked. Even if they weren't hits, I knew that they would be the ones to get airplay.

So one thing was impressions of Detroit. Another was variations on the blues. Another, a suite written for the sixteen-track tape recorder we'd just gotten at Atlantic. Still another was radio fantasies, *Part of the Search*, where he was in a time machine. A lot of people hated what I did, but in retrospect, you couldn't force Yusef or Rahsaan to do something they didn't want to do, even if you hit 'em with a fungo bat.

Sometimes, Yusef was open even when he didn't know what the project was. He let me do shit. Rahsaan was stricter. Yusef sometimes said, "Let's see what happens." There were some things I did with him that seem forced, some things that weren't successful, but there were also some great paintings.

He's an interesting guy and a thrill to work with. My dream was to make an album with Yusef and Rahsaan together. Rahsaan was into it. Yusef wasn't. I didn't know what it was. Rahsaan was crude sometimes, talked about drugs onstage, and Yusef was a very traditional Muslim. He adhered to the Word, 100 percent.

Later, he said he didn't remember the duet project, and I'm sure he didn't. He was honest. By the time Yusef said he wanted to do it, Rahsaan had suffered a stroke. That's the only album I regret not making. There were others I wanted to make that never got made, but that was really the one that I think would have been un-fucking believable—no matter how it turned out.

I was hanging out one night with George Harrison and Lamont Dozier, of Holland-Dozier-Holland. We had one of the farthest-out conversations. At one point, it was really wild, we said simultaneously, "Didn't you think it was never going to end?"

I thought that, when I was sixty-five, me and Rahsaan, Yusef, and Fathead [David "Fathead" Newman] would still be making records at Atlantic in the studio next to the office. Lamont Dozier said, when it was over in Detroit, he thought somebody had pulled out the fucking rug. For me, when I saw that, it was different. There were people working at the record company who had jobs. I didn't know what a project coordinator did. Producers used to do everything. So it became a different place. There was no room for me, and I was gone. I left before they threw me through a window.

By the mid-seventies, the guys who knew how to do this shit figured out that it was a business. Conglomerates started coming in the late sixties. They were buying futures. So TransAmerica bought United Artists Records. Seven Arts bought Warners, and this parking lot bought that pharmacy company. It started getting gobbled up. By the mid-seventies, it was the "music business." It was no longer this hip cottage industry full of colorful characters. There were cats graduating from different law schools coming in as entertainment lawyers. There were guys with MBAs who were coming in to run the companies. It wasn't a bunch of Jews with cigars anymore.

CHARLES EARLAND, *BLACK TALK!* (1970, PRESTIGE)
Bob Porter

When Don Schlitten officially became recording director at Prestige, after the departure of Cal Lampley, he hired me to work the soul jazz roster. He wasn't interested in it. He had his own artists: Jaki Byard, Booker Ervin, people like that. I started in 1968, but the first record date I ever went to was one of Esmond Edwards's [early sixties] sessions. I was a twenty-two-year-old college kid, and he treated me like an equal. I think it was largely because I was probably the only white guy who asked him about Gene Ammons. Esmond was a real mentor to me.

I signed Rusty Bryant, Billy Butler, and an organist named Sonny Phillips, but we needed to find another good, solid organ player. I still had Johnny "Hammond" Smith on the roster, but we needed a powerhouse. Charlie [Earland] was working with [saxophonist] Lou Donaldson, and at one point Schlitten and I went to a benefit, and Lou played there. Earland was in the group, and Schlitten mentioned to me that Charlie would be a good organ player I should check out.

I had become very tight with [tenor saxophonist] Houston Person. I was recording him. He lived in Newark. I lived in Bergenfield. We hung out a lot when he wasn't working. We went down to the Key Club one night to hear Lou Donaldson's quartet. He had trumpet, organ, and drums. He had no guitar in the working band, although they used guitar on his records.

Charlie Earland blew my head off. He was in the Groove Holmes tradition, a real powerhouse player. But he was even more so, I think, than Groove. I talked to him that day and said, "Let's do a deal." He was up for it, and we recorded him, I believe it was December '69, the first time.

Let me say one thing about producing jazz records. There are a lot of different ways to do it. In my way, most of the work is done before the session. That is to say, you come up with a band; you come up with a concept. The concept was Charlie bringing in a few tunes. I suggested Houston Person, who Charlie had known and worked with on some gigs, and Virgil Jones, who had worked with Houston on Johnny "Hammond" Smith records and would become like the house trumpet player at Prestige for two or three years. Then we used Lou's band, the one Charlie was recording with: Melvin Sparks on guitar and Idris Muhammad on drums.

My contribution to *Black Talk* was two things. I asked for a short, fast blues for radio play. That's where "The Mighty Burner" came from. Charlie came up with it on the date. The other stuff, he came in with. The big tune turned out to be "More Today than Yesterday," which ultimately was eleven minutes long. My contribution to that particular track was to say, "Let's have no horn solos. The horns have lines to play, and Virgil has a muted thing on the intro. But solos might make it be too long." I was right. With just guitar and organ solos, it was eleven minutes long.

One other thing is that "More Today than Yesterday," great as we all knew it was, wasn't our first shot. We put out a single with "The Mighty Burner" on one side, and on the other side was an edited version of "Black Talk." The title track—"Black Talk"—is actually "Eleanor Rigby." It came about because Charlie and Houston had worked a gig down on the Jersey shore, I guess, the weekend before the record date. They came in and we were very positive about the way it worked on the gig. So we did it on the record date.

In reality we had [pressed] a single at the same time the album was happening, but the single wasn't getting played. What was getting played on radio was the eleven-minute version of "More Today than Yesterday"!

I should mention that "The Mighty Burner" was named for a Philadelphia disc jockey named Sonny Hopson, who was very tight, not only with Charlie but with Charlie's manager, Leon "Cannonball" Fisher. Hopson broke that record—wide open. From Philly, it spread to Chicago to L.A. and Detroit. Those were our breakout markets. If we were selling records in any two of those markets, we could have a hit. They had radio that sold records in those towns. That's how it got off the ground and really launched Charlie.

I don't know what it sold. I left Prestige at the end of '71, and it was at about one hundred twenty thousand then, and it was still selling. My guess is that it probably ended up over two hundred thousand. Studio costs, musician costs, even mastering costs totaled twenty-one hundred bucks. Sounds wild doesn't it?

FREDDIE HUBBARD, *RED CLAY* (1970, CTI)
John Snyder (CTI)

I didn't see Creed much in the studio, but I saw him a lot as he dealt with artists. He was the quintessential auteur. He controlled everything. Musicians were hired for a particular purpose, and they were respected. Many times, when I was sitting in my office, George Benson, Deodato, Freddie, or somebody would come in and complain. "Creed doesn't give me enough attention. Creed makes me play songs I don't know, don't like. Creed won't let me choose musicians."

On Creed's behalf, I'll say that all those records sold well. He made a gigantic success of that label. The reasons it failed were not musical. They were strictly business reasons, bad choices. Musically, Creed created a very homogeneous approach. It was not so much about the essence of jazz. It was an idea about taking some of the characteristics of jazz and polishing them—really perfecting them. Having a production that provides consistency and accessibility doesn't really stretch your mental capacity too far, but it is done by all experts.

He developed his point of view over time. Also, when you're working on staff for a record company, you play the cards you're dealt. I'm sure those cards were dealt to him. I'm not sure, but I assume it.

I don't know exactly what role he played in the studio, but he was, generally, a calming influence because he didn't get rattled easily. He didn't raise his voice, and he had great taste of a specific sort. There are people who will argue with CTI forever, but for example that first record Freddie made, *Red Clay*, became an essential jazz record. It was, therefore, not that much different from the record Freddie made on Blue Note probably six months or a year before that. He saw the Blue Note record sell fifteen thousand units; on CTI he could sell a hundred and fifty thousand. So that's not all Freddie. That's packaging, that's attitude, and it's respect. It's also part of a bigger picture, and Creed was the one painting that canvas.

HOWARD ROBERTS, *ANTELOPE FREEWAY* (1971, IMPULSE)
Ed Michel

At Impulse the guy across the hall from me was Bill Szymczyk, who was a rock 'n' roll engineer starting out as a producer. Hanging with Bill made me tremendously aware of the sound of things in a way I hadn't been aware before.[8]

I came up hanging out with musicians and going to record dates with musicians sitting around and saying, "How come I can hear the cymbals real good in the studio, but when I hear the tape played back, I can't hear them?" They'd ask the producer the same question.

Szymczyk influenced me in a way that no jazz producer ever had. The substantial way that recording changed in the mid-sixties, with the Beatles, really opened me up. You could hear parts better on rock 'n' roll records than you could on jazz records. Why? A lot more time was spent on the recording.

My idea of what records should sound like was Les Koenig's Contemporary Records, which were very carefully done, beautifully put together. I grew up in Radio Recorders in L.A. which was a great studio where they did all kinds of production work. I thought I knew something about sound, but rock-'n'-roll recording was better in a lot of ways. More time was spent. More care was taken, especially on bass and drums. I learned something from that.

Antelope Freeway happened because Szymczyk wanted to coproduce an album with me. It can't make up its mind whether it's a jazz album or a rock-'n'-roll album. The Firesign Theatre was not far from our minds at any time. It was actually done fairly quickly.

I loved Howard. He was such an experienced studio guy that I said, "The only way to make a surprising album with you would be to drop you and a microphone out of a plane and record what happens before the parachute opens up."

For *Equinox Express Elevator* [1972], we had recorded the tracks, but they sat in the can for about a year and a half or two years before we took two days to finish them with overdubs. That was the politics of what ABC wanted to release. Howard said at one point, "It's fun to make records like these because after twenty-five thousand record dates, there are very few

8. Szymczyk's productions include hit albums by the Eagles, Joe Walsh, Elvin Bishop, and Bob Seeger.

surprises left." He was a guy who had the ears and the chops to respond to whatever was going on around him. The more you gave him something he'd never heard before, the more he'd pull out something that you'd never heard before.

MILES DAVIS, *A TRIBUTE TO JACK JOHNSON* (1971, COLUMBIA)
Teo Macero

Miles comes to me. He says, "Lookit, I'm going to California. I've got $3,000. I'll give you $1,500. You put together some music from the vault."

I said, "Fine, okay." He left for California, and I went to the vault, found some music. I pasted it together, edited it together, and we turned it all around. There're a lot of repeats. It's like the beginning of the fusion thing—the repetitive sounds that they're doing today. It repeats over and over and over and over. Jesus!

All those things we bridged together in the editing room; later on he did them in concert. He'd run in from one tune to the next. He'd start one tune, and the band played it out. Meantime, he'd start another tune. One of the critics interviewed me, "I thought Miles did that deliberately."

I answered, "Probably, the only reason he did it deliberately was because we used to do that in the editing room." When you hear *Jack Johnson* and some of the other records that we made, you'll find that there's no pause between some of those edits. It cuts from one thing to another, which is like a classical composition. Harmonic structures that lap over one another were all done by Miles.

I knew what we could do on those later records because I experimented all of the time with different tracks, for example with tone generators. We used them on the *Jack Johnson* record. That "woo-woo-woo" sound. They made quite a bit of the equipment for me to use with my jazz artists, especially with Miles's records. I involved myself in the music because, sometimes, you need another pair of ears. A good editor can make a great book even better. A lousy editor can ruin a book.

MILES DAVIS, *ON THE CORNER* (1972, COLUMBIA)
Teo Macero

I understand from some people who've gone back into the vault that they would come up with a tape, compare it with the recording, and say, "It doesn't sound like the same tune." Of course it doesn't. Not by the time

we used reverb, loops, and all kinds of things we thought his music should have to make it contemporary.

You listen to *On the Corner*. It sounds like it was done today. It's got a freshness about it—the funk—all the things with the wah-wah pedal. Miles was just learning to use the pedal. I remember—the first day he had it in the studio—it was terrible. I said, "Don't worry about it. We'll wah-wah it in the editing room." And that's what we did. If he made a mistake, I'd take the tapes, and when I did the editing, I'd use the wah-wah pedal and punch it in.[9] Wah-wah them to death. People didn't know that.

If something didn't work, I'd take it out. When I made a record with Miles, I tried to make it as if it were my own. Miles was a great artist. I'd check with him on everything that we were doing. I used to say to Miles, "How do you like that?"

[*Imitating Davis's whispered rasp*] "Yeah, all right!"

And I'd say, "We're going with it—coming out in a month."

After that first album, though, he became very proficient with the wah-wah. He'd do it over long vamps.

After a while, I used to record Miles on two or three microphones so that I could take one program and wah-wah the shit out of it and, at the same time, keep the original program in. It would create a whole different sound. Also, it would go through an amplifier. We'd pick it up direct from the amp. He had a little mike on his bell. We had the natural microphone. Then, I might have had another one nearby. He had a tendency to walk away from the microphones that I used to mark. So we were covered anyway! That's a simple technique, and a lot of producers won't even talk about that. They think it's a phony way of working. But if you go back and listen to it, you'll hear. In those days, if you had a solo of the trumpet with a mute, the clipper would automatically reduce the impact of the trumpet. I turned the thing around and made it a monaural and a two-track, so that you get a strong trumpet sound in the middle, the rhythm on the left and the right.

9. Punch-ins were an electronic means of substituting a new audio signal for one previously recorded on the master tape.

JIMMY RUSHING, *THE YOU AND ME THAT USED TO BE* (1971, RCA)
Don Schlitten

A friend of mine, who was working for RCA, was a great jazz fan, and it was a time of the popularization of nostalgia. Middle-aged people were starting to say, "You've been leaving us out in the cold. What about our music?" Everybody was jumping on Glenn Miller again.

Eliot came up with this great idea: "Why don't we take an old-time blues artist and a contemporary blues artist?" Blues was also making a showing at the time. His idea was for me to get Shuggie Otis and have him play behind Jimmy Rushing. Jimmy was old enough to be Shuggie's grandfather.

I said, "Eliot, that's a very nice idea, but I don't want to do that. It's the wrong idea. Jimmy Rushing may be famous as a blues singer, but if you know Jimmy, you know that his heart is in singing songs, and nobody ever lets him do that. On most of his records there's maybe one standard like 'I Cried for You,' or something like that. But it's mostly blues. Nostalgia is coming back. Why don't you let me do an album with Jimmy Rushing singing great old songs?" Somehow I convinced him, and somehow he convinced the powers that be to let me proceed.

When I called Jimmy, he was like, "Oh, man!" He was in seventh heaven. We decided to do it in three sessions. The first thing I did was split up Al [Cohn] and Zoot [Sims]. With Zoot, I got Ray Nance, who I've always loved and who is a forgotten artist. Not only would he play trumpet, he would be able to play violin. I'm almost a schmaltz lover. And rather than sax and trumpet in the other band, I thought it would be nice to blend tenor and soprano. I got Budd Johnson to play soprano and Zoot to play tenor. Those were the two horn lineups, with the same rhythm section in both. I needed an accompanist who would be like Teddy Wilson on the Billie Holiday sessions. He'd be like the musical director, who knew and understood Jimmy and also loved old songs. Dave Frishberg was perfect for the part and also for doing a couple of plain piano-voice duets. We did it in three sessions.

I thought a lot about which songs we should do, which groups should do them, and which songs should be done as slow ballads with the piano. I try to put all that together in my head before talking to the artist. If he disagrees with me, we'll go to the next step. If he agrees, we go straight ahead. That's what we did. I tried to pick songs from the period that Jimmy would sound good singing. Like "Thanks a Million," a Louis Armstrong thing. For example, when I asked, "Would you like to sing 'Bei Mir Bist Du Shein'?"—I am a sucker for Jewish songs—Jimmy said, "I love that song!" It made me feel good that we were on the same wavelength.

When the final session was over, Jimmy was sitting in the studio. Everybody else had packed up and gone home. Eliot, Dave, and I were there, and Jimmy was apologizing for messing up some words, which he had done. But Nat King Cole did it; everybody's done it a couple of times. So what?

He said, "I'm really sorry, but I was so worried about my baby." As we talked, we realized that his baby was his wife, who was old and not feeling well. Then he started to talk about his baby and how much he loved her and what a beautiful life he'd had with her. We were just enthralled by his feelings.

After about ten minutes, he said, "I guess I better go now." At RCA Studios they had very big swinging doors. It was wintertime. He put on his little hat and coat, and he had, not a cane, it was more like a shillelagh ["shalaylee"], a knobby [Irish] walking stick. He starts walking toward the door, and he starts singing, "Thanks a million, a million thanks to you." He's singing the song, twirling the stick as he goes through the swinging doors. It was like the perfect ending to a film. I said, "Oh my God, people would never believe this." It was the last time I ever saw Jimmy. Whenever I tell the story it really gets to me.

It was his last session, but the fact that he chose that song, "Thanks a Million," he was so thankful that we'd listened to him. He'd been almost in tears talking about his baby, his ninety-year-old baby.

SONNY STITT, *CONSTELLATION* (1972, MUSE)
Don Schlitten

A lot of these guys I grew up with, hung out with, and got high with—all that nonsense. Sonny's problem was that he wanted a quick dollar. He was bored—bored with himself and with everybody else. So he needed some kind of stimulation. He had just finished working with the Giants of Jazz when they were touring the world. Because of who he was with, I guess he couldn't stay as drunk as he usually stayed. During that period, he was sort of not a total drunk most of the time.

Prior to that, in the Prestige days with all of the organ players, he was always drunk. Between you and me, I'd rather work with a stone junkie than with a drunk anytime. I did manage to get him on a Don Patterson session that I did for Prestige when I linked him up with Charles McPherson and Pat Martino. For some reason, it's a very scarce recording—I don't know why—that was called *Funk You*. Something at that session turned Sonny on about Charles. He started to give Charles a whole lot of pointers and little tips. I guess it gave him a little more self-respect that he was able to help this talented person.

The next time we met, after the Giants of Jazz, I said, "How you feeling?"[10]

He used to stutter. "You know me, man."

"I have some ideas," I said. "I want to work with you, but on one condition."

"Okay, man, you know me."

"Smoke and coke, that's fine. Nothing else. No juice." The first time we went in the studio, he had no whiskey at all, and he played his ass off. Second time, he had a tiny bottle, but it wasn't bad enough to get in the way. The third time, the bottles were bigger, and I had to drink with him so we could finish off the gin before he finished it off himself. We did about four sessions. The first was the best, and then it went down the line. Although all four of them were good—better than anything else he had done—I saw that he was going in the wrong direction.

He asked, "When are we going to do this again?"

"Sonny, I said, "I can't work with you when you drink. You know that. If you can promise me before . . ."

"Well, you know me, man."

He was calling me from Dolo Coker's home. When he got off the phone, I asked Dolo, who said, "You know Sonny!"

So at that point, I passed on it. I was finished with him. Besides, how many great portraits can you paint of the same person? On the sessions, I'd kept the bass player and piano player the same. I changed around the drummers, which lent an entirely different feeling to each session. That's a little trick. People don't understand that. Everybody's different. Everybody lends a different feeling.

10. The Giants of Jazz were a touring group composed of Art Blakey, Dizzy Gillespie, Al McKibbon, Thelonious Monk, Sonny Stitt, and Kai Winding. In 1971, Atlantic Records issued *The Giants of Jazz*, an album of the group recorded at a concert in England.

AL COHN AND ZOOT SIMS, *BODY AND SOUL* (1973, MUSE)
Don Schlitten

It was my idea to use the rhythm section. It's the bed you're going to lie in. It has to be comfortable, and it has to be inspiring. Whenever I do a record, I handpick the band. Nobody comes in and is surprised. If I'm doing Al Cohn, like in this particular case, I said, "How about Jaki Byard [piano], George Duvivier [bass], and Mel Lewis [drums]?"

"Fantastic. Fabulous."

I've never once ... That's not true. I once picked somebody where the bandleader said, "I'd rather not work with him." But I manage to hit it on the head because I've studied these people. I've been digging them since I was thirteen years old. I know what's right. Obviously, the artists have agreed with me; we've never had any dissension there. But the proof is in the music.

I thought of a Count Basie kind of swing rhythm section. Also, I wanted to use somebody who would go in and out, like Jaki Byard, and do other things as well so that there'd be constant surprise to encourage and inspire Al Cohn to do something different.

It's very interesting when you study Al and Zoot. They were buddies for years. They played together hundreds, maybe thousands of times, but when you listen to them and work with them in a recording session, you find that Zoot perfects his solo from take to take. For example, on take one somebody dropped an ashtray or something. You had to do the tune again. Take two, Zoot always managed to use the same solo but somehow or other change it just a little bit. Al was a real honest-to-God jazz musician. He came from left field every time out and did something completely different. You really had a problem figuring out which take was best. They were so different.

Like when I did the Jimmy Rushing session, one of the things we did was an old Jewish song, "Bei Mir Bist Du Shein." It opened with Al playing a four-bar introduction. Every time out it was entirely different. I was ready to put out five introductions to "Bei Mir Bist Du Shein"! If you think about all of the great jazz musicians, and there are lots of them, there weren't that many who fell into that category of being honest-to-God creative improvisers from the get-go. He was one of them. Zoot wasn't, not to negate him. He did not have that quality that made Al one of the true greats.

DEODATO, *PRELUDE* (1973, CTI)
Creed Taylor

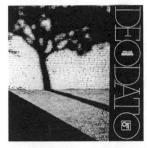

Deodato [*Prelude*] was many times "gold." It actually caused us to overexpand. We went into self-distribution and got knocked in the head. A hit is a very dangerous thing because it creates a false sense that you can do no wrong. You made one; you can keep doing it. Your perspective gets a little out of whack, to tell you the truth, because it's not that easy, obviously. In this genre of music—I hate to use the word *jazz* all the time, but that is what we are talking about—it's not easy to take an improvising musician and put him in a context that's going to make him, not only palatable, but enormously pleasing to an awful lot of people. Then you try to do it a second time, and it's very dangerous. If it doesn't work, it backfires.

While I'm on the subject of becoming more popular, you know how *Billboard* and the trades have categories and statistics attached to various genres of recorded music? Jazz winds up with 5 percent market share. I've never made an issue out of this. But what happens when—let's take Grover Washington Jr.'s *Mr. Magic* [1975]—the album starts out on Kudu [CTI's sister label]. It's a jazz record. It's listed on the jazz chart. Gradually, it explodes onto the R & B chart, and then it migrates onto the pop chart. It sells gold. It has become popular music, and its statistics go to the credit of popular-music volume. The same with Deodato and Stan Getz.

When someone breaks out of the 5 percent category, you go into a store and say, "What's new in jazz?" and you've got George Benson's *Breezin'*. He's somehow no longer jazz. All of us connected with jazz get cheated out of the crossover advantage of statistics that go to popular music. It's a false, insidious kind of statistical thing.

ART ENSEMBLE OF CHICAGO, *FANFARE FOR THE WARRIORS* (1973, ATLANTIC)
Michael Cuscuna

What I learned at Atlantic was the idea that a song builds from the rhythm track up. I suppose, if you had asked me on the street, I knew that, but I really saw it firsthand.

I had been dealing with other stuff: Chris Smither and Bonnie Raitt. I couldn't do her first album because I was on the radio; it was a conflict of interest. But I did her second album [*Give It Up*]. With Bonnie and Chris

you take each song individually, and you write a whole new script for every song.

At Atlantic, I saw people thinking about albums, thinking about the whole song list and developing a stable of rhythm sections that would be right for certain artists, really working from the rhythm track up. That's a different way of working. It's also absolutely what made Atlantic great: what made it great in the sixties and seventies. That's the single most important thing I learned from Atlantic, and I learned it from [keyboardist] Richard Tee—one of the most remarkable people I ever watched work.

All the stuff that Ahmet and Jerry had done in the fifties was rhythm driven, but not rhythm track driven. The difference is hard to explain. With rhythm and blues records the rhythm wasn't necessarily unique. The records were unique, but the rhythm wasn't. What really became the Atlantic style in the sixties was a very unusual way of mixing, building a rhythm track, and then building all the rest of the record off of that. Jerry [Wexler], Tommy [Dowd], and Joel [Dorn], and Arif [Mardin]—they all worked that way.

While at Atlantic, did your work with the Art Ensemble of Chicago benefit from what you were learning about building recordings "from the rhythm track up"?

Not at all. The Art Ensemble of Chicago was a self-contained jazz group. They constructed their own music prior to recording anything.

How did you come to produce them?

I produced a live recording of the 1972 Ann Arbor Blues & Jazz Festival. I'd known [Joseph] Jarman, Roscoe [Mitchell] and [Lester] Bowie since I first visited Chicago in 1967 or '68. At Ann Arbor, they did an amazing forty-minute set. When I got back to New York, I convinced Joel Dorn and Nesuhi Ertegun to let me sign them. Nesuhi, after all, was a big champion of Ornette and so was open to the avant-garde. *Fanfare for the Warriors* was the next album. We did it in a Chicago studio that Ben Sidran had recommended, which was run by former Jimmy Giuffre 3 bassist Jim Atlas. What I didn't know was that it was a fourth- or fifth-floor walk-up—no elevator. The Art Ensemble arrived with literally a school bus full of instruments. We had to cancel the first day and hire movers to bring all the gear up for the next two days of recording. I loved recording what impressed me, and this group was clearly in that category.

In the studio were members of the band isolated and the album multitracked, or was everybody all in one room?

It was a big room with nice sound. So we spread everyone out, but they played live together in an open room. We did record multitrack, which the guys liked because they enjoyed capturing the textures they heard when we got to the mixing stage.

SAM RIVERS, *STREAMS* (1973, IMPULSE)
Ed Michel

 My sense is, if you trust the musicians, it's their judgment that's important. If you don't trust the musicians, why are you recording them? What I try and do beforehand is have an understanding of what the guy's music is about, *guy* being a nonsexist term: how the structure of it works, and have the studio set up to handle about any set of conditions that the leader is likely to ask for.

You can really control what goes onto tape and what comes out on record. First of all, just by the guys you sign. That really controls the overall aesthetic: the people you go out of your way to sign. What's interesting about the way I've worked is I've never had a label. I've always worked for somebody, running their label for them. Generally speaking, they signed the artists. There've been very few times when I could go out and sign the artist I wanted to, when somebody said to me, "Hey, why don't you go record three or four people you think ought to be recorded?" Mostly it's somebody else's idea of who should be recorded. I don't mind that. I don't even mind being an aesthetic samurai, doing somebody's aesthetic dirty work for them because they've made decisions about it. That's the basic kind of decision that you make about music or any other art form: Who is it that you are going to give the available space?

About the only time when I could sign artists was when I was at Impulse. It was possible to sign Sam Rivers without getting permission from anybody. It was possible to sign Dewey Redman because he was recording with Keith [Jarrett]. Keith had come to Impulse because of Steve Backer, who was running promotion at that point. Steve really argued for that signing. It was an absolutely great move.

GATO BARBIERI, *CHAPTER ONE: LATIN AMERICA* (1973, IMPULSE)
Ed Michel

With the Barbieri recordings, Michel was the thinker; Gato was the player. Those guys [in the band] were very involved in movies. They thought cine-

matically. That's why it was *Chapter One, Chapter Two, Chapter Three*: it was a serial. In some ways, they were almost more interested in movies than they were in music. A lot of their friends in Argentina were involved in the movie business. They were pals. They hung out. It was quite a triumph when Gato got to do the film score to *Last Tango in Paris*, instead of Ástor Piazzolla. The two of them had a serious rivalry over that.

Gato had left Argentina because the playing opportunities were better in New York. So everybody was very pleased that he'd come back to Buenos Aires to record, but at that same time, elections were being held to see if [Juan] Perón could come out of exile. There was a lot of union activity. The first night we were going to record, the electrical workers' union turned off all of the electricity in one-quarter of the city that included the studio in which we were recording. There were other unexpected difficulties that I couldn't prepare for.

The first album was recorded in Buenos Aires and Rio. I got to the record company down there, talked to producers, and asked, "Where's a studio?" In Buenos Aires, there was a studio that had recently installed eight-track equipment. It was the first one to have that available. I thought that would be a great advantage with the kind of band I was recording. I got to the studio, went and met the engineer, and talked to him through a translator—the girl who made the coffee.

He said, "We have an eight-track machine, but we've never used it because we can't get 1-inch tape into the country." We actually smuggled in a carton of 1-inch tape. They had the mikes, but that's not something I cared about. That was the engineer's business. I'd tell the engineer if I didn't like the sound he was getting. I could tell him specifically what it was, but I don't think I ever specified a mike in my life. I had enough trouble being the producer; being the engineer was another job.

SUN RA, *SPACE IS THE PLACE* (1973, BLUE THUMB)
Ed Michel

We had a distribution deal with El Saturn Records, which grew out of what was going to be the signing of Sun Ra [aka Sonny Blount] by Impulse. But that signing never happened. It was just too far out.

Sun Ra was like nobody else. Negotiations weren't absolutely normal and straightforward. There were always clauses in the contract that didn't show up much in anybody else's contracts.

Sun Ra story number one. As soon as Bob Krasnow found out that the Impulse deal wasn't going to happen, which he found out before I did, he signed Sonny. The Sun Ra / Blue Thumb contract, to which I am a close signatory, in paragraph five gives the places where the company has the right to sell records: that is, all of planet Earth—every place on planet Earth. Paragraph six says where Sun Ra has the rights, which is every place off planet Earth, which includes but is not limited to and then names all of our solar system's other planets.

I wasn't there when Krasnow first saw the contract, but he told me, "I swallowed and asked, 'Hey, who's your distributor on Jupiter?'" Which was about the only way to respond.

Another Sun Ra story. We were mixing the *Space Is the Place* album. At that point I liked to mix at the pain threshold. We were mixing it quadraphonically in a relatively small room. And it was loud! You felt everything in your body. Sun Ra was sleeping! He was sleeping deep and snoring loud. For some reason, I stopped the tape in the middle of a tune. He woke up and stopped snoring—came awake. He looked around, wheeled his head like an owl does all around the room, checking everything out. He looked at me and said, "You Earth people sleep too much." He put his head down and started to snore again. He was a great man.

SUN RA, ASTRO BLACK (1973, IMPULSE)
Ed Michel

The first time I got to record that band Sonny walked into the studio. Nobody had been sent to pick him up. He took the band to task in a twenty-minute lecture about [responsibility]. "Every species has its leader who tells you what to do, and Earth doesn't have one. Human beings don't have one. I was sent here by a higher order of intelligence to serve as the leader for you people, and nobody saw fit to pick me up to bring me to the date. You don't understand your responsibility to your leader."

I stood there in the studio stunned, trying to telepathically will my engineer to turn on a machine and get this on tape. I really wanted it because my mind wasn't going to be able to hold the whole thing. Baker [Bigsby, the engineer] told me, he'd received the thought waves directing him to turn on the machine, but he knew that, if he did, Sonny would turn on him and eat him alive. That was a religion. It was a matter of deep faith being involved with that band.

Did band members wear full regalia when they recorded?

We recorded in the only studio in Chicago that had a sixteen-track tape machine, which meant they had sixteen feed lines from the studio into the control room. We had to borrow a lot of submixers. They had four sets of drummers, four full drum kits, [and] a percussionist. The reed section doubled on everything known to man; the brass did the same. And they had five dancers, who danced through the studio while we were recording. Not one of them tripped over a mike cable.

Everything was ready. The guys showed up. They brought in two of those 3-inch-thick ring-binder books. Every guy had two books, two ring binders of parts. They never knew what Sonny was going to call. He said to me, "Before we record, we'll run a tune down once. You can change the mike settings and everything. But we're just going to run it down once, and then we're going to play it once."

In a day and a quarter we did four LPs. Two came out on Saturn [*Crystal Spears* and *Cymbals*], one came out on Blue Thumb, and the other one that belonged to Blue Thumb sort of vanished mysteriously into the mists of time.[11]

DAVE HOLLAND QUARTET, *CONFERENCE OF THE BIRDS* (1973, ECM)
Dave Holland (Bass, Leader)

It was a great time in the music because there was a very open attitude, at least amongst the people that I was associated with. The lines weren't drawn so acutely between the different genres: blues, rhythm and blues, rock 'n' roll. All this stuff was crossing, and jazz was crossing lines.

I wasn't really thinking about this at the time, but looking back on it, I think the musicians were looking for a music that would somehow represent the flows and the currents that were going on through society and through the American scene. Because you know it was a time of great social upheaval as well.

---

11. In 2000, Evidence Records issued *The Great Lost Sun Ra Albums: Cymbals and Crystal Spears*. Ed Michel wrote liner notes. As for the lost, never-released Blue Thumb recording, Michel surmises that it must belong to Tommy LiPuma.

MILES DAVIS, "HE LOVED HIM MADLY" (1974), *GET UP WITH IT* (COLUMBIA)
Bob Belden (Columbia/Legacy Reissues)

When the music got to where it was so abstract there was no melody, Teo would sometimes create the melody. He would go in, like on "He Loved Him Madly," and loop. There, he did it inadvertently because the tape he was using was defective. He just joined the first half of the reel with the second half of the reel, and looped the main melody. Teo was working with loops in '67 and '68.

His version of "Circle in the Round" has a few little loops. That was really his first editmania piece.

Throughout the seventies and into the early eighties, Miles was approving tracks for release due to his having to maintain his lucrative advance. Miles's deal at Columbia was two records a year, no matter what. When he wasn't feeling good, it was up to Teo to put out the records.

CHARLES MINGUS, *MINGUS AT CARNEGIE HALL* (1974, ATLANTIC)
Joel Dorn

Ilhan Mimaroğlu and I coproduced the reunion record, *Mingus at Carnegie Hall*. Let me be totally honest with you. I sat in a truck with Tommy Dowd and made sure that we grabbed everything. I saw Charles for a few minutes before the show. "You my producer?" he asked.

"Yeah."

"Nice to see you again." I just made sure the music was nailed.

Mingus came by the office sometimes, and every time I met him, he was another guy. I saw him be really nuts. I saw him at Pep's in Philly, screaming at the audience, the owner of the club, and the guys in the band. Then I had conversations with him. He'd say, "Hey, how you doing, man? How are your productions going? How's Roland? Heard you're working with Yusef. How's it going?" Or, "Is Aretha around?"

Other times, I'd say, "Hey, Charles."

He'd look at me like he was going to spit on me. I never knew. He was Mingus! I've got a theory. Anybody you call by one name—when you say

Rahsaan, Mingus, Miles, Monk, Trane, Duke, and Bird—one-name people are special people. If you call me, you go, "Joel Dorn." He was Mingus.

HUBERT LAWS, *IN THE BEGINNING* (1974, CTI)
Creed Taylor

Two things [account for the drum sound on Laws's version of "Airegin"]: it was the way Rudy [Van Gelder] miked the drums, and it was the sensitivity with which Steve Gadd recorded. Gadd was not just a great drummer. He was a great recording drummer. Using his headset, he knew what sound he'd get if he tapped a certain way. He could talk to Rudy, have him make slight changes, and then it just went down. There are some great drummers, too, who are not great recording drummers. I wanted to point that out about Steve Gadd. What you observed on that particular recording was a lot of Steve Gadd's attention to the microphone.

BILL EVANS, *SYMBIOSIS* (1974, MPS)
Helen Keane

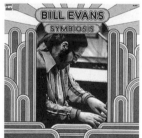

I came to it [record production] through Bill Evans. I actually had produced other records, but I hadn't been given credit. I was given "consultant" credit or something like that, but never full producer credit. With Bill I was so much a part of his life as his manager, it was a natural step to have me produce the records.

[Writer] Gene Lees introduced us, though I had met Bill once before. A Chicago singer named Lucy Reed was doing a record date. She was a very close friend of mine and asked if I would come and help. I had this ability and didn't know it. People were always asking me to sit in on sessions and make suggestions. I used to end up practically producing the session. That night, I met Bill for the first time. I had been a fan. I loved his music, although he was virtually unknown. But that's how we met the first time.

The second time, Gene Lees, who was very close to Bill, had written about him in *DownBeat*. He felt that Bill needed professional guidance. Gene and I were together romantically. He said, "You should be managing this man."

I came into the picture right after Orrin Keepnews. I was always there.

Creed [Taylor, Evans's producer at Verve] would ask my opinion on many things and tell me to take tapes home. When he was leaving Verve, he got me a contract as Bill's producer. I learned on the job.

Was Evans insecure, as Orrin Keepnews claimed?

I don't think he was insecure at all. He was very secure. He loved to record. That's when he was happiest. Bill knew exactly who he was. His addiction problem had nothing to do with insecurity. Ninety-nine percent of the time it was impossible to tell if he was strung out. The last ten years of his life he'd stopped using heroin. When he was cleaning up, he said, "I know it's going to be hard to do, but I never really enjoyed heroin in the first place." Then, he got into cocaine the last year he was alive.

Would the two of you sit down to preplan albums or was the process more spontaneous?

We did it both ways. The live dates were more spontaneous. *Quintessence* [1976], *We Will Meet Again* [1979], and *I Will Say Goodbye* [1977]—records that for the most part had an additional musician on them—were planned more carefully than trio records.

Do you recall the development of the orchestral album Symbiosis?

Symbiosis it was sixty-five men, and it was a live date, totally live, which is unheard of nowadays. Occasionally, classical records are done this way, but not very often. In other words, all sixty-five musicians played at the same time, and were recorded at the same time. Which is really amazing.

This was done for a German company. We were right between signings then, and so we were available, contractually, to do this for a man named Mr. [Hans Georg] Brunner-Schwer who had this record company called MPS. He also liked to play with engineering. That was his hobby. He was a multimillionaire, and he had his own studio in Germany.

So what he did, after Claus Ogerman and I spent twelve hours one night mixing the album, when it was released, Brunner-Schwer had remixed the whole thing himself—added echo and reverb. He ruined it.

Claus started a lawsuit. It was taken off the market and then reissued the real way.

But you can't do that. A record appears, disappears. When it reappears, nobody pays any attention. The one that's out now is the real one. So that's the *Symbiosis* story. Everybody was all together. We had multitracks, but nobody was isolated. It was something to see. And there were amazingly few takes for something as complex as it was.

Did both you and Evans listen to playbacks?

In the beginning, but after a while, he wouldn't. I did it all. He'd said, "I've done the playing. Now you do the rest. It's all yours." He once said to me, "If I come in and I'm going to be overseeing the mixing, all I'm going to be doing really is listening to myself and wishing I'd played something differently. You can hear everything. That's what you're there for, to hear everything."

Did you favor particular studios?

Columbia Studio, Thirtieth Street, we liked very much. It's no longer there. They used to do a lot of the classical records. We'd record there and have a special piano brought in. I would say it was our favorite. It had been a church, and, acoustically, it was really great. Then, we recorded a lot at Fantasy Records when we were signed to them. That was in California. They had great studios. They had Bill choose the piano that they bought for him to use when he recorded out there.

BILL EVANS, *THE TONY BENNETT /*
BILL EVANS ALBUM (1975, FANTASY)
Helen Keane

It was my idea. Tony and Bill had been casual friends for a long time and great admirers of each other. Tony, who became a very close friend of mine, was always a jazz fan. A man named Jack Rollins became Tony's manager. He was also Woody Allen's manager. Jack and his wife are my closest friends. And I guess that's what brought the idea to mind.

Because Jack was managing Tony, I said to myself, "Wouldn't it be wonderful if they recorded together?" So I called up Bill and said, "What would you think?"

"I'd love it!" he said, but he added, "I'll tell you how I'd want to do it."

"How?"

"Just the two of us."

So that part was his idea. Their recording together was my idea. Then I called Jack, and he called Tony. Tony said, "Absolutely." And that's how it happened. They did two albums together.

Did you discuss repertoire with them, or did they work that out?

The first album, I picked all the tunes. The two of them were so nervous about pleasing each other that neither one would say what they wanted to do. So I said, "Here's a list. Take a look." The last tune that I picked was a tune called "We'll Be Together Again." The night before I flew to the Coast to do the date, I went to see Bette Midler in her one-woman show called *Clams on the Half Shell.* In one section she came out alone—she and Lionel

Hampton—and sang "We'll Be Together Again." I said, "We have to do this tune." So I had a lead sheet messengered to me the next morning before I went to the airport. When I got out there [to California] I didn't know if either one of them liked it, knew it, or anything. They both reacted very positively and said they would love to do it. And then the second record, of course, was called *Together Again.*

And they recorded together in the studio, no multitracking?

Are you kidding? They were standing right there in the studio together—both times.

JIM HALL, *CONCIERTO* (1975, CTI)
Creed Taylor

[Arranger] Don Sebesky and I talked a great deal before we went in to record. I made suggestions about how to format a very simple and almost no-arrangement kind of context, but where each player would come in, and then there would be that kind of interplay, for instance, between Chet [Baker] and Jim [Hall]. Then Paul [Desmond] would do that kind of contrapuntal stuff that he was so famous for. There was never a problem with Sebesky, because he was an absolute, polished professional. If I asked him to take out four bars of "Letter A," take out that figure and then change anything, he'd do it immediately.

There were a lot of very simple changes that you don't hear in the bumps of that record. (It was just [a matter of] making more space than he had actually provided for, once we went into the session.) I am not explaining it very well, but that's such a classical recording. For instance, once a solo begins, with those particular artists, nobody, including myself, made any suggestion as to whether or not a solo should be extended or whether it should be shortened. Those guys—Chet, Jim, Paul, and everybody—had such a magnificent sense of form.

Rudy [Van Gelder] recorded it. All the horn players loved to record there because they could hear themselves. The natural reverb of the room comes back at them. And actually, string players have told me many times, "That's my favorite studio."

Did you do much punching-in and editing?

Not to the extent that has now become the case. There were no punch-ins on that recording. Actually, the punch-in thing never came into much of my production because, aside from everything else that Rudy did so well, he was an absolute whiz at splicing. I don't think anybody could make an edit on Elvin Jones the way Rudy could, and Elvin played across the beat. He was an absolute nightmare for somebody to edit unless you understand the music. Rudy was so good that he did a lot of intercutting, not punch-ins. The punch-ins really didn't start happening until we got into the eight-track, sixteen-track, and then digital, of course.

John Snyder (CTI)

I got Chet on that date because I always thought that Chet, Jim Hall, and Paul were the perfect compatible players. I pushed that right from the beginning and, somehow, Creed bought it. That version of "Concierto de Aranjuez" is pretty. Though it was no Gil Evans [arrangement], the way those guys play, the solos on that record, oh my goodness. Chet's solo on that record is startlingly beautiful. Roland Hanna's solo—at its ending where it goes up the scale—it's fantastic. That's a beautiful, beautiful performance. Although it's rhythmically static and its arranging is not challenging, from an improvisational standpoint, those guys play beautifully.

Esmond Edwards (Argo/Chess)

I really admired Creed Taylor, because I felt that maybe he got close to my philosophy. I wanted a wider audience to be touched by my recordings, rather than only the strictly esoteric jazz audience. Creed put his stamp on "commercial jazz recordings." He did it very well. I don't think he's going to be remembered for discovering any fantastic new talent. He came along and cherry-picked from the guys who, obviously, had a lot of talent, and who had already made it on straight-ahead jazz recordings. He put them in a context with Don Sebesky or whomever. He always chose the best sidemen. He made some excellent records.

I never had the freedom or the budgets to do what he did, but I always felt that I wanted to straddle that fence: do some things that were artistically viable and, maybe, important but still have a tune or two that the wider public could associate with.

I think Blue Note did that to a great extent also. Alfred Lion did a number of successful things with Lee Morgan, Herbie Hancock, Horace Silver, and Art Blakey. I always thought that was the way to go. I didn't feel that jazz artists should be restricted to "esoteric areas." I felt, if the guy who knew only three chords could make a million dollars, the guy who knew one hundred chords should be able to make a hundred thousand dollars, at least, without compromising his talent or his art. I always thought that was something to strive for.

Ed Michel (Impulse)

There are schools of production that are anything but an invisible style. Creed is the clearest example of that. Creed designs a suit and then puts his artists into it. That works great if you like that sort of thing. There are directors who are complete auteurs of their films, and there are producers who are complete auteurs of their records. That's okay, but by my choice, I'll record musicians who amaze and delight me, and I'll try and give them the wherewithal to be able to do that. In fact, they're out there working in front of the public. They're playing every night. They have a chance to check out their repertoire and find out what works. I'd always rather record a working band than put together an ensemble that just met for the first time in the studio.

MARION BROWN, *VISTA* (1975, IMPULSE)
Ed Michel

Marion was very easy to work with because he knew what he wanted to do, and that album works the way it does because of multiple keyboard players [Stanley Cowell, Bill Braynon, and Harold Budd]. They are pretty amazing players. The textures they got were pretty amazing. Marion was aware of that. He would say, "I don't know why Miles Davis gets all of the attention, and I don't I make more interesting music than he does, and I dress better." I liked working with Marion because he liked the idea of storytelling records.

KEITH JARRETT, "PRAYER" (1975),
DEATH AND THE FLOWER (IMPULSE)
Ed Michel

Keith was very much determined who and what he would record. He could do all kinds of music and liked to do all kinds of music.

Artists are very different. No two are the same in any way. Some people want to hear playback of everything. Most people want to hear playback of the first tune and maybe the second tune, and from then on, they know it sounds right. They'll ask for a playback if they're not certain. Once you've worked with somebody, they'll say, "Do I need another one?" I'll say "yes" or "no." In that context I'm always ready to do another take, no matter how good it is. There've been colossal takes that I would have thought, "God, this is one of the high points of Western culture." And the guy will say, "Can I do another one?" I'll say, "Certainly." There might be a better one behind it. Why not?

For example, on a Keith Jarrett date, the *Death and the Flower* date, there's a duo he does with Charlie Haden—"Prayer." They played it, and I thought, "Jesus, that's good."

"Let's do another one," Keith said.

I said, "Absolutely." They did another one. Keith played an even better solo, and then it broke down. It just stopped at about five minutes, and I said, "Well, we've got the first one. There's no problem. Why not do one more just for the hell of it because it's going so well?" The third one was the take. When I'm teaching a production class, sometimes I do that at schools, I'll play that as an indicator of "Don't stop just because it's good."

RAHSAAN ROLAND KIRK, *THE CASE OF THE 3 SIDED DREAM IN AUDIO COLOR* (1975, ATLANTIC)
Joel Dorn

We wanted to leave Atlantic to go to Warner Brothers, but we owed Atlantic two albums. So we went in the studio and recorded. I ended up with three-sides worth of material. What to do? One day I was sitting, and it occurred to me: "Wait a minute. I'm going to make this almost a double record."

Rahsaan asked me, "What do you mean?"

"I'll do a three-sided record, and we'll call it *The Case of the 3 Sided Dream in Audio Color.*" So I created the montage material in between songs for the dream effect. But it also has another meaning.

Then, another day I was sitting and thought, "How many people are going to listen to a blank fourth side? Let's see." I had my secretary, Kathy, call Rahsaan. I recorded the bit, their piece of the conversation. I put it smack dab in the middle of the fourth side. Having explained to the world that it was a three-sided record, I wanted to see if the Rahsaan freaks would go and understand that there was no such thing as anything you could trust on those records. People actually dug it. I started getting calls. There's a regular group of Rahsaan people that call me, that find out my home number. It's not listed under any set of circumstances anyplace. I don't contact them. They contact me.

Fantasy is always a reflection of what reality is. You know that great line, "Show me with whom you sleep, and I'll tell you what you dream?"

Rahsaan was the encyclopedia of jazz, and he's the fucking surrealist of that era.

ART PEPPER, *LIVING LEGEND* (1975, CONTEMPORARY)
John Koenig

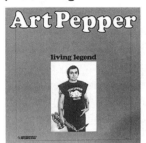

When I was in my very early twenties, I worked for Contemporary, after graduating from UCLA. I met Art before he made his comeback record, which was *Living Legend*, on which I worked with my father. That was a quartet date with Art, Hampton Hawes, Charlie Haden, and Shelly Manne—an interesting group.

[In the late fifties] Charlie came to Los Angeles, basically to meet and to play with Hampton Hawes. And so that quartet—Art had played with every one of them in the fifties—went to the concept that I hold of having people who are comfortable with each other and can anticipate how others are going to play.

My father was the one who would talk to Art. If he had an idea for Art, he'd ask him. I prepared a lot of the music: wrote out charts and things like that. I was in the studio and helped set up microphones.

On that particular session, Art was a little bit nervous because he hadn't recorded for quite a while. There was always a certain level of being-on-the-edge with him in terms of whether it was going to happen or not. It always did happen. I very rarely heard Art play badly on a date. But the stakes were different on that record because he was, essentially, making a comeback. He wasn't sure if he still had it, but of course he did.

The next record was *The Trip* [1976], which was with George Cables, Elvin Jones, and David Williams. That was an easier session. They were all such nice guys, and their grooves were so natural that Art fell into it. As I recall, he was faced with musicians who were first-rate, and he reveled in it.

I didn't know the subtext of a lot of Art's titles at the time—I didn't know the whole Art Pepper story—but *The Trip* referred to his stay in San Quentin. Guys would sit around, and they'd tell each other, "Take us on a trip." Somebody would tell a story, maybe about what they had done earlier in life, maybe how they ended up in prison. Art had these—I'll call them literary—associations with his music. He was inspired by those things.

MCCOY TYNER, *TRIDENT* (1975, MILESTONE)
Orrin Keepnews

The idea of having him [McCoy Tyner] play the celeste and harpsichord came out of a conversation about an accident on a Monk session, "Pannonica," one of the numbers on *Brilliant Corners*. There was a celeste in the studio left over from a previous day, and Monk said to me, "Hey, set that up over here by the piano." That way he could play both, simultaneously, one hand on each.

So the conversation that I had with McCoy involved satisfying his curiosity and giving him a historical fact. That, conversationally, led its way to the combination effects, piano and celeste, on *Trident*.

The idea of doing a pure trio record emerged from the fact that our last few projects had been rather complicated, involving large groups. So it was certainly a natural enough point to say, "We've been doing complicated things for a while. Let's get back to basics, take the best available bassist and the best available drummer and go into the studio." Frequently, great ideas are simply applications of a little common sense.

JIM HALL, *JIM HALL LIVE* (1975, HORIZON)
John Snyder

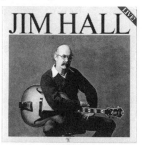

Not a lot of production involved. That album, though, happens to be some of the best Jim Hall playing on record. You take what you get, and what you are going to get is whatever they usually play as a group. They have their repertoire, and you're just capturing it on tape. That was a live trio recording, and my first record at Horizon.

I was a music major in college—a trumpet player—and had been in band since I was thirteen or fourteen. I had my own band in college, and for some reason, I went to law school. That combination of things made me attractive to Creed Taylor.

While in law school, I wrote him a letter and told him that I loved his work, had a music degree and a law degree, and asked if he could use me. He called and said, "Sure, let's talk about it." So I went up—came up from North Carolina—and he hired me the first day I talked to him—which was a big thrill. I went from listening to Freddie Hubbard, Hubert Laws, and Ron Carter to working with them.

I stayed with Creed for a couple of years, and then I went to A&M, where

I started the Horizon series in 1975. We did maybe twenty-five records or so, from '75 to '77. I left there and started my own company called Artists House. That lasted until '81. I worked as director of jazz production for Atlantic from '85 to the beginning of '87. Then I became an independent record producer with A&M, RCA, and Telarc as my main clients.

JIM HALL, *COMMITMENT* (1976, HORIZON)
John Snyder

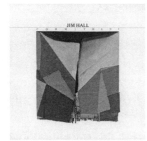

The *Commitment* record was a different idea and combined a lot of the friends of Jim. My input into all of those records [on A&M Horizon] was really as a series: photography and how they were packaged; all those things, I really got off on. I made records and packaged records as if I were going to buy them. I used to go into the record stores, and I loved picking up a record that I couldn't wait to get home and listen to. I loved the feel of it, and that's what I wanted to do. I wanted to make a record that people would pick up and say, "Wow." They would know that somebody put a lot of thought into it. It shows a certain respect for the music, the musicians. Also, once the musicians see that you're going to do that, they're going to perk up a little bit, too. It's kind of a bootstrap effect. You can each reach a higher level by being influenced by the other. It's like a receptive audience or an enthusiastic audience pushing an artist to a greater performance. There is magic in that. If you can achieve that result in your efforts, you've done something.

In that sense there is a consistency in all those records [for A&M Horizon], but *Commitment* was more hands-on. I was involved in the choice of material, artists, and studio—all that. The Horizon packaging was my idea, and it turned out to be very difficult. It was almost harder to get the records packaged than to make the records themselves.

GEORGE BENSON, *BREEZIN'* (1976, WARNER BROS.)
Tommy LiPuma

Overall, I think the jazz police never forgave me for taking George Benson from the jazz area to where he became a pop artist. I was always a pop music freak, but I was a big jazz fan. I was a saxophone player. I played professionally for years, until I got into the record business. I was also a big fan of Creed Taylor. He was a big influence on me and on how I made my records.

I worked for Liberty Records as a promotion man from 1961, I believe,

until late '65, when I went with A&M. In between, I worked for Liberty's publishing company. They'd bought Lew Chubb's Imperial Records and had the O'Jays signed. My first production was with the O'Jays, their first record. Jerry Moss and Herb Alpert were close friends of mine, and I joined them at A&M in October of 1965.

I was a fan of George's going way back. The first time I saw him was with Jack McDuff in 1963 or '4, at the Jazz Workshop. At the time, I didn't know who he was or his name. So the first time I really heard him was on a record he'd done on Verve that Esmond Edwards had produced [*Giblet Gravy*, 1968]. I remember Herbie Hancock was on the album, on a version of "What's New." I was really taken by George. I was a big Wes Montgomery fan, among other great guitar players. But this guy really grabbed me.

I bought his albums on Creed's label [CTI]: *White Rabbit, The Other Side of Abbey Road*, and so on. But for some reason or another I'd never heard him sing. I missed those cuts. Somewhere around 1973, I was in San Francisco doing an album. Al Schmitt, who was still producing at the time, he hadn't gone back into engineering, he and I were close friends. We shared a hotel suite at the Miyako Hotel in San Francisco.

Al was working with the Jefferson Airplane; I was working with Dan Hicks and His Hot Licks. After work one day, we were riding by the Keystone Korner. I looked up, and the marquee read "George Benson." I stopped the cab and said, "We've got to check this out." We went to hear George play, and that was the first time I heard him sing. He sang "Summertime," which he'd done on a Columbia album that I didn't know. It struck me, "This guy can really sing." We stayed for the set. I didn't introduce myself. I split.

At that time in 1973, I was partners with Bob Krasnow in a small record company called Blue Thumb. We sold the company in late '74. I went to Warner Brothers, and about six months later, Bob joined us there as a talent scout. Maybe it was 1976. He called me one day, and he said, "I have a thing here that was made in heaven. I just got a call that wanted to know if Warners was interested in signing George Benson. I thought of you." I had introduced Bob to George Benson's music. I had played him a lot of George's things. So he asked, "Would you be interested?"

"Absolutely."

Bob set up a meeting, and I got together with George. The first thing I asked him was how come he hadn't sung more on his albums? He told me—it was, of course, his conjecture—that Creed was trying to make him the next Wes Montgomery. Wes had died by that time. Creed wasn't enthusiastic about recording him as a vocalist. I said, "I saw you about three or four years ago at the Keystone Korner. I thought your voice was fantastic. I think you should sing more on your albums."

As it turns out, he signed with us, and then we got together. The amazing thing is he left the looking for the material and the casting of the material up to me. I came up with all of the songs. It just so happened that I knew Leon Russell very well, and I was familiar with his song "This Masquerade." I told George, "Look man, it's a great song. If we're going to do something . . ." But even before that, I'd said, "I don't think that we should go in and do just a bunch of vocals. If we find something that's really great, we'll do it." I'd found one. He loved the song. We recorded it.

There were six cuts on the *Breezin'* album. Five were first takes. I'd also done some stuff with Bobby Womack and Gabor Szabo. This was when I was with Blue Thumb. There was an album I did with Gabor called *High Contrast* [1971], where a friend of mine, Jim Keltner, a great drummer, he mentioned, "You know, there's this friend of mine, Bobby Womack. You ought to check him out." I did, and I thought, "This guy's a great rhythm player, and he writes good stuff." So I had him on this Gabor Szabo date, playing guitar. Bobby wrote this thing called "Breezin'," which we recorded with Gabor. Nothing happened with the album, but there was something about it that kept my interest. It turns out we ended up doing that tune again. I had Bobby Womack come down and play rhythm guitar. But *Breezin'*, the whole album, took only three days.

Claus Ogerman, the gentleman who did all of the string arrangements, was also a close friend of mine. He was spending six months of the year in Munich, Germany, at his home, and six months in New York. When I called him to do the arranging, he said, "Geez, I'd love to do it, but I'm leaving for Munich."

"Hey," I said, "we'll come there."

By that time, Al Schmitt was doing all of my engineering. Al and I took the tapes, flew to Munich and did the strings there.

To what do you attribute the quick recording time?

George nailed it, but we did have several days of rehearsal before recording. I'm really—I don't want to use the word *stickler*, but in a sense I am. Preproduction is very important. We rehearsed and went in ready.

I don't necessarily have rehearsals on every album that I've done. But we do have preproduction meetings. Everyone, or at least the artist, has a good idea what we're going to do and how we're going to approach it. A lot of times when we go into the studio, we don't have arrangements so to speak; in fact, very seldom do we have rhythm arrangements. We go in with a sense of what we're going to do, though we may have only a chord sheet to follow. Then, once we get in there, we work on how best to do it, but we have a good sense of the road we're going to take when we start.

Esmond Edwards (Elektra)

I had a terrible experience doing a Jimmy Smith and George Benson album. It was Jimmy's date. George was doing it as a favor. He was riding a crest of popularity after "This Masquerade." We set up, with everyone's concurrence, like a live date. The guys were pretty close together, a minimum of baffling around the drums and so forth. There was a lot of leakage. You had the Hammond [organ], mikes on the Leslie and the guitar amp.

George came in while we were mixing to hear the tapes. He didn't like any of his solos. Problem was, there was almost as much guitar on the drum tracks as on the guitar track. That's the way we'd decided to record.

We spent a whole day trying to overdub George's solos, and it didn't work. Eventually, the session was scrapped. They ended up rerecording the whole thing in New York with Tony May [as *Off the Top*, 1983]. But that's just one of the things that can happen. At the time, if George didn't like his solos, the record wasn't coming out.

DAVE BRUBECK, *ALL THE THINGS WE ARE* (1976, ATLANTIC)
Michael Cuscuna

[This Brubeck album is distinguished by a most unusual pairing of personnel. The title track features both Lee Konitz and Anthony Braxton on alto saxophones.]

It was my idea, and I had to talk Brubeck and Konitz into it. Anthony idolized both of them and immediately said, "Yes." By the end of the date, everyone was happy. I don't think I'm the first to say it, but very early on, I realized that—before any other skill—producers have to be diplomats and psychologists in order to get records done. And that idea goes, very much, hand in hand with the idea of invisibility.

I feel very strongly that, as a producer, you should be as invisible as possible, to the extent of working with artists and, sometimes, planting ideas in ways that let them think it's their idea. You really should be wallpaper, if you possibly can.

The Leiber and Stoller and Phil Spector schools: they're really arrangers. They're almost the artist with a hired singer. I love what Spector and what Leiber and Stoller did, not so much as producers but as arranger-architects of records. They don't make careers. They don't enhance individual artists. They were the artists.

Basically, you're trying to accomplish a record. And when you're trying to do that, there's an incredible amount of ego dynamics: sidemen who don't think they should be sidemen, engineers who hear things a certain way, and a musician coming in who wants to hear it his way. There are a million kinds of things going on, dynamics going in a hundred different directions.

If you as a producer are stupid enough to interject your ego and add that to the mix, then you've become a burden instead of a solver of problems. What you actually have to do is streamline everything to a point, and soothe everybody to a point, where they can get down to making the best possible music. Then, hopefully, you've got the best possible record. It's as simple as that.

But it is an effort. You have to remove obstacles blocking an artist from getting his work committed to record. You have to run interference, head off anything that ranges from temper tantrums to confusion over technology, anything that will upset an artist and throw them off to the point where the mood is over, as it were.

Often, [as an artist] it's annoying to go about your business and have other people suggesting stuff or trying to tell you what to do, whether it's an engineer or bass player or producer. It's so much smoother when there's a flow to what's going on—if things can be suggested in a subliminal way over a period of time. That enhances the whole project, and it also means fewer things can go wrong in the studio. You want an easier flow for the artist. I don't care if it's Bonnie Raitt, Anthony Braxton, or Buddy Guy.[12] It has nothing to do with any particular kind of music. The studio environment should flow almost as much as somebody's living room or a concert stage.

I remember Walter Davis laughing at me once in the middle of a session. He'd come by just to visit. "I've been looking in your eyes," he said. "It's amazing that you project a calm exterior while there are all these thunderstorms going on inside your head."

I guess that's the absorbing process necessary to properly supervise a

12. Cuscuna produced Braxton for Arista Records, a label formed by Clive Davis after Columbia had fired him. In 1972, Cuscuna produced both Bonnie Raitt's *Give It Up* and Buddy Guy and Junior Wells's *Play the Blues*.

date. You've got to put out fires, preferably before they get started, and if they flare up, you've got to put them out very quickly before a whole session is trashed. It's a delicate balance.

ANTHONY BRAXTON, *CREATIVE ORCHESTRA MUSIC 1976* (1976, ARISTA)
Michael Cuscuna

I felt hemmed in at Atlantic. I'd wanted to sign a lot of people, and Nesuhi was the kind of guy who said, "We'll put money into the records, but I don't want to give big advances."

For plus or minus a thousand dollars, I was not able to sign a lot of people who went to other labels and did very well. That was a creative time in the fusion area. This is '72. What Joe Zawinul and a few other people were doing was startlingly interesting, and also something of the future, something that was going to be commercially viable. There were a lot of things that I wanted to do but couldn't. I got frustrated and I left.

Steve Backer and I had become friends. He'd gone to Impulse and was talking about bringing me over, but before anything materialized, he left the label. Or Impulse ground to a halt, and Steve ended up at Arista. He was looking for a label to distribute. I had met with Alan Bates, who had Freedom and Black Lion. We struck a deal for that, and then we started.

I had convinced Anthony Braxton to come back to the States. I thought the time was right, that his time was here. I'd heard Atlantic was interested in signing him, but suddenly Arista got into the mix. Steve wanted him pretty badly. So gradually we developed a system of putting out a lot of records through [Arista] Freedom and, also, making productions directly for Arista. That was an exciting and fun time.

Basically, at Arista, we'd do a few small-group records. In those days they were selling relatively well. Then, we'd do a large-budget production of something that Anthony [Braxton] really wanted to realize. We would be very lean on the small-groups records, watch the dollars, carry those budgets—the left-over money—over into doing something big. I think *Creative Orchestra Music* certainly was the most ambitious, probably the most expensive record that we did.

We had reached a point where we had built up the bank account in terms of stealing from one budget to give to another. In those days on Arista—a large independent—Anthony was selling very well. I don't remember the exact numbers, but it was well over ten thousand. That was certainly very good for an experimental artist in 1976.

When an artist like that is on a major label, the main long-term goal is to get a lot of those things done that you would not be able to do otherwise. Most of the time, artists have their moment in the sun on a major label at a couple of periods in their life; the rest of the time, they record for independent labels—for people who do it because they love the music. So that was all the more reason for us to really accomplish something. Up to that point, Anthony had been recording for Delmark and a few small French labels—recording for a pittance.

I guess it comes off more serious than the tone of the project itself, but we had a really great time. I hired Seldon Powell to play first tenor, because of his doubling ability and his reading ability. It was a lot of fun to watch him interacting with Roscoe Mitchell: New York versus Midwest; young generation versus old. We did the rehearsals at a place called Bill's—a big rehearsal hall in New York—and then we recorded at Generation Sound. It should've been a very pressured time. We had some wrinkles along the way. But it was a very celebratory time.

Anthony is like a journalist. A lot of the compositions were things that had been written over the ten years leading up to it—not all necessarily for big band. But there's never a project where he's not writing the last of the arrangements at four in the morning, six hours before rehearsal. So there was a mad dash to get everything arranged and copied before the beginning of the rehearsals. But once it started, it was wonderful.

Anthony has a great sense of humor. If you interview him, he goes into automated academician and theorist, but that's this other person. Really, Anthony is a very funny guy and loves to laugh all the time.

WEATHER REPORT, "BARBARY COAST" (1976), *BLACK MARKET* (COLUMBIA)
Joe Zawinul

I learned how to love music and a groove from trains in Europe when I was a kid. On "Barbary Coast" I set the music to the train sound. It was in the same groove. If you play that tempo, you can bring in the train whenever you want.

I used it several times. On *The Immigrants* (1988), one of my best albums with my band, the Syndicate, there's a song called "From Venice to Vienna." I have this serious, serious train coming in there.

SAM MOST, *MOSTLY FLUTE* (1976, XANADU)
Don Schlitten

For him, it was just a matter of getting the right microphone. He was a guy who was so nervous, you really had to hold his hand. Somebody else could be totally in charge and borderline egomaniac. Then you've got Sam.

We went to Montreux. Ten musicians were on the stage. Whereas with most stages you come from stage left or stage right, in Montreux the curtain opens in the middle. So you come out of the middle and walk to the left or the right, to wherever you want to stand. Sam came out and stood there. He looked to the left; he looked to the right. He looked to the left; he looked to the right. He didn't know which way to go. It was so typical of him not to be able to make up his mind. Finally, somebody said, "Sam, go to the right please." Still, for me, he's the best jazz flutist there ever was.

DEXTER GORDON AND AL COHN, *TRUE BLUE* AND *SILVER BLUE* (1976, XANADU)
Don Schlitten

Dexter and I were good friends from way, way back when. He was just coming back from Europe; he hadn't yet signed with Columbia and become a matinee idol.[13] One of the first things he was going to do when he arrived was a recording session with me. I'd set up a situation where everybody who knew Dexter was going to be on the session, but Dexter didn't know who was going to be on the session.

So here's Dex, and he's waiting around. As each one of the cats came into the studio, there was great love and hugging and all that sort of stuff. It became almost like a party without candy and other refreshments. Then in comes Al Cohn.

One of the things I wanted to do was to record "Lady Bird" and "Half Nelson" together, which I had done with Dexter and James Moody for Prestige. I wanted to do it with two tenors and two trumpets and make it sound like a big band. So I got Dexter and Al Cohn, and I got Sam Noto and Blue Mitchell on trumpets. The rhythm section was Barry Harris, Sam Jones,

---

13. Schlitten is referring to Dexter Gordon's role as Dale Turner in Bernard Tavernier's 1986 film *Round Midnight*.

and Louis Hayes. Because of the number of musicians, we ended up doing two albums. You do a blues for fifteen minutes, that's one side already. So we did two albums called *True Blue* and *Silver Blue*. It was a very exciting afternoon and a historic occasion for us all.

VARIOUS, *THE CHANGING FACE OF HARLEM:*
THE SAVOY SESSIONS (1976, SAVOY)
Bob Porter (Savoy Reissues)

 There are several different kinds of reissues. In some cases you simply reissue an album as it was originally issued. That's the easiest thing. All you've got to do is new cover, new liner notes, boom, go. I had done a few reissues at Prestige, and I had done a couple for Esmond [Edwards] when he was at Chess, but I really got into it when I went to Savoy in 1975 [when it was purchased by Arista].

Steve Backer hired me for that job. I was rather astonished at the amount of stuff Savoy had. They had acquired a lot of different labels. Sometimes, as I said, you just put out the record as originally issued. But one of the problems with Savoy was that people didn't like Herman Lubinsky [the man who created the company in 1942]. You found a lot of artists, especially in the 1940s, when Teddy Reig was there, who would do one session—four tunes. Because you didn't have enough material for an album, you had to come up with concepts that combined a bunch of different artists, who had a relatively small number of sides for Savoy, and put them into a project.

With the Savoy reissues the concept was double albums. I came up with concepts like *Brothers and Other Mothers*, essentially the white tenor players: Getz, Cohn, Allen Eager, and Brew Moore. Another one was *The Changing Face of Harlem*. Savoy was always into black jazz. They were into it early, and they recorded a lot of guys. We took sides by Pete Brown, some of the Tiny Grimes stuff, some Lips Page things—where you didn't have enough for an album—and combined them in this concept album. The essential idea was to show—by moving through side A, number one, to side D, number eight—how the music changed over a couple or three-year period. We did two double albums of *The Changing Face of Harlem*, and probably could have done a third one without much trouble. I'd say we got to about 95 percent of the catalog, though I wish I could have done whole albums on Leo Parker, Allen Eager, and Pete Brown. There were two *Black California* albums. The final volume of California stuff was called *Cool California*. That was the white guys: Shelly Manne, Cal Tjader, the Johnny Richards Orchestra with Dizzy, and the Georgie Auld Band (which was actually recorded in New York but with enough California players to make it work).

It's the kind of thing where you have to know the music, know which artists are compatible with one another, know how much stuff you've got, and know how to fit it and sequence it.

Hopefully, with those anthologies you get writers talking because it gives them something to say. If you reissue an album as it was originally released, you're not going to get anybody talking. It's not news. Even a great record, like the Milt Jackson recording with "Opus de Bop" on it, which was a hit when originally issued. When we reissued it, nobody cared. When the record first came out, the idea of flute and vibes was an interesting concept, but by the time we got to it in the mid-seventies, it was routine.

With the big projects—the Charlie Parker and the Lester Young—we were fortunate that we had enough material. It took me a long time to do the Charlie Parker box because I could not locate original source material on some things. The one session I didn't have on acetate disc was from December in Detroit, the one with "Blue Bird" on it. I finally found the recordings. They weren't on 16-inch acetate discs, which is the way disc sessions were customarily recorded. They were on 10-inch blanks, with one tune only on each side. We finally got it all together, and the box-set sound was better than *The Savoy Recordings (Master Takes)* (1976), which were taken from tape dubbed in the fifties. We were able to get much better sound on the box set [issued on LPs in 1978 as *The Complete Savoy Studio Sessions*].

ALICE COLTRANE, "SPRING ROUNDS" (1976), *ETERNITY* (WARNER BROS.)
Ed Michel

On Alice's Warner Brothers dates, we used a large chamber orchestra. It wasn't quite a symphony-sized orchestra, but thirty or forty players. We did an excerpt from Stravinsky's *Rite of Spring*. Alice's music depended on everybody's presence in the room, and so that album—like all the ones I recorded with her—was recorded live. The give and take was a lot of what was happening. The freer the music, the more it's dependent on that.

In the studio we'd run down a piece one or two times. But we had a concert master, Murray Adler, who was very tuned in to what Alice wanted. He could convey to classical string players the ideas that she had for them. There's nothing like hearing a room full of studio fiddlers—symphony players on their day off—learning how to play free jazz, and hearing Murray trying to explain the music. It was very confusing and very exciting for them. Once they started playing, they got it very quickly.

CHARLIE HADEN, *CLOSENESS* (1976, HORIZON)
John Snyder

Ed Michel introduced me to Charlie. I got the job to run Horizon, to create the label. Ed was up for that job, but he had long hair, thick glasses, and a very determined point of view. He'd been through all the political bullshit at ABC [Impulse], and he didn't have much tolerance for it. I was younger and blonder and southern. I looked different so they hired me for the job.

But I didn't know what I was doing, and I knew that. So the second day, I called Ed and said, "Come on in. Let's talk about what we can do." He taught me a lot, and he got me into a lot of trouble, too, introducing me to Charlie Haden. I'm just kidding. Charlie was a full-time job. I got involved in Charlie's life, and that led me to Ornette, which led me to five years down the road where I managed Ornette for a long time. My whole life changed as a result of that one meeting.

But also, as a result of that meeting, we made that duet record. Charlie came in. He sat on the couch. I was using Herb Alpert's office at the time. Charlie says, "You've got to do this, man. I have this great idea. Man, this is really going to be great. I'll get Ornette Coleman. I'll get Keith Jarrett. I'll get ... [Alice Coltrane and Paul Motian]."

"Charlie," I said, "if you can do all that, you've got no problem. We'll do it."

He asked, "How much money?" And I told him. "Man," he said, "I've got to have more than that." So I gave him the money he asked for.

We made the record. I worked with Ed on it, but I forget how we split it up. I think I did two tracks, and he did two. It wasn't all done on the same day. Keith Jarrett came in. Charlie and Keith played. Alice came in, and Charlie and Alice played. I picked up Ornette at the airport. He came in from Paris, wearing a full-length mink coat.

He's quite the clotheshorse.

Ornette hates to perform. He thinks of himself as a composer, and that's why he doesn't move. When you go hear him play, he is not going to move, and he's purposely doing that. He doesn't want to do anything to draw attention to himself. On the other hand, he'll wear a suit that the only human being in the world who could wear it is him. He has specially made suits for concerts, truly beautiful silk suits with patterns all over them. He's like most of us. He's contradictory sometimes, but as far as his heart goes, there is none bigger.

On those records at Horizon I called myself "creative director." That was because I saw myself having an overall view, but I was in the studio and very much involved. Also, I was going to take that record out of the studio, going to play it for the people who could sell it, going to package it, and going to see that it got marketed. That was my job and, gradually, by working with Ed and watching and taking some projects on myself, I got better and more interested.

ORNETTE COLEMAN, *DANCING IN YOUR HEAD* (1977, HORIZON)
John Snyder

Ornette changed my life. I spent a lot of time with Ornette. I lost my job at A&M because of Ornette. I started my record company [Artists House] because of Ornette, and I lost my record company—not because of Ornette, for sure—but because we were all working on Ornette. It was Ornette, Ornette. I had twelve people working for me at one time, and we all had some segment of Ornette's life on our desks. It was a big job.

Ornette was the only musician I ever worked with who made me play trumpet with him. He made me organize a band, which he would give music to and rehearse. He called us the White House Band because we were all white. "If I can teach you guys how to play this music," he said, "I can teach anybody how to play it."

"Well, thanks Ornette. We're glad to be of some service." But it was cool. He'd put us in a circle and hand out music. Then he'd tell us to play. It was pretty chaotic, but it certainly was fun. He'd stop us, once in a while, tell us what we were doing wrong, or he'd tell each individual. He said things to me that made great sense.

The first time I played with Ornette, I was down there talking about some problems. I spent a lot of time at his loft on Prince Street, trying to keep him from getting evicted. I was ultimately unsuccessful, but I came in at a very late stage. I was able to get him some money out of it, but he had to leave.

I was down there talking, it was late, and he handed me his trumpet. He said, "Play this line that I wrote for [Don] Cherry."

"Ornette," I said, "I haven't played for five years. I can't play this."

"Play it."

I played it, got through it. It was not a big deal. "Now," he said, "play it with me." He picked up his alto, and I swear it was the most amazing musical experience. It was like he pulled this line right out of me. I had no place to go but right with him.

All of a sudden, it hit me: "This is how Cherry and Ornette are able to do all that stuff that doesn't seem possible, exactly together. They aren't playing metrically consistent, and yet they're playing hard, fast lines like they're one person." It made perfect sense to me. He has some kind of power that allows him to have that effect on you as a musician. You lock into it, and you're on the track because you go right with him. It truly was amazing.

I had to admit that Ornette was not only concerned about the money, selling records, and all the other business things, he was concerned about my musical, spiritual well-being. He was certainly the most generous and kind person I have ever met. He was the only person I have ever known to actually pick up a drunk off the street, take him home, clean him up, and take care of him: help get him back on his feet. He doesn't give money to the United Way; he picks the guy up off the street. That's a real fundamental thing about Ornette. He is very direct. That's why the world is so mysterious to him.

Time had passed, and he needed to be more cognizant of how fucked up things are. I am sure he is, but he was always surprised that the world could be a certain way and that he was somehow different. He never understood why he was treated in certain ways.

I needed to catch a cab late at night. He was there, and I had my hands full or something, and he was trying to hail the cab. And cabs are flying by. They had their lights on, but nobody was stopping. I put out my hand, thinking maybe they didn't see Ornette, and a cab stops. He said, "You see that, right?"

"Oh yeah, I see it now."

"I deal with that shit every day," he said. Ornette is a great man. There is no question about it.

How'd you lose your job at Horizon?

As I said, I originally got involved with Ornette because I asked him to record with Charlie on *Closeness*. Through that we got to know each other. I told him, "I'd like to make a record with you."

He said he'd just finished a tape that he felt very proud of, but he really didn't want to let it go. He'd been working on it for three or four years. Eventually, we got together on it. We [A&M] bought that master tape from him: *Dancing in Your Head*. It was different, definitely a big change in his style; it was considered something of a breakthrough, like it or not. That was a good thing we did. We paid a lot of money for it, but a couple of months later, he sent me back for more money. I went and got it. When Jerry Moss fired me, he said, "You know, towards the end there, John, I think you were working more for Ornette than you were working for us." It was true. I was. I was spending all my time down at his place. I was focusing on his loft problems and his business problems. I never realized that things could be so screwed up in somebody's life. He just lived a certain way, no lamp shades around Ornette. It was all bare light bulbs.

ORNETTE COLEMAN, *SOAPSUDS, SOAPSUDS* (1977, ARTISTS HOUSE)
John Snyder

I didn't own those tapes. In those days, I was motivated by the fact that Norman Granz had sold Verve for seven million dollars or something. It always bothered me. He got rich, and Charlie Parker didn't. I said, "I'm not going to be that way." So I leased the tapes from the musicians. I didn't have any rights to them.

With Ornette it was all preproduction. That's one thing that set him apart. Dare I say, he was like Gerry Mulligan, where everything is also preproduction. Creed Taylor, too, was all preproduction. We [at CTI] knew exactly what we were going to do before we went in the studio, but I've made a lot of records with jazz musicians where we don't know.

The first thing out of Ornette's mouth was that he wanted to do "Mary Hartman, Mary Hartman" [the theme to a popular television show]. "You've got to be kidding," I said. "Why?"

"Look," he said, "that is the most popular show on television. Everybody knows it. This is what people are listening to now. I want to be in with them. It's the way to get the people to buy the record."

I didn't believe that for a minute, but I thought it would be funny and interesting. I also thought his idea of how to be commercial was really interesting: how to be accessible and how to comment on the society, how to make his own statement about what was going on. I thought it was a typically insightful idea. Most jazz guys wouldn't think that way. They're not going to think politically or culturally in that sense. Ornette was always into that.

Ornette would talk your ass off. It took me a year or so just to understand his syntax. He has a different language. When he would try to solve a legal problem, that's the first way I got personally involved with him, I'd say, "Ornette I don't understand what you are saying. We're talking about specific, factual matters. Can I tape it?" Then I'd set my little cassette recorder down and listen to what he'd just spoken, trying to figure out what he said. Consequently, on cassette I have one hundred hours of Ornette talking.

In any event, he used to do that to his band, too. He'd talk at them, talk at them, and talk at them. While we were on tour, they were all sitting in one of the train compartments. I went in to hang out, and I said, "Do you all have any idea what Ornette is talking about?"

Every one of them said, "No. We just play. When he says change it, we change it." Talking to Ornette later on, I said, "You know those guys don't know what you're talking about."

He said, "They may not understand everything that I say, but by the time I get through with them, they are going to be sharp as tacks." That's what he did. By the time he got through with them, they could do anything he wanted. During that tour of Europe, we drove more people out of halls than you would believe. It was too loud and too inaccessible. People would stream out of those concerts. I said something to Ornette about it. He didn't seem to be concerned about it at all.

CHET BAKER, *YOU CAN'T GO HOME AGAIN* (1977, HORIZON)
John Snyder

 When I asked Jerry Moss [cofounder, with Herb Alpert, of A&M] if I could make a Chet Baker record, he said, "Yeah, but try to make it something that's a little more contemporary. I don't really want another jazz quartet." So that's more of an arranged record. There was a good deal of unreleased material that later came out. It featured Paul Desmond on his last jazz record (he played a short solo on an Art Garfunkel record), Tony Williams, Kenny Barron, Ron Carter, John Scofield, and Michael Brecker. It's very different from the record that we released, which was more high energy.

Chet was a sweet person. He really was, but it was sad. He'd call me every day for fifty or sixty dollars, which was kind of a refreshing change. Most of the guys would call for a thousand or three thousand—something ridiculous. You could almost afford Chet.

I really loved Chet from the time I was ten or twelve years old. I loved Miles, too. I used to compare their records, and I heard things that I thought were very similar: the solos they played on "But Not for Me." So I loved Chet, and somebody sent me some tapes when I first got to CTI in '73. They said Chet was out in New Jersey playing in a little club. "He can't play, but he's trying to get back. He's struggling. Can you help him?"

"You came to the right place," I said. I'd go see him, I'd listen to tapes, and I'd go to Creed and say, "Please, let's do Chet."

He'd listen and say, "He can't play anymore."

"He's coming back," I'd say. "He's getting stronger every day."

One day Creed called me. "I was at a party last night and this beautiful woman came up to me and said, 'Whatever happened to Chet Baker?' Why don't you see if you can get him in here?"

So okay, whatever it takes. Chet came in, and we signed him. I gave him my flugelhorn, which was gilding a lily. He didn't have his own horn. He got a Conn sometime around that same time.

I took him to A&M when I went there, and I took him to Artists House when I left A&M. I was very much involved in his life. I knew his wife, his girlfriend, his kids, and his mother. I employed his son, and I used to write letters to his daughter, a beautiful twelve-year-old, back then. She wrote the saddest poetry. It just brought tears to your eyes because those kids were so neglected by Chet, yet they were so needful and missed him. It was indescribably sad. But Chet couldn't handle that; he wasn't into it. He knew he was irresponsible, and that probably contributed to his self-abuse. Chet was always interested in one thing first.

DAVE BRUBECK QUARTET, *25TH ANNIVERSARY REUNION* (1977, HORIZON)
John Snyder

25TH ANNIVERSARY REUNION

This is the last recording of that group. During that tour, [drummer Joe] Morello's eyesight became progressively worse. We had to cut the tour short, and then do further recording. We were a little bit short of material. In fact, some of the material on that record didn't come from the sessions that I did but from another concert recorded by a radio station.

JAMES BLOOD ULMER, *REVEALING* (RECORDED, 1977; RELEASED, 1990, IN+OUT)
James Blood Ulmer

That was my first record, even though *Tales of Captain Black* was released first. I was studying with [Ornette] Coleman at that time. He fired the band just before he got Prime Time. I said, "Oh my God, I've got to start doing something." A friend of mine had a studio in his house, and we made some songs with Cecil McBee, George Adams, and Doug Hammond.

I thought it was a good tape, and I brought it to Coleman. I said, "Coleman, I want you to hear this."

Coleman listened. Boy, he listened to it about three or four times. Then he said, "Well, Blood, I'll tell you what I'm going to do. I'm going to make you a record. I'll play on it, and I'm ..."

It made me feel like he didn't want to be left out. After we'd studied so hard, he must have said, "What's this motherfucker doing now?"

"Don't worry about this tape," he said. "I'm going to produce a record for you, and I'm going to play on it with you, too."

I said, "Oh shit! That's good!" So that's what happened. He got me that record. I put the tape in a box, put it in a drawer. He made *Tales of Captain Black*. I sold *Revealing* thirteen years later.

JAMES BLOOD ULMER, *TALES OF CAPTAIN BLACK* (1978, ARTISTS HOUSE)
John Snyder

When we made this record with James Blood [Ulmer] for Artists House, *Tales of Captain Black*, Ornette [Coleman] rehearsed those guys—Blood, Denardo [Coleman], and Jamaaladeen [Tacuma]—every day for a month. We came to the studio, and we made the record in three hours. It was just a question of putting it down.

When I convinced Ornette to record the old quartet—[Don] Cherry, Billy [Higgins] and Charlie [Haden]—he brought them in, kept them up for weeks and rehearsed them every day.

He came to the studio, and he said, "Okay, we are going to go through it. We are going to play these songs"—eight songs, I think it was—"and we are going to play them straight through. We are going to stop a minute between every song, but we are not going to stop more than that, and we are going to play them straight down."

He did that, took an hour. And he did them in the order they were going to be on the record. He came back into the control room, listened to the whole thing straight through one time, didn't stop, and said, "Okay fellows, let's go do it again." Right back out to the studio, did all eight songs again, one after the other, stopped one minute between each song, and the record date was over. And he made a great record that never came out.

James Blood Ulmer (Leader, Guitar)

Coleman used to drill me, and I used to play for him so much! He used to get his horn and say, "Play B-flat. Play E-flat. Gimme this. Gimme that."

I went through about six months of that. I said, "I'm going to find out the way to play the guitar where, when Coleman asks me to play E-flat or B-flat, I ain't got none." I went to sleep, and I dreamt the tuning—the whole tuning the guitar that totally eliminated scales and chords. I woke up, took my guitar, and tuned the notes to all of the notes that I had dreamed about and started playing it. And it worked!

I went to show that to Coleman. I sat down and said, "All right now, let's play."

"Play B-flat," he said.

"I ain't got no B-flat! In fact all of my strings are tuned to one note. I have one note here with six strings tuned to the same sound." And it got us music!

Coleman's harmolodic and my harmolodic are totally different except for melody. He writes the symmetrics of harmolodics. I make sure to deal with the diatonics of harmolodics. I'm inside, and he's outside. (It's not inside/outside, but you know what I'm saying.) One is symmetrical; one is tonal. I'm in the key signature, and he's out of the key signature. I make sure to write all my stuff in a tone center, or inside of a tonal drone. By playing from a drone, I can play all twelve notes, instead of eight, and still sound like I'm in a key. You can take the whole orchestra and set it inside of that drone—no matter what the notes are.[14]

14. Ornette Coleman coined the term *harmolodics* to refer to his philosophy of improvisation that fosters free exchange among members of a music group. The term combines *har*(mony), *mo*(vement), and (me)*lodic*.

Ornette Coleman

I found that every person has their own movable C—do [as in "do re mi"]. When you put your sound or your idea into an arena mixed with other things—if what you're saying has a valid place—it's going to find its position in that total thing, and it's going to make that thing much better.

I think that every person, whether they play music or don't play music, has a sound—their own sound, that thing that you're talking about. You can't destroy that. It's like energy. Your sound, your voice, means more to everyone that knows you than how you look tomorrow. You might grow a beard or shave your hair. They say, "I didn't recognize you." But as soon as you talk, "Oh yeah, it is you!" It's the same thing. If it's that distinctive, then there must be something there.

JOE FARRELL, *SONIC TEXT* (1981, CONTEMPORARY)
John Koenig

For years, I was a classical musician. I was the solo cellist in the Jerusalem Symphony and played in the Swedish Radio Symphony in Stockholm, which is one of the major symphony orchestras in Europe.

My approach to musical expression is always from a very human perspective. Everything I've done as a producer has been geared toward capturing that. If you're going to make a good record, there are a number of elements that you must have. They are essential. *First*, you have to have good material. Ahmet [Ertegun] and I used to talk about this. There's no such thing as a good record without good songs or compositions. It can't happen. *Second*, you have to have feeling. The way I always tried to get that to happen was by using rhythm sections who had played together a lot. And we'd rehearse. That's something I learned from Joe Henderson, when I produced him. We talked about his days at Blue Note and how Alfred Lion paid guys to rehearse. Then they knew the material. They weren't on the date, tape recorder running, and them trying to learn music. One thing about a record, when it's done it's done. You have to live with it forever. Either you put it out, or you shelve it. Nobody wants to hear somebody who was uncomfortable or insecure. That goes to feeling, which partly comes from musicians' familiarity with each other. When possible, I tried to get material that suited people, rather than attempting to record someone's grandiose idea of a magnificent, complex work. The *third* most important element of production is having a strong lead voice—whether an instrument or a singer—that is compelling, that has interest to an audience on a human level.

My primary goal musically is to try and get that feeling. Take, for example, the album I produced with Joe Farrell. It was a quintet date with Joe, Freddie Hubbard [trumpet], George Cables [piano], Tony Dumas [bass], and Peter Erskine [drums]. The rhythm section—George, Tony, and Peter—had a trio called Cable Car which had played frequently around town for a couple of years. They were in tune with each other.

I'd done one album, a quartet date, with George [*Cables' Vision*, 1980]. Based on that, when Joe had a gig, he wanted George, and George said, "Why don't we use Peter and Tony?" Joe was fine with that. Then I ran into Freddie Hubbard, who said he'd love to record something with Joe.

Actually, I heard Joe Farrell and Freddie playing together at a club in Malibu. They were sensational, but the guy who booked the club was also the house bass player. So as great as Joe and Freddie were together (and I think George was with them that night, as well), I didn't think the rhythm section was quite right. But I was very enthusiastic about having Tony and Peter play.

The first time I ever heard Peter was at the Lighthouse when he was playing with George and Tony. Peter knocked me out. I didn't know he was in Weather Report at the time, but he was. I'd been away in Europe in a symphony orchestra cello section, and the Weather Report I remembered had had Eric Gravatt or Freddie Waits as their drummer. Peter was a revelation, and I approached him on his own terms—not because he was a member of a famous group, which I'm a little embarrassed to say, I didn't know then. So we had all of the elements. In preparing for that record, I went over the anticipated repertoire with Joe. He had some tunes that I listened to and liked, and I had a couple of suggestions. We went in and did it.

My feeling was to do something that suited Freddie, and a lot of people have remarked to me that they've rarely heard Freddie better than on *Sonic Text*. That goes to preparation: making sure the rhythm section is comfortable and in tune with each other, and that they have the same sense of groove; and that there's good material. Plus, it was hard to go wrong with Freddie Hubbard and Joe Farrell.

MATERIAL, *MEMORY SERVES* (1981, ELEKTRA/MUSICIAN)
Bill Laswell

I, first, was a musician, and I learned the hard way about being on the other end. I came to production through making records, from being re-

sponsible and by coordinating things out of the necessity to have a bit more control over what I thought was valuable or my opinion. I acquired control, more and more, out of the need to be responsible for what I was doing. I learned step by step all the ways to make things happen: whether to force something, whether to mutate it, manipulate it, or destroy it. Or whether to let it grow organically. It all comes down to a spontaneous or basic intuition about performance and sound. There's a magic there that people won't be able to appropriate unless they've had a certain kind of experience.

As for postproduction, there are lots of levels of manipulation, and to me that's all very much a part of composition. In the past, composition was notation. To me, it's memories. To me, tape is composition. That replaces notation because it's all memory. Once something is on tape, it's no different than having it on paper.

Composition is expanding every day and all the time. And it's being redefined. Many years ago, [John] Cage said that in the future records would be made by records. DJs have proven that in genres like hip-hop—which arc made from older records.

As far as writing something down on paper and calling it a composition that can be played and repeated, to me it's not that different than recording something, memorizing it, and repeating it. Whether you memorize it, then, by notating it is one way. Or whether you do it with a computer or whether you do it with a sampler or whether you use the actual piece and reproduce it the way DJs reproduce records to create records, they're all new ways. There's always a new way to create music, and it always comes down to collage because you are always fitting things together.

The more sort of desperate and far-fetched concepts that do fit together as collage, if you can make them feel like music, then that's an achievement. All of these things didn't come in styles. They didn't come in forms. It all started with the person who had an idea, who was copied and copied and copied. Then it's preserved by people who know very well they can't do better.

With sound as an idea, you keep delving further and further into it. At some point, lines or themes disappear, rhythm disappears. It all gets sort of washed away by just sound. You start to deal with areas of sound that can be manipulated and processed and changed. It's endless, and sometimes it takes over. Sometimes you appropriate it with other sorts of sounds which could be rhythmic, which could be melodic, which could be conventional instrumentation. But when you start to work in that area, you step into a space that's endless.

VARIOUS, *AMARCORD NINO ROTA* (1981, HANNIBAL)
Joel Dorn (Atlantic)

When Hal [Willner] was fourteen, I lived in a place called Lower Merion, outside of Philly. Hal lived on one corner; we lived on another. I was pushing, maybe, thirty. Hal's father owned a delicatessen in the neighborhood. So we'd go in there. Hal was the busboy. He introduced himself and started saying, "I dug what you did on the Joe Zawinul record. I heard what you did on the Yusef—that bell underneath the subway train."

"Who the fuck is this kid?" I kind of wrote him off. But he'd come to the house, knock on the door, and say, "I just got Yusef Lateef's *Part of the Search*. Man, I dug ..."

I don't know exactly what it was. I was so far out, a little onto drugs—crazy. I was *really* producing records. So I didn't get him. One day, Hal came by, and some friends of mine were over. We were sitting in the backyard, eating hamburgers, barbecue, or some such shit. Hal came by to talk about—I think it was Rahsaan or Joe Zawinul. I was getting ready to brush him off again.

One of my friends, an older cat, said, "Hey, what are you doing? Take this kid in! He's into it. He's you, schmuck!"

So I dug it. He became my Tonto. Like I used to bother Nesuhi, Hal used to bother me. He's a brilliant guy. Nesuhi passed me the baton; I passed it to Hal.

Hal Willner

When I started out, active producers didn't stick to one kind of music. As a kid, I saw names on records, like John Hammond, Tom Wilson, Joel [Dorn], and all those. Take Tom Wilson. His name was on records by Sun Ra, Cecil Taylor, also Simon and Garfunkel, Dylan, Mothers of Invention, Velvet Underground. And Joel was on records by Rahsaan [Roland Kirk], Yusef [Lateef], the Allman Brothers, and Bette Midler. I thought producers were supervisors, responsible for how the record was, which went all the way from taking over and being hands-on to, if need be, leaving it alone. Knowing what the record was supposed to be—what you're going after—and then making sure it's realized, that determines how much hands-on or hands-off it will be.

At that time many, many producers couldn't even play an F on the piano. Of course, that's changed. Most of the guys now are glorified engineers or glorified something else. In general they're more in charge, it seems to me. Most of the records I've been doing are more conceptual. I maybe do one artist a year.

At one point, the styles of producers were practically invisible, like the styles of Hollywood directors during the heyday of the studio system. Then styles became opaque. For example, you could pick out a Creed Taylor production. What you do think accounted for that change?

A lot of those guys formed their own labels. They heard a certain sound, a certain kind of record that they wanted to make. And they found artists who could relate to their concepts, to that sound, and followed through with it. I don't know if John Hammond really had a sound. He sort of documented things.

When I started out, I basically wanted to be a staff producer because, to keep the analogy to films going, it seemed that it created some amazing things. When there were staff directors, things happened—people got assigned. You had Victor Fleming, who got to direct *The Wizard of Oz* and *Gone with the Wind* in the same year. It made for some incredible combinations. At the time I started, record producers were well versed. They had to be into every type of music. Generally, they were able to keep hands-off directly and still go after capturing their artist. I guess I got to see the very end of that era. It's really unfortunate that it doesn't still exist. We now have producers who get great drum tracks, that sort of thing. Then, you have guys whose careers are a flash in the pan. We could go on about that for hours.

I know how I found my role, and it wasn't going to go that way. I drifted into doing my own concept things. The Joel Dorn school was an amazing thing, just incredible. You'd have Roland Kirk, Don McLean, Leon Redbone, and Little Jimmy Scott walking in the studio around the same time. Joel used to mix up these people, put Yusef on the McLean record, put Roland Kirk on the Bette Midler record, and then the other way around. And Joel's interest in surrealism, Fellini, and Laurel and Hardy: it was an amazing school to attend. Plus, I was really lucky to catch the end of personality radio—commercial radio where you got a station playing Dylan, going into Hendrix, then into Captain Beefheart, Orson Welles radio shows, and Ornette Coleman. It all related. I wanted to make the kind of records that I wanted to hear. I started to do things like take a body of work—say, Nino Rota's—and get interpretations from Carla Bley to Blondie. My thing grew from there.

On Amarcord Nino Rota, did you hook up with Jaki Byard through your work at Atlantic?

No, I didn't. Joel had already left Atlantic. When I was gophering for him, I was a kid. I was in my early twenties. I was going to see everything, and Jaki Byard was pretty active at that time. Somehow, I pictured him doing *Amarcord* and *La Strada*. He had never heard the music, but I thought, "Wouldn't that be interesting?" and it just so happened that ended up being amazing.

You're a cinephile. Do film concepts carry over into your production work, for example, into more conventional projects like Marianne Faithfull's Strange Weather?

It all relates. The same with listening to old radio. I developed a big collection of everything from the Mercury Theater to the *Goon Show* and Ernie Kovacs. I visualize music. It's what videos ruined. I put in my own images. Joel learned about making records from paintings and from Nesuhi Ertegun and then took it to another place. I took it to my own.

Marianne Faithfull was a different thing. You're looking at a record. *Strange Weather* [1987] was an extension of the track that I did with her for the Kurt Weill record [*Lost in the Stars*, 1985]. It used the same approach. That's where my series ended up going. After the second record, I realized I had a series. The second record [*That's the Way I Feel Now: A Tribute to Thelonious Monk*, 1984] was made because I felt Monk was slighted in all the tributes being given to him. NRBQ deserved to be in a Monk tribute more than Oscar Peterson. That's where that came from. I've tried to make really cohesive records by taking wonderful bodies of work and then going through the motions.

Marianne, at that point in her life, wanted to make a record where she became an actress, played a role. Once a week, I'd go up to Boston, and we'd listen to music. Some songs came from different periods of my past, and then, talking to Marianne, songs came from her past, like "Penthouse Serenade." The musicians used were a mixture. Bill Frisell—who had made his recording debut on *Amarcord Nino Rota*—had by that point started to become very well known. I thought he would provide the right colors. And also Michael Gibbs. It was just taking things from different worlds. But that was recording an artist. It was very different; it wasn't my album. The trick there was capturing Marianne where she was at, at that time in her life.

A real record is like having a great meal. From appetizers through dessert, you really feel like you've been through something. You've gained—as with reading a book. At the point I started listening to records in the late sixties, the records that did that—from *Sketches of Spain* to *A Love Supreme* to *Trout Mask Replica*—caught up to literature and films. Record-making became a way to make art. Somehow it has taken a step backwards. We're back into batches of songs. Some rap artists are doing interesting things as far as albums-as-minimovies are concerned.

ART PEPPER, *WINTER MOON* (1981, GALAXY)
Ed Michel

Here's the whole genesis of that album. When Art signed with Fantasy, the deal was he was mostly going to do small-band records. But he asked [label president] Ralph Kaffel, "Can I do one big project?"

Ralph said, "Sure." So this was the big project. We had talked about several possibilities. We'd wanted to do a fairly big Latin album, and we talked about doing an R & B album. Art was a great R & B player. He'd sit around, listen to records, and play tenor—great R & B tenor. He really loved, at least, the Ray Charles side of R & B: jump-band music. He'd come up in it. Those were a couple of thoughts. Then he decided he really wanted to do a strings album. Like all saxophone players, he was crazy to do one. That was absolutely fine.

We talked about who should write it. He knew Bill Holman and Jimmy Bond very well. Jimmy had been a bass player in his band for a while, and he and Holman went way back in L.A. I thought very highly of them as string writers. So it was line up the arrangers, tell them the general parameters, and let them write it. Get a good rhythm section. Then it was very easy. To be safe, I had told Art, "Why don't I put you in a vocal booth, booth you off from the band so I get clean tracks in case you want to play over them again? If you don't like a solo, you can take another whack at it without having the string players sitting around."

"Sure, sure. Absolutely, we can do it that way." Then, the night before the date he said, "No, let me go out in the studio and do it with them."

"Fine," I said. We were going to record in San Francisco, and I think the biggest decision was, "Would the quality of San Francisco string players be equal to what we were used to in New York?" And it was. After the first rundown, there were no problems. They were fine. In fact, they were trying much harder. L.A. and New York string players really have attitudes. They spend a lot of time looking at their watches, complaining about humidity in the studio, asking when their next break is going to be so they can call their brokers. In San Francisco they were so pleased to come in and play on a jazz date that they could hardly stand it.

I regarded Art as one of the great ballad players. He was gifted. He knew how to play in front of a large ensemble, and he knew how to be a soloist. What's to worry about? I was, however, worried about whether the strings were going to be able to do it right. They were the missing element. I knew the rhythm section was trustworthy. They'd make it happen. Strings make for a more expensive time in the studio, and there isn't the looseness there would be if they went away.

Did Pepper's well-known personal problems make for challenges?

He was one of the most famous crazy people in the history of the planet. My job is dealing with people who are artists first and human beings second. It's my job to keep things rolling. Art pitched an amazing, uncalled-for tantrum after we did two takes of something that didn't get on the original album. He was just out there, and for no reason at all. But that was okay. It wasn't the first time. Art wanted to have an "out there," and so he did. He stalked out of the room, and I had the string players run down the next two charts. That's kind of what you do.

I always like to set up a date so that the leader doesn't have to do anything but come in and play—nothing to worry about. But Art's drug of choice was adrenaline. If things were too easy for him, he found a way to up the adrenaline level. The first date we did, I figured, "Oh, why make it hard for him? I'll make it really simple. All he'll have to do is pull out the alto." There wasn't enough to keep him nervous, so he banged his toe into a mike stand and thought he had broken it. He was in great pain. He said, "It's okay. I'll play anyway." That's what he wanted to make it work.

I had to give Art at least the illusion that he was walking into a dangerous bar in a frontier town and was going to saxophone his way out of it. He liked that. And great fondness resulted. Art and Laurie and I were old friends. We were teenagers together in L.A. In the late fifties, we worked at the same folk club in L.A., called the Ash Grove. To pick ballads, I said, "Art and Laurie, come up to my house." I lived in a little town in central California on the ocean. "Come up for three days, and we'll listen to ballads, pick thirty or forty tunes that are knockouts." So we did, and it was nice.

Did you discuss whether he'd play alto or whether, on a cut or two, he'd play clarinet?

I said, "Bring the clarinet." I always wanted him to play clarinet. But I didn't much care. It was his dream album, and I didn't want to make a lot of choices for him. He knew what he wanted to do. I was very pleased that he wanted to write a couple of tunes for the album.

We picked the takes after the sessions were done, although it wasn't very hard. We usually knew when we had it. If he'd done a take one and then a take two, then we'd probably done take two because we expected to get a better track. And we did. I always picked takes with artists, unless someone wasn't interested. If he said, "You pick them," then I would.

GANELIN TRIO, *ANCORA DA CAPO* (1982, LEO)
Leo Feigin

The music I choose for my label is, of course, a matter of my taste or a matter of my intuition. My understanding of the music is purely on this intuitive level. I never try to explain the music which I hear, but I think I understand it.

As far as coming to terms with difficult music, I don't understand what you could mean, because I don't think I've ever come across difficult music. Do you mean music of some African tribes or Stockhausen? I think there's music which one likes and music which one doesn't—the music which draws some response from your whole aesthetic vocabulary and the music which doesn't. What really matters is how wide your aesthetic vocabulary is. The bigger or wider it is, maybe, the greater your potential response.

A common preconception says that in order for musicians to play good music they must love each other, or have respect for each other, and so on and so on. The Ganelin Trio is a living example that this is totally wrong. You don't have to love or respect each other to play great music. [Vyacheslav] Ganelin and [Vladimir] Chekasin come to the stage every time for their final musical battle. They can't stand each other. Musically, they are trying to bugger up each other, to put each other into the corner, to finish, to ruin the other musically. Of course, this fight goes on within the limits of structure, of some tonalities, of musical laws which are followed or to which they adhere. This is what I mean by music which takes ultimate chances: that is, this musical attempt to conquer one another.

As far as the future of Leo Records is concerned, I can't be that optimistic. In order to run my label, I have to work full-time somewhere else. I am very tired. I have so many debts that I can't go on. I'll tell you honestly that now I cannot even sell one hundred fifty copies of a new release.

I press five hundred copies of a new release. Two hundred I send away to radio stations, critics, magazines, and to some fans in the Soviet Union.[15] I send about one hundred to my small distributers in Switzerland, Austria, Germany, and Italy—and that's that. They can't order more than ten copies of each new release. The rest—about two hundred copies—are still on my shelf collecting dust. A label can't go on like this. The point is, I am really disillusioned with the lack of support from critics, radio stations, magazines, and publications. I know that sooner or later Leo Records will be recognized, and this music will be known by a wider audience. But as very often happens, this will come too late.

How do I retain my zeal for new music? The question is wrong. I don't keep my zeal for new music. New music helps me to live. I have to work twenty-four hours a day. I've taught myself to sleep no more than six hours and, sometimes, I sleep three or four hours in a day. Whatever concerns the label, I do myself. It's not that I keep my zeal for new music. It's when I am dead, when I feel that I am finished, when I feel I can't go on anymore, I put on some unreleased tapes by Ganelin, Arkhangelsk, or another musician. When I put on a special record, I recover. New music helps me to recover. It keeps me alive.

HERBIE HANCOCK, "ROCKIT" (1983), *FUTURE SHOCK* (COLUMBIA)
Bill Laswell

The people around Herbie were looking to change him, and I think he was open to anything that happened. Success wasn't a bad way to go. It certainly wasn't a case of working directly with him where you play and then record. For example, with Shannon [Jackson], there was dialogue. With Herbie, it was really sort of a hatchet job. It was more, "Bring a concept. Bring an idea. Do everything. Then he'll drop a few notes on it." Then it's a hit record, Herbie's a star, and it's a big success.

It was recorded incredibly quickly and spontaneously, and with a crew of people who had a kind of alliance together [i.e., by Laswell (bass),

15. This interview was conducted in 1987, before the collapse of the Soviet Union. Feigin mailed me taped responses to questions I had mailed him. At this time he specialized in issuing experimental music from the Soviet Union. Leo Records is still in business.

Michael Beinhorn (keyboards), and cohorts]. It was really all done in New York and then taken out to L.A., practically finished before anyone there even heard it. If I remember, Herbie's parts were added and done in a couple of hours, and the actual mixing of the one piece that became this big hit ["Rockit"] was done in less than two hours. It was done without any thinking. It was spontaneous: ideas went on tape, done very quickly and mixed very quickly, and that was that.

It was a single idea. It was a tempo and a bassline and a way of appropriating that. It was like decorating a metronome to suit the times. That's all it was. It was done without a lot of research, a lot of work. I mean bassline, one take. Turntable thing [GrandMixer D.ST]. You'd be amazed at how quickly it was done. Car-service driver waiting on the couch. Daniel Poncé [percussion], one take. Take the tape out to L.A. Everybody says, "What is this shit?"

I said, "No, it'll work. It's okay." Play a couple of notes on it, mix it, and that's that. That's a freak record. It had everything to do with timing. It probably had a great deal to do with some debt at Columbia, somebody trying to get some money back. It had a lot to do with using a DJ in that context. There certainly wasn't any brilliant production, or it wasn't any great piece of music. It was a freak incident.

JAMES BLOOD ULMER, "ARE YOU GLAD TO BE IN AMERICA?" (1983), *ODYSSEY* (COLUMBIA)
James Blood Ulmer

My song "Are You Glad to Be in America?" was a very good song in England, where I made it. I made some money. I sang, "Are you glad to be in America?" in an ironic way that [suggested] you might not have to be glad to be there.

So after we released *Black Rock* [1982, Columbia], Joe [McEwen, associate producer] brought in Junior Morrison, the guy who used to produce Funkadelic, to make "Are You Glad to Be in America?" real commercial, like "Oh boy, aren't you glad to be in America?" The background was like everybody was happy to be here.

They tried to get me to do that, and I said, "I wouldn't even have nothing like that playing."

"If you don't do it, this will be your last record."

I said, "Not only am I not doing 'Are You Glad to Be in America' like that, I'm going to make my last record with no bass." And I made that record with drums and violin. That guitar tuning had the bass, everything in it. So I hooked it up like that. For three years after that, I played without tuning up regular. I traveled and played what I call diatonic harmolodic tuning.

KIP HANRAHAN, *DESIRE DEVELOPS AN EDGE* (1983, AMERICAN CLAVÉ)
Kip Hanrahan

When I played percussion in high school and junior high school—I was playing in some Latin bands—I know I didn't think of myself as a musician. Later on, I realized there was a way—not by playing it but by directing or writing it—that would be my clearest way to articulate or to make happen something that needed to happen; that if it didn't happen, it would be painful.

On a level, which I think is not actually dishonest but is a kind of funny way to look at it, [I make records] because it gives you more of an internal gleam than you deserve—you hear music that needs to be there. You don't actually hear the notes—not necessarily, but sometimes you do. You certainly hear a mood, and you need to hear that music mood realized on a record. You envision. I don't think you conceptually envision a record. You just need to make it happen. It's a kind of addiction, and you're not comfortable until you hear those emotions in music made audible. I know that sounds a little bit too noble; it sounds strange. You have an image of yourself, and it's like a way of breathing. It's really just something I can do.

I never want to do the same project twice; I never want my relationship to the work to be the same. If the record is under my name, my stuff is supposed to describe a series of emotions inside me, or between myself and other players. I write almost all the words, I write almost all the music and arrangements, and I direct the band note for note. Or if I choose not to, for one particular piece, that's a choice, although it's rare. On my own records I'm really tight about what goes down there. All mistakes are there for a reason. I take full responsibility for being the source and the editor of that aesthetic, the source and the director of the sound of that aesthetic, or the sound of those emotions. I'll take the blame for them also, if people don't like them.

VARIOUS, *CONJURE: MUSIC FOR THE TEXTS OF ISHMAEL REED* (1984, AMERICAN CLAVÉ)
Kip Hanrahan

With *Conjure*, I commission work from people, and I record it.[16] Generally, people look to me to be a musical director, but depending on whether I think I'm good or bad for a particular piece, I can defer or I can pass the musical directing job on to somebody in the band—whether the composer or the main voice—if I think they're going to be more dynamic and more clear about it. *Conjure*— it's more fun. It's not my aesthetics. It's not my words. It's not my music. I'm just the musical center of it—sometimes. Or if I'm not, it's my choice.

VARIOUS, *LOST IN THE STARS: THE MUSIC OF KURT WEILL* (1985, A&M)
Hal Willner

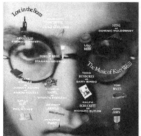

Aaron Neville, who I've worked with a few times, was put in a very comfortable situation for the "Mickey Mouse March" [*Stay Awake: Various Interpretations of Music from Vintage Disney Films*, 1988]. It fit into a concept. I put him with Mac [Rebennack aka Dr. John], who Aaron knows, and made him feel at home.

    With the Kurt Weill record, I put him in an uncomfortable situation. The only recording of the song "Oh Heavenly Salvation" was in German. Then, I was going for something else. Those are two completely different types of performances. Artists try a different kind of way if they are not as comfortable.

    Another example is the work I did on the TV show *Night Music*. I had people do stuff together that on camera you'd never see. Probably the best collaboration I ever did was on a show with Leonard Cohen and Sonny Rollins. You talk about a situation you wouldn't normally see! It was, of course, very strange at first, but then they locked in. The key was the song that was chosen, "Who by Fire," which Leonard wrote based on the He-

16. Three *Conjure* albums—all employing texts by Ishmael Reed—have been released: *Music for the Texts of Ishmael Reed* (1984), *Cab Calloway Stands in for the Moon* (1988), and *Bad Mouth* (2005).

brew prayer for the dead. It was something that Rollins could relate to: the prayer aspect of it. Making them uncomfortable led to the creation of something unlike what you'd ever heard before—a certain kind of performance. Audiences had never heard anything quite like Leonard Cohen with Sonny Rollins, or Aaron Neville singing Brecht and Weill.

I don't know if I used the right words with "comfortable" and "uncomfortable." Maybe "challenging." You've got to create a situation where something is going to happen and not be boring. If it's comfortable—like having Aaron singing the "Mickey Mouse March"—at least make them do something they wouldn't normally do. It's often hard to come up with the words.

I follow my instincts, whether they make rational sense or not. More often than not, at least it will be interesting. That's what I think you have to go for. Stay away from being boring at all costs.

Was Sergeant Pepper's *important to you aesthetically?*

Other things are more influential: records that inspired *Sergeant Pepper's. Absolutely Free* [Frank Zappa and the Mothers of Invention] meant a little more to me, and as an adult I probably followed the Velvet Underground more, and how that stuff came out of Varèse and out of *A Love Supreme* and *Sketches of Spain.* Those are amazing concept records. They came from classical music. Stravinsky and Charles Ives did very conceptual things. That's what the LP gave you the chance to do.

George Avakian told me that he sequenced albums so that the first cut would grab people and the last cut on the first side would make people want to turn the record over.

I often go the opposite route. I see it like a Venus flytrap. You invite them in, eat them, and spit them out. I often prefer to start out records kind of quiet—kind of inviting you in—and place my strongest thing at the end. I do agree with wanting to have it so people want to turn the record over. But I've found that when you grab people, especially with CDs, a lot of people won't get much past that. They'll play that track over and over again. CDs are a one-sided thing. If you talk to a lot of people, they'll tell you they don't even get to the end of a CD. They don't hear the whole thing.

On your projects do you make assignments? For example, did you say to Lou Reed, "I want you to sing 'September Song'"?

Not necessarily, not all the time. Sometimes I do. On one of those records, I might go from being hands-on, involved with tracks, to saying, "Would you like to be on the record? Pick a song." But I'm always there supervising, watching the sounds, with mixing and everything. Each track is its own story. I did, however, suggest "September Song." Lou actually got mad at the time, but he thought about it and said, "This is a great song for me." We recut it for a TV show, years later—a new version with a different tempo.

ÁSTOR PIAZZOLLA AND THE NEW TANGO QUINTET, *TANGO: ZERO HOUR* (1986, AMERICAN CLAVÉ)
Kip Hanrahan

Piazzolla's project, that was a treat. Working with Ástor, as a producer—"treat," that's a thin word, but I can't summon a strong enough word. I worked differently on each record. Each one was different; it required a different producer. When you're working with Ástor, you're basically agreeing to be subordinate to his crystalline aesthetics. That makes it easier to have faith in his project. It's somebody else's aesthetics, and somebody else's stakes you have a real deep faith in.

In his case you know what his thing is. You look at his paperwork and everything makes sense. It constructs his aesthetics. Your gig is to make it the best possible. On *Zero Hour* I worked for weeks, going over every possible tempo, going over which song should be tighter and which song shouldn't be—before the band even got there. We wrote for about a year before. We decided what compositions from the older stuff we might want to rework, what sequences might work, and what changes we'd make, what new pieces would make sense for it, and how we could use more complex and less complex times.

I worked with Piazzolla as a servant to his aesthetics. That was beautiful; that was comfortable. I really lost myself in that. At the end, when Ástor was happy and I was happy, it was a moment almost like—because everything is qualified—but it was as close to unqualified satisfaction as you could come up with. Yes, I got what Piazzolla was able to deliver. And working within his rubric, I was able to take it further, make it better. That was fantastic. But in that case, I rehearsed the band, we went over pacing, we went over rewriting parts.

The second record [*The Rough Dancer and the Cyclical Night*, 1988], he had like twelve minutes of music. He wanted to do something really rough; he didn't want to make it complex. So he dumped it in my lap to make it into a record. He liked what I did on the first one. So I was able to complete the pieces for him: never really adding repeat signs, but take it and make it into a record.

As a result, it was a fun record, but I don't think it was as deep as his other stuff. He gave me the reins as copilot. He said, "Here, you take it." I overdubbed some of the stuff, but that wasn't as deep a record.

The last record [*La Camorra: La Soledad de la Provocación Apasionada,* 1989] was different. The band was just about to break up. "The Camorra Suite" Ástor wanted intense and rough. Also, it was a dare. After we finished *Zero Hour,* I kind of dared him to come up with something more beautiful and more complex than *Zero Hour,* and when you dare Ástor, he'll come back. At times *La Camorra* is more complex and, at times, more beautiful, but I don't think—except for the "The Camorra Suite," which is incredible—I don't think it is as consistently good as *Zero Hour.*

MILES DAVIS, *TUTU* (1986, WARNER BROS.)
Tommy LiPuma

Miles's new manager, David Franklin, brought him to Warners. That was a great experience. Miles was a unique character. I went in with much trepidation, to say the least, because I'd heard horror stories about him, which were all bullshit. One thing about Miles, there were no gray areas. He either liked you or didn't like you. Fortunately for me, we hit it off and became close friends.

I made a couple of calls that he liked. I brought Marcus Miller into the picture [as bassist and coproducer]. I'd been working with Marcus on numerous things. I knew he was a great writer, and Marcus had been part of Miles's band for a short time. So when I first mentioned him, Miles said, "Oh yeah, man, I know Marcus. Great." I did other albums with Miles, but I have to say *Tutu* was the best one.

There were some interesting choices of material. Music by Scritti Politti?

Miles Davis loved pop music. I never forget when I played him the Scritti Politti thing, "Perfect Way," which we ended up doing, he recognized it. I told him, "If you ever needed a job as an A & R man, I'd hire you in a minute." He recognized all that shit. He knew when something was great. I'll never forget, I turned him on to Mr. Mister. Remember that group? They had this thing called "Broken Wings." It was a big hit. I said, "Hey man, you've got to check out this thing."

He called me after a gig in Miami. He said, "Hey man, I just heard that Mr. Mister. That's a motherfucker."

He knew good stuff. He had no prejudices. That went all the way. People thought he hated white people. No, he didn't hate white people. He hated assholes. If you were an asshole, it didn't matter what color you were.[17]

STANLEY JORDAN, *STANDARDS, VOLUME 1* (1986, BLUE NOTE)
Stanley Jordan

I had a good time in the studio, because I was producer. I was in control, able to do whatever it took to get the job done. Because of that, I was much happier with this album than with *Magic Touch* [1985]. There were times when I felt a little bit rushed, but that was because I'm living in a real world, and the record company needed an album.

We recorded everything direct—clean guitar. The actual EQ was done later. Afterwards, we could refine the sound because we had the original guitar. I stay away from overdubbing for a couple of reasons. The main reason is I wanted to show what could be done without it. A lot of people use it to cover up for what they don't have, as far as musical ability. I don't like that, because it's like joining the track team and, when it comes time to run, you jump in a car and try to beat everybody. Part of it is the human effort of trying to achieve the impossible. When something comes along that brings new possibilities, then it should be presented, and people should see it for what it really is. It's not like I'm against overdubbing. I've done it. But by not overdubbing people can hear what I really can do as a musician.

The other thing I like about not overdubbing is that it makes the recording a true musical moment—something that really happened. It makes it easy to relate to. I studied high-tech and computer music enough to know we're getting to a point where we can synthesize any sound. So music can't be just about sound. In order to be true it's got to be something human that people can relate to.

Still, I was not trying to say, "Hey everybody, this is me!" On *Magic Touch* that was what I was trying to do. I was breaking out. On this album

---

17. Davis's pop-jazz orientation on this comeback album could be seen as directly related to his contract with Warner Bros. It gave him a signing fee of over $1 million, but it assigned publishing rights on new compositions to Warner Bros, hence formalizing a disincentive to write. See Ian Carr, *Miles Davis: The Definitive Biography* (New York: Thunder's Mouth, 1998), 441.

I said, "Here are some songs that I grew up with and that I love. Let me share them with you."

The album is not flashy. Technically, I did a fraction of what I was capable of doing. The album is about bringing as much musicality and expression as I could into the songs. I put a lot of attention on phrasing. I tried to take the existing language of the song and bring out more in it. For example, on "Moon River" I tried to improvise a totally new melody, not just state the melody and then play my solo. My improvisation was as mellow as the original song.

SONNY ROLLINS, *G-MAN* (1986, MILESTONE)
Sonny Rollins

I like to reach an audience. Everybody does. But I find that when I'm really playing myself, that's when I reach the audience. Trying to do anything else, I realized a long time ago, is counterproductive.

I'm playing mainly improvised, spontaneous music. Everything depends upon what has preceded it directly. If I'm in good musical form, I'm able to utilize my timing—which is very important. I also utilize my sixth sense, because a lot of things I do are intuitive. If I'm in good shape, then I usually find some way to communicate with the audience. If I'm struggling any particular night, then this can all be lost. That's what makes playing so much fun. You want to jump off the roof sometimes. It's not set; it's very problematical. It's so scientific and it's so artistic at the same time.

I just try to be in good shape, and other than that, the way I play—my natural talent, whatever you want to call it—that's what the people react to. It's not a conscious effort to get to people. I don't want to alienate people. No, of course not. But I like to think that it's something in the music beyond my comprehension that the people link with.

HENRY THREADGILL SEXTETT, *YOU KNOW THE NUMBER* (1986, RCA/NOVUS)
Steve Backer (Executive Producer)

The jazz community often gets the idea that corporations are this big, evil ogre in the sky, but they're nothing but individuals grouped together. Sometimes they're good at what they do, sometimes they're mediocre, and sometimes they're bad—the same as in any field.

For the last five or six years [1980–86], jazz has been in a retrenching

period where a lot of people are looking back instead of looking forward. I don't see how some of the players who are a part of the current neo-classicism are going to want to do that much longer. A number of wonderful musicians have now gotten caught up in neo-this and neo-that. People need to start looking forward and moving their music forward. A fairly subjective example of that is Henry Threadgill, who never looks back and is always moving forward.

Henry was introduced to me by Anthony Braxton. At that point, I had done maybe seven albums with Braxton at Arista, which is quite a feat in itself, dealing with a major corporation, recording music as outré as Anthony's, and being able to have the continuity of doing seven, eight, nine albums. We ended up doing nine albums before it all dissolved. But Anthony introduced me to Henry, and I started listening to Air, and they blew me away. The first two albums that we did with them—[*Open Air Suit* and *Montreux, Suisse* (both 1978)]—were, pretty much, open-ended free improvisations. They got a good deal of critical acclaim. But when we settled in on the concept album—which was *Air Lore*—that really brought it home for them.

Unfortunately, it happened around 1980, and I couldn't go forward any more from there because the entire industry was purging itself of anything that was aesthetically and not commercially inclined. It's like regime to regime. Those cycles make a lot of difference in the timing of recording jazz. So we left off with *Air Lore* (1979), which ended up being the album of the year in 1980, and we picked up again.

Ed Michel

I'd been hired by Steve Backer, who was running the jazz operation at BMG. There'd been some real problems with reissues, and he hired me to come in and "unproblem" a couple of things. I wound up doing a lot of re-issue work and new work. I was there, and I had a reputation for getting things done on schedule and on budget.

Henry and Keith Jarrett are very much the same, but only in the sense that they both know what they want to do before they go in the studio. It's not going to be an accident. So it was fairly easy to record Henry. In both cases [*You Know the Number* (1986) and *Easily Slip into Another World* (1987)] there were working bands. The problems were, in one case, a vocalist not used to working with the band, and one of the guys in the ensemble couldn't play a lot of the parts. One of the other guys in the ensemble had to overdub the guy's parts for him. It worked out fine. What can I say? Henry is, first, a composer. When you're recording a composer who's performing his own stuff with his own ensemble, it is generally going to be lined up ahead of time. He is also very demanding, which is nice. He'll ask for another take before I will.

Since you asked about Threadgill and about suggestions I made that turned out well, here's one that didn't. I said, "Henry, shit, I think the most interesting music you can write is music for marching band. I know you've got a big library of marching band music. But it wouldn't really be practical to get a bunch of guys to come into the studio and sight-read that stuff. With marches you've got to rehearse and get the feeling, get the sense of how they go. I think we ought to find some friend of yours who's teaching at a band camp, a summer band camp, and give him a dozen charts, a CD's worth of charts, and have him rehearse them with a band. They could go out and march every day and play them until they really had the ensembles happening like marches. Then, we'd bring in the band to record with you and a couple of key soloists."

Henry got really distressed with me. He thought I was putting him on or being condescending. I wasn't. I was being pragmatic. I thought and still think it's a good idea. I'd love to hear a band-camp thing, marching-band music by Henry Threadgill or Anthony Braxton. They could do that, and nobody ever plays it in that context.

DUKE ELLINGTON, . . . *AND HIS MOTHER CALLED HIM BILL* (REISSUE, 1987, BLUEBIRD; ORIGINAL RECORDING, 1967, BLUEBIRD)
Steve Backer (Executive Producer)

I'm not a hands-on producer who works the board in a recording studio. I'm a combination of things—a production company and an executive producer—which is quite different. I don't have the time to stay in the studio, so I try to match the artist with the most harmonious individual on a production level to oversee a project.

If you will, describe as specifically as possible the executive producer's job.

You make projects possible by your role in the executive end of the corporate structure. You create opportunities: from conception through to contractual negotiations with the artist; to communicating the project the artist has in mind; to overseeing, conceptually, the actual recording process. Once the album is delivered, you advise and consult with the company on many levels, such as marketing, merchandising, promotion, advertising, touring, and so on. It's a multifaceted role.

In regards to Bluebird, it means that I'm the person that made it possible for the vaults to be reopened at RCA. On a business level and on a creative level, prior to the actual remastering and reissuing of the projects, the executive producer decides which projects to do or not do.

What are your criteria for choosing albums to be reissued?

I want them to have as much impact as possible on the consumer and the jazz community (which includes critics, radio, and all the people that help you as midwives between the reissuing of albums and them reaching consumers). I look for balance between aesthetics and commerciality.

Give me some free-associative characterizations of the material you've recently reissued.

Fats Waller, *The Complete Fats Waller*, volume 4. We're attempting to complete some of the things I feel ethically obligated to complete, projects that RCA started in the seventies. They end up being completest-oriented endeavors, geared more to collectors than to general consumers.

Originally, Bluebird was RCA's jazz budget line. But the last [pre-CD] incarnation of Bluebird was in the seventies when, working on a completest level, they concentrated on the swing bands of the thirties and forties. We're trying to take a more thorough and comprehensive attack than just the swing bands.

I didn't go to CD on some recordings for a very practical reason. The technology for moving some of the material from the pretape era (pre-1948 or 1949) was really not there until recently. We've now [in 1987] found a company in California whose software reduces the surface noise—the pops, clicks, and hisses—of the pretape era without altering the high end of (or compressing) the music. Now, I'm able to move more things to CD.

Duke Ellington, *The Blanton-Webster Band*. I have dual feelings about this reissue. Conceptually, it is a brilliant project. *DownBeat* awarded it reissue of the year. Obviously a lot of critics feel as I do. Musically, it's wonderful to get material from that particular band collated in one package for the world. From a sonic point of view, however, it has given me a lot of heartache. It was one of our first packages. We've now redone the recording entirely. It will be the same package without sonic mistakes (and without one musical mistake that drove me up the wall).

Duke Ellington, *... And His Mother Called Him Bill*. Here, you're talking about the post-tape era, which is a piece of cake compared to the pretape era, in terms of digitally remastering and moving things to CD. With this album you have an amazing set—the whole band played with an intensity that was remarkable. It was recorded only three months after "Bill" Strayhorn's death. It's a beautiful CD, musically and sonically. We found four previously unreleased cuts. Two had been issued overseas and two had never come out anywhere.

Gary Burton, *Artist's Choice*. Gary recorded for RCA for a number of years, and this is a compilation for which he chose the cuts. It features a lot of really great players—Steve Lacy, Gato, Carla Bley, Jim Hall, and Larry Coryell—in a lot of different settings; the most exciting, for me, is from the *Genuine Tong Funeral* period. This incorporates maybe two or three cuts from each approach Gary took with the label.

Paul Desmond, *Late Lament*. We promised to lease some tracks to Michael Cuscuna at Mosaic for a Desmond box, but we didn't want redundancy. The only thing we didn't lease—most of the things we leased to Michael were quartet things—was this session with strings.

Artie Shaw and His Orchestra, *Begin the Beguine*, and Charlie Barnet and His Orchestra, *Clap Hands, Here Comes Charlie*. Because I didn't want to dig deep into "major," early material before sorting out sonic issues, we stayed within the swing and big band era for our first batch of [digitized] releases. And that's the reason we compiled the best of Shaw and Barnet in a best-of manner.

Most all this material has not been available domestically for between a decade and two decades. So it feels really good to be able to unlock the padlock on the vaults.

JAMES BLOOD ULMER, *AMERICA—DO YOU REMEMBER THE LOVE?* (1987, BLUE NOTE)
Bill Laswell

Blood was someone I'd known from way back. I'd played with Shannon [Jackson] and him on different occasions. We shared the same environment, playing live and playing festivals in Europe and playing clubs. We sort of came out of the same scene here [in New York] where people from a more jazz or avant-garde background began to play in punk clubs and attract a different audience. We came out of that ["no-wave"] scene. Shannon Jackson, Blood Ulmer, even to some extent Henry Threadgill, Olu Dara, Ornette Coleman's Prime Time: all those groups were active in the late seventies, early eighties.

Blood wanted to do the project, and the person who was managing him wanted to go that way. It was kind of a natural thing to do. At the time I had some support from [Blue Note president] Bruce Lundvall, who I knew because I'd worked with him at Elektra. Since then, I did another project with Blood: [Third Rail's *South Delta Space Age*, 1997] with Ziggy Modeliste from the Meters, Bernie Worrell, and Amina Myers.

Usually, with Blood there's a lot of playing and then going over ideas with instruments. There's not a whole lot of conceptualizing verbally about what's going to happen, but there's certainly a lot of playing. He likes to be comfortable with the playing side of it. And then you record. On the overdubs he lets me do what I want, but he had to be sure about the basic structure. He's someone looking for other sounds and always looking to sound different. He doesn't mind drastic change. He's not necessarily preserving any tradition. He's coming in at another angle.

WAYNE HORVITZ, BUTCH MORRIS, AND ROBERT PREVITE, *NINE BELOW ZERO* (1987, SOUND ASPECTS)
Wayne Horvitz

It was done in a really inexpensive studio [Newtex]. There was no producer, per se, though the engineer, Steve Gaboury, had really great ears. It was done live to two-track, and it was done that way because that's all we could afford.

Another thing that made that record have something in common with so-called pop production had nothing to do with production at all, in the sense that we normally think: ideas about miking and mixing things. It had more to do with the fact that, when you're working with songs, everything serves the songs, whereas jazz seems to have stayed in this sort of world where you get the head over with and then it's the guy's solo. One of the things I like about *Kind of Blue* is that the solos never stop serving the compositions. It's all about what serves the song. It makes the tune a piece of music instead of a structure where someone plays a theme and then someone has a chance to blow. I mean, I love hearing Sonny Rollins's *Live at the Vanguard*. But personally, in my own music and what I'm attracted to when I produce is not that area. Your average contemporary jazz record works exactly the same as records from the fifties and sixties. You play the head; you have an arrangement. Then it's about people's solos.

What made it [the album] kind of unique was that it was this kind of chamberesque use of sounds, like DX-7s and the earlier drum machines, that at the time people heard a lot but, typically, loud. We used them soft, to put that as stupidly as possible. And we improvised with them. We improvised with drum machines onstage, which people started to do, except they tended to do it in a totally free, avant-garde, noise way. We used loops and drum machines to make pretty melodic music. Yet it wasn't like new age. We really believed in letting people play instruments.

I didn't know anything then about producing. I had this group, and I wanted to record. It could not have been more low-key. Luck must have had a lot to do with it. If you called me up now to produce that record with that instrumentation, I'd probably go, "Oh well, we can't do it that way." It's funny. Sometimes a little knowledge is a dangerous thing.

THE PRESIDENT, *BRING YR CAMERA* (1988, ELEKTRA MUSICIAN)
Wayne Horvitz

I did a lot of work in advance. I put sequences down, or when we were in the studio, I played a keyboard part that was totally written. With that band, I didn't improvise much. I created these little worlds, and I usually took either the sax or the guitar and made them the principal soloists. It wasn't that hard. I could stand away from it a little better. Then, as soon as we got to the solo-ing, which often was done as an overdub, then I wasn't a musician anymore. I could go in and put on my producer hat.

Actually, *Bring Yr Camera* had a producer, Artie Moorhead. At the time, he worked for New World Records. That's kind of how I got into producing. When we did *Bring Yr Camera*, we went into Power Station. It was a full-out twenty-four-track recording. And Artie is not a musician. Most of his production experience was straight-ahead jazz or classical stuff—not stuff that really used the studio. Artie took a back seat to what I was doing with the recording, which was to his credit. He didn't let his ego get involved. He liked what he heard. But he was the person hired to produce the record. Afterwards, he started talking to me about producing other projects. He's a good friend of Bob Hurwitz, who runs Nonesuch. They talked to me about producing Bill's records [Bill Frisell].

Did you choose Power Station?

No, but I was thrilled. The label said, go in here, and they picked the engineer. I had very little experience with that kind of thing. Previously, I had done everything either at home in my eight-track studio or in little rooms. By the way, that has a lot to do with why the musician/producer is a contemporary fact of life. So many people have home studios. Even if you're not an engineer in the real sense, if you know what mikes to use for your own stuff, you've got some engineering skills.

Sometimes, on that album, we'd do a solo live. There was one case in particular. We said, "Okay, we'll do the sax solo again." But we ended up keeping the original. We spent half a day trying to get a better one and never did. This certain thing had happened on the live one. It had a kind of imperfection but spirit that we decided to keep. Everything else started to sound too slick. Then other solos were overdubbed. We'd almost always do a solo live, but sometimes we'd replace it.

Many rock bands for many years recorded the tracks live. They're, once again, doing that. There were a couple of years there where people put down the bass drum and the snare in two separate takes. Fortunately, people started to get away from that method really fast. It kind of reached this logical absurdity in the mid-eighties. Everyone realized it was idiotic.

Basically, we used the normal process of doing it live and then replacing things we didn't like. We added some overdubs to flesh things out a little. When I went to do *Miracle Mile* [the President's second album], I actually did a twenty-four-track version of what I'd previously recorded. I used material from my eight-track albums, which came out on little obscure labels. I put down a lot of stuff using drum machines and sequencers and then had people overdub one by one. I also did that on *Bring Yr Camera* with a couple of tunes we recorded as sort of an afterthought.

We'd made a record and then decided it wasn't quite working. I came up with three new tunes. For example, the opening track on *Bring Yr Camera* was drum machine, synth bass, and the organ parts. Then I had [saxophonist] Doug [Wieselman] play the theme. Next I had Eliot [Sharp] come in and do his guitar parts, including the solos. Last, [drummer] Bobby [Previte] put on his track. He didn't play to a click track; he played to everything so it could be musical in that other way. He responded to the solo, and he responded to the whole. I love working that way. It's really fun.

BIRD (ORIGINAL MOTION PICTURE SOUNDTRACK) (1988, COLUMBIA/LEGACY)
Joe Fields (Savoy)

I had bought the Savoy label—everything that wasn't gospel—from Arista, who had originally bought it from Herman Lubinsky, the original owner. We got a call from Clint Eastwood's people, and we sent them an analog

tape of "Parker's Mood," "Ko Ko," and "Now's the Time." I don't even remember if it was a copy Jack Towers remastered. But it really didn't matter because they fired the band. [Through the use of digital technology] they substituted new players for Parker's band.

I'm happy in one regard. For the first time, you're going to find people sitting in the dark entranced with this lovely, romantic movie, the story up there, and they're going to hear an awful lot of good music, and walk away getting a nice dosage of it.

For the music, that part is a plus. But make the parallel to fine arts. You can walk in [a museum] and look at your familiar Van Gogh. The central character may be right, but the rest is paint-by-numbers that somebody else filled in.

When I put on the soundtrack LP, John Guerin is on drums. On the original recording, it's Max Roach, who literally reinvented drumming to fit that situation. It was spare; it was very tight. Guerin, in turn, drummed in, more or less, today's style. They should have gotten Kenny Washington, who can imitate different styles, or for that matter Max Roach himself. And Parker was pushed too far back on the recording.

So my thought was a lot of people are going to go out, see the film, and buy this soundtrack. And that's wonderful. But to a certain degree, you're tampering with masterpieces, and people are going to perceive the music as being what was done to it. They should have the understanding that, if you want to transcend or go beyond the colorization of the music, the real things are out there.

ILLINOIS JACQUET AND HIS BIG BAND, *JACQUET'S GOT IT!* (1988, ATLANTIC)
Bob Porter

In the early eighties, Illinois was a guest lecturer at Harvard University for two years. He found that the kids were so responsive to what he was teaching that he said, "I should form a band of professionals." That's what he did. For the last twenty years of his life he led a big band.

That album came together for the simple reason that, when I was with Atlantic, I worked directly with Ahmet Ertegun. I didn't have to go through anybody else, which was absolutely great. I said to Ahmet, "You want to record Illinois Jacquet?" He perked up and said, "Yeah!" because he had heard that band live. He knew what they were capable of, and he knew the history of that kind of music. Basically, it was his project. I was just the guy who supervised the sessions.

Ahmet was a Renaissance man when it came to American music. He was into everything. He knew more about gospel, he knew more about blues piano players than anybody. He and [Jerry] Wexler together were an unbeatable team. By the time I got to Atlantic, though, Wexler was gone, Ahmet was doing things on his own, and the label was hot as a firecracker with rock stuff. But Ahmet was one of these guys who wanted to record certain people whether or not the record sold. In some cases he would record people, and the records wouldn't even come out. He just wanted to record somebody and put some money in their pocket. That's an aspect of the business that existed at Atlantic and almost no other place that I have heard of.

The Jacquet album cost a lot, more than twenty grand, because you had union rules and the band rehearsed like crazy. When they came in to record, it was rare that we had to do two takes on anything. It was *bim, bam, boom*. We sat down and got it done. Illinois was a very good bandleader in the sense that he knew what he wanted, and he was tough on the musicians until he got what he wanted.

We brought in some ringers on that date. Duffy Jackson was not the regular drummer, but Illinois decided he would be the best. I was thinking about Butch Miles, but Illinois decided on Duffy. He wanted to use Milt Hinton on bass, because he and Milt were neighbors out on Long Island, and despite the fact that Mona [Hinton] insisted on double scale for her husband. We brought in Marshall Royal to lead the reed section and Jon Faddis to lead the trumpet section. The other guys actually worked with the band: Eddie Barefield, Joey Cavaseno, Rudy Rutherford, and Frank Lacy, who played a couple of great trombone solos on the record. Irv Stokes was another trumpet soloist. Faddis was great on that record.

The only new dates that I did at Atlantic were Illinois's album and a session recorded live at the Village Vanguard with Fathead Newman. At the time there really wasn't a lot of enthusiasm for jazz at Atlantic from anybody. Ahmet used to say, "Between Porter and Ilhan [Mimaroğlu], if we're going to do some jazz, we'll do it with those guys." Which was okay with me. I had plenty of work just doing all of the reissues.

BOBBY PREVITE, *CLAUDE'S LATE MORNING* (1988, GRAMAVISION)
Bobby Previte

A sound popped into my head a couple of years ago. It took me quite a while to decipher what that sound was, as far as instrumentation goes, even though I was hearing the sound in all different moods and shapes. This is without having any music written. Finally, I deciphered the instrumentation. I kept replaying it over and over in my head: "Oh yeah, that's a pedal steel."

Then, at the same time, right when I was doing that, I started to write one of the pieces, "One Bowl." And that was the kernel for the whole thing. It has everything I wanted on the record, which is a band concept, not an overdubbing situation. I wanted very much a breathing band, in terms of tempo. It also has all the ideas—the sounds—that I'd heard. Basically, it was a kind of a big machine, but I wanted it to be, in a sense, light, because there was no bass.

I was hearing this big machine that was able to move, partially because the bottom frequencies weren't taken. I'd always wanted to do a record with me playing tom-toms as a bass function. It didn't quite work out that way, but some of that is there. I had a lot of instruments that could serve a bass function. I had the accordion, the Hammond [organ], the harp, and the tuba. All of those instruments go very deep and low, but they're not a bass. I think by taking instruments and changing their function from tune to tune, I accomplished what I wanted to do.

I like to orchestrate. Trying to use each instrument to its maximum potential is a fascinating problem. I had eight instruments. You realize, they could play a head and then somebody take a solo, and have the other guy smoke a cigarette, or whatever. But I prefer to have him as an integral part of the composition at all times. Even if he's not playing, he might have an integral part because he might have the next cue to get out of the section, or something of that nature. So he's always in the music—something I think makes for good ensemble playing.

BILL FRISELL BAND, *LOOKOUT FOR HOPE* (1988, ECM)
Lee Townsend

Bill was at ECM before I was. I was there from '84 to '88. Bill made his first record the year before I came. It was *In Line*—solo and duo material with Arild Anderson. He'd been recording as a sideman for a couple of years

even before that. But I was at ECM when he did *Rambler*, his first record as a real leader. I didn't produce it, Manfred [Eicher] did, but that's when I first got to know Bill.

When the band was born, luckily for me, it was deemed a project that I should do. They had done their first European tour. We went through all the live tapes and picked out what we thought were the right songs to tell that particular story. I still have a real soft spot in my heart for that record, *Lookout for Hope*. There's a freshness to it that still comes through.

Manfred knew that Bill and I had hit it off well, and that I was very interested in Bill's work. We recorded at Power Station. What people purport to be the "ECM sound" was a bigger influence on me before I went to ECM than when I was at the label or thereafter. When I was younger and figuring out that there was a craft, if not some kind of art, to making records, ECM really stood out, not only because it was obviously very quality-oriented, but because there was somebody with vision in back of it. That, in and of itself, was an influence on me—just the fact that somebody took that kind of care and had a point of view. The specifics of it were less important to me than what the overall or the underlying message was. I think it's fairly easy to come up with your own sound. The great producers take care—and have a point of view about—how to frame an artist's work and have it tell a story.

Artists at different stages of their development need different kinds of assistance or guidance, depending on the situation. What I try to achieve is to create an atmosphere that's (a) truly collaborative and (b) not threatening, yet somewhat challenging so that the music doesn't come off as safe or complacent. To me, what's most important is for everybody to treat the work as what's most sacred, not have it be about the producer or the artist, but try to clear the way in personal investment as much as possible so that you get out of the way of the ideal that's being created. That means really being familiar with what the artist's work is and what the artist's goals are, and instilling some trust there.

BILL FRISELL, *BEFORE WE WERE BORN* (1989, ELEKTRA MUSICIAN)
Lee Townsend

Bill had left ECM and started with Nonesuch. Bob Hurwitz wanted a record that could show a lot of the different sides of Bill, not only what his

band was doing but some of his work with people who were known at the time as Downtown artists. The task was to make a record that showed the breadth of music Bill was involved in. We did the band stuff augmented by a horn section with Julius Hemphill. It was sort of like Bill's tribute to Julius. Then we did a long piece arranged by John Zorn, and stuff with Arto Lindsay and Peter Shearer. I'm sure for Nonesuch the idea was to signal that Bill had left ECM and was starting this new era, but for me in terms of producing—the tracks that I did and then sort of overseeing the rest of it—I wasn't concerned with that aspect of it.

I'm not interested in making records only for aficionados. I'm interested in music that's engaging, challenging, and not some sort of decoration. The people in the jazz realm that I work with have all grown up on pop music, and the people in the pop/rock realm that I work with have all dealt with jazz and improvising. To me it's a completely natural marriage of sensibilities.

FRANK MORGAN, *MOOD INDIGO* (1989, ANTILLES)
John Snyder

He got out of San Quentin, and one of the Fantasy labels produced three or four records with him. When he signed with Island, a guy that used to work for me called and said, "We signed Frank Morgan. Would you like to produce him?"

I said, "Sure. Who is Frank Morgan?" So they hired me, and I met with Frank and his manager.

It was a truly bizarre record date. Frank was totally scattered. He was very nervous, or at least appeared that way. I'm talking more about my response; I don't know what he really was. But he didn't seem happy. Nobody quite knew what was going to happen, and Frank was not good at talking to musicians. If they didn't hear it in his playing, then he got pissed off at them. He was loath to instruct musicians. A lot of jazz players are that way. They won't talk to each other. Anyway that's the way he was, but Wynton [Marsalis] came in and played. He was great. He played because he wanted to be there. He thought very highly of Frank.

There was a lot of tension on those dates. It was a mess really. The last session, the third day, the last two hours is when it all came together. We started getting complete takes. We got maybe an hour and a half of solid music.

I still thought it was a big mess. I didn't know what the hell we had: bebop, ballads, a little bit of this, and a little bit of that. There was no focus. I took the tapes home and spent all weekend sequencing different versions.

I remember when it happened: seven o'clock on a Sunday night. I hadn't even gotten out of my bathrobe that whole day. I just listened to Frank Morgan tapes. I realized the answer was to leave out stuff; the answer was to make it a more mellow record. All the fast stuff—the jaggedy kind of drug music—that had to go. All the bebop was taken out. I started the record and ended the record with the same song: "Lullaby" [by George Cables].

As a result, the record became accessible. My mother called me and told me that she liked the record. I didn't know she had it. She didn't listen to jazz. She didn't care anything about it. That record sold seventy-five thousand units very quickly which was a big success. We went on from there and made a few more records.

CECIL TAYLOR, *IN FLORESCENCE* (1990, A&M)
John Snyder

 My second tenure at A&M, there was a different A & R guy, Steve Ralbovsky. He'd had some successful records, and he wanted to make a statement in the jazz world. That meant the jazz giants: Sun Ra, Cecil, Max Roach, Dizzy, Art Blakey, Gerry Mulligan, and Stan Getz. When he told me what he wanted, I said, "You know, I lost an awful lot of money doing that. I see where you're coming from aesthetically, but they fired me for my aesthetics and for not making money. The lesson I learned was if you don't make money for these guys, like right away, you don't get a chance to do what you think is right. You've got to make money before you can be aesthetically correct. If you're aesthetically correct and you lose money, you will not get to second base."

Steve said, "I can make one pop record, have a hit, and that'll take care of all of this."

"Okay," I said. Of course, sooner or later they got rid of him and discontinued the series. In the meantime, though, we got to make some awfully nice records.[18]

18. Nevertheless, Ralbovsky did all right. He subsequently helped develop the careers of the Red Hot Chili Peppers, the Strokes, and Ray LaMontagne.

I was trying to get shorter songs from Cecil, concise statements, and then I got the idea of putting vocal stuff on the album. It was a most amazing record date. He came in an hour and a half late. We had set up everything. The musicians, the bass and the drummer [William Parker and Gregg Bendian], sat there next to their instruments that whole hour and a half and didn't say much. It was like a church. There was a very respectful feeling in the studio. Cecil came in, and I swear it was like a tornado blew through the door. He swirled through the door and kind of circled the piano. He'd sit down and not even say anything to the bassist and drummer. Then, bang! He was off. He had furious energy. When the song was over, he popped off the piano bench like a rocket. He'd circle it, walk around kind of like a cat. Then he'd sit back down and do the next take. We did probably three-fourths of the record in an hour and a half. Next he took a break for like two hours and told us how much he loved *I Love Lucy* and other stuff. Then, we slowly finished recording a couple more songs. But it was that burst of energy that was so surprising.

That was an incredible experience, to have Sun Ra in one room mixing and Cecil in another room at the studio complex. We talked and then drank; talked and drank. I went back and forth between Sun Ra and Cecil. After many bottles of champagne, I finally got Cecil back into the studio at midnight. We'd been there since seven o'clock or so. I had convinced him to do a little spoken introduction or an ending to the record. He came in and said, "I want to do something before every song."

"Great!" Cecil was finally going to walk up to the mike and start. I had no idea what to expect. The first thing he did was scream as loud as he could. The meters jumped to the right into the red, and they stayed there. We had to get somebody with a screw driver to unpin them. Everybody was blown away. It was like, "Whoa!" I said, "Cecil, what that hell was that?"

"I am just getting warmed up."

"You scared my engineer to death. You can't be doing that." He laughed. We'd listen to each song and discuss what might go before them. He'd try things. It was fun, and it came out the way it came out.

I expected Cecil not to have any interest at all in what I had to say. He told me what an inspiration I was to him. He asked me questions, and I would tell him what I thought. He'd say, "Okay, okay." I remember leaving there thinking, "Well, he made me a record producer today." He let me do it, and then he not only encouraged me, he took my advice and was gracious about it and appreciative. It was a great experience.

What sorts of things did you tell Taylor?

It might be about the structure of a song or the solo order. I might notice something about Gregg, the drummer, that I thought was particularly interesting. I might suggest that, maybe, Cecil play to that. We discussed the idea of playing to people's strengths and avoiding weaknesses, and how you might inspire other people around you to greater heights. I remember very clearly being in this particular room hanging out with Cecil and talking about what had just happened. It was just the two of us, and he was asking streams of questions. He was very interested in what I thought. How he internalized it and what it meant to him, I can't really say, but he was very appreciative and kind.

SUN RA, *PURPLE NIGHT* (1990, A&M)
John Snyder

I remember Sun Ra. We rehearsed for a week because I wanted to see what that would be like. I made one record with him for A&M where I just kind of showed up [*Blue Delight*, 1989]. But we got along real well. On the [first] date he didn't know me, and so he just did his thing. It was like riding a bronco and holding on.

The second record, I said, "We're going to budget for rehearsals for Sun Ra, and we're going to bring everybody in, and we are going to work everything out." *Purple Night* was three drummers, a percussionist, dozens of musicians, his usual band plus Don Cherry, an extra percussionist, and more keyboards.

Okay, so we know what songs we're going to do. We go do the rehearsals, and we've got the record date. We had three nights for recording. After the first night, I said, "Sonny, you didn't record any of the songs we rehearsed."

"John, look at it this way," he said. "Suppose I was a football coach, and we had a big game on Sunday. We practiced all day, every day for the week before that." He said, "We never played that game we played on Sunday during practice on Monday or Tuesday or Wednesday. We just practiced for it."

"Well, okay," I said. "But that's not quite the same thing is it?"

"No, it's the same thing. We got used to playing together and playing in certain ways, in certain feelings, and I am just taking those things and plugging them into another format, another structure."

That's what he did. In a sense it was the ultimate in improvisatory music, but it was as rehearsed as you could get it. They had rehearsed being ultimately improvisatory. They had never rehearsed exactly the same thing that they played. That's the difference.

During recording, he'd point to things and make motions. He'd direct by playing. In a sense Gil Evans did that, too. Sun Ra would kind of work it around and work it like he was stirring something. There was one particular thing, early in the session, where it was mixing and mixing, and all at once it started to boil. It was like a big round rocket ship that was moving slowly off the ground with great power and then, all of a sudden, it went. I looked at Jay [Newland, the engineer] and said "Wow! This is incredible." He was wide-eyed like, "Man, this thing that just happened was something!" The band kept playing. The tape ran out, and even then, on another tape seven more minutes went by before they stopped. It was quite a trip, a good experience.

One time when he was playing at the Vanguard, I went down to the millinery district in the City and bought a bunch of feathers and beads to give to Sun Ra. He was into that, colorful materials. I went back in the kitchen, and there was Sun Ra with no shirt on, looking like a rather out-of-shape Buddha. There were people around him, dressing him, shaving him, attending to him: his musicians and June [Tyson]. He had that kind of effect on people. He was the guru, and they took care of him.

I thought it was fascinating. He mistreated them, didn't pay them very well. One time I said to him, "Sun Ra, all your guys are so shaggy, living in your house. What is up with that?"

"John," he said, "all musicians are in some kind of jail. My musicians are in the Sun Ra jail."

"Okay." That's the way he thought. He knew his position. He'd also talk about being from Saturn. I didn't even take note of that, didn't say anything about it. Sherman, one of the guys who worked for me, asked him, "Hey Sonny, tell me something. Do they have pork chops on Saturn?" That pissed him off. He didn't like being made fun of like that. He didn't even answer.

Sun Ra wasn't born; he was dropped. He was dropped in Birmingham [Alabama]. He's probably up there on Saturn right now saying, "I told you so."

I don't really know what causes people to be the way they are. He certainly manifested himself in interesting ways. His detachment from Earth was reflected accurately in his music. What people choose to be inspired by is a strange thing.

MAX ROACH AND DIZZY GILLESPIE, *MAX + DIZZY: PARIS 1989* (1990, A&M)
John Snyder

When I first heard Dizzy talk, I couldn't believe it, that that voice came from that face. We were fortunate to be able to hear him and Max Roach talk about their lives. Besides, on that recording there was the technical problem of having more music than would fit on one CD but not enough for two.

I didn't want to lose a note, because it was all free-form playing. I wouldn't edit it down. That was the bold thing about that record. There were no songs on it. They didn't have a thought in their heads when they went onstage. Even though we discussed at length what they might do, they went out and walked the high wire for an hour and a half, and it more or less worked.

Dizzy was an original avant-gardist. At the end of that concert he walked offstage, and backstage his horn fell off a chair. We tried to get the mouthpiece out of his horn. It was stuck. We could live with that, but the first valve was also stuck. We tried to unscrew it, to get it out, so we could fix it. At the same time, there was a documentary film being made.

Max and Dizzy were getting paid for the concert, the recording, the documentary, a TV show, and a radio show. There were five sources of income for the artists, all going on at the same time. It was a zoo backstage. In the dark—with this big, bright light from the documentary crew shining down—huddled a lot of people. It looked like an operating room. I wish I had a picture: twenty people surrounding a trumpet, trying to make it well so that the people in the audience, who were stamping their feet and shouting "more, more, more," could get more.

Dizzy said, "You're going to have to go out there and tell them."

"Tell them what, Dizzy?"

"That I dropped my horn and can't play."

I said, "That's not going to work. Why don't you go out there and sing something?"

He looked at me and said, "Okay." He walked out and asked, "Ladies and gentlemen, is there an instrument repairman in the house?" Since nobody raised a hand, he started singing "Oo Pa Pa Da," the only song that's on the record.

ABBEY LINCOLN, *THE WORLD IS FALLING DOWN* (1990, VERVE)
Jean-Philippe Allard

In the late eighties, I ran Polygram in France. Because of CDs, it was a good time for jazz, and we started to do some production in France. One of my favorite artists, ever, was Abbey Lincoln. We'd had no news of her since *Talking to the Sun* [1984], her Enja album. My colleague, Daniel Richard, and I shared the same love for what she did. So I decided to call her, despite a lot of people telling me that she was a "difficult person." They in fact warned me.

I phoned her, and we got along right away. She always talked about this first call. We started to speak about what she wanted to do, what she had in mind. We talked about concepts and musicians. I said, "With whom would you like to work, if you could choose anybody?"

She said, "Alain Jean-Marie," a French pianist.

I was very surprised and said, "Okay, great, I love Alain Jean-Marie. What about Charlie Haden?" They'd never worked together. I don't think they really knew each other.

"Yeah, okay," she said. "What about Billy Higgins?" Then she talked about the songs, her new songs.

I'd found a song of Charlie Haden's called "First Song." I thought it would be great for her to write lyrics for it. She loved the song and wrote lyrics right away. When we thought we were ready, we booked a studio in New York. It was my first time to go to New York, and in a short time I was walking into the studio with an artist. It was a very difficult session, but Abbey and I always got along very well; so that part was easy. She was always creating, writing new songs.

Why was the recording not easy?

First reason, Jackie McLean didn't show up. The week before the sessions, he said he was booked, couldn't make it, and would have to record his parts later. I knew he really wanted to record. So we got Jerry Dodgion to do the alto parts which were, later, replaced by Jackie's. It's hard to handle that sort of situation. You can't postpone the recording. Everything was planned. I came from France. It was complicated.

Then, the second reason was Abbey got really sick in the middle of the session—some kind of flu or something. She had a high fever. She was very weak and couldn't sing. She was totally devastated by that. I remember her crying. We had to make the session work without her; then, when she could walk, we finished.

Also, she wanted Ron Carter to write the arrangements. I thought that was a little strange. He could do the job, obviously, but he's more known as a bass player than an arranger. Plus, we already had Charlie. To have Charlie and Ron Carter in the same room was not great. We had some conflicts—some personality clashes—and had to handle that. For all those reasons, it wasn't easy, but at the end everything was cool. Jackie came and did his parts. Abbey recovered, and everybody was really happy. I learned a lot from that session.

What was the setup in the studio?

We always worked with the band. They were isolated, but they were always in the studio. Sometimes, Abbey would change a word or correct a mistake—just little things. One time, she wanted to change a whole vocal part because she had another idea for how she wanted to interpret the song.

You've worked a lot with Jay Newland. What do you look for in an engineer?

He was on Abbey's first [Verve] recording because he was the house engineer at BMG [RCA Studios]. I noticed that he was really into the music. David Baker was the main engineer. Jay is very quiet. We formed a relationship. After that, I worked with another engineer, but I wanted Jay to be the assistant. Then I started to notice that, for me, he was the best engineer for this kind of project.

When Jay is not the engineer, I'm always frustrated. He does exactly what I want to hear without talking a lot. He's really quick. He's one of the fastest engineers. With him, you never have a sound check. The musicians come, and when they're ready, they can play.

When someone comes into the booth to listen to a take, it sounds good already. It's not unbalanced. It's inspiring. When I work with him it's really easy to keep the energy going. We don't waste time and energy making takes and takes because we don't know if we have what we need. We always know sooner with Jay, because of his ability to do really great rough mixes.

Abbey liked him a lot, too, and felt confident with him. Jay never gives singers any attitude: "I am the engineer. You don't know what you're doing."

BILL FRISELL, *IS THAT YOU?* (1990, ELEKTRA MUSICIAN)
Wayne Horvitz

Hopefully, with jazz records you're really trying to capture something not too far from the way the band plays live. There are exceptions. I think Weather Report—I'm a pretty big fan of their early records—those records show a studio sensibility applied to music we call jazz, but with strong pop and rock influences.

In my experience, Bill Frisell is known as a jazz artist. I've produced three of his records. One of them falls into one category; the other two fall into the other category.

Is That You? was very much a multitrack record where hardly any musicians played on it. If they did, they often played after Bill and I laid down the basic tracks. In other words, we'd put down drum machine, sequence things, and then have Bill do a bunch of overdubs. Then, at the very end Joey Baron came in and played drums on some things. That was more like producing a songs kind of record. We came up with lots of the ideas in the studio or in preproduction. We went into a cheaper studio first and made a little mockup of the record. For me, that was a blast.

The other two records I did for Bill—the covers record, *Have a Little Faith* [1993], and *Nashville* [1997]—I enjoy listening to them just as much as to the first record. I enjoyed producing them. But they weren't near as interesting to produce because, essentially, you get great musicians, a great engineer, a good studio, and there's still some work for you to do. But not a whole lot. The guys play great, and the sounds come off great. It's more a matter of making sure the flow happens and making sure that the people stay focused, stay having a good time. If one of those things isn't happening, you try to create a situation where it will. But there's not more to it than that.

Could you contrast your approach to producing Frisell with Lee Townsend's?

I wouldn't want to do that. Lee's a good friend. If you take the way Lee produced Bill's record with horns, *This Land*, with my approach to those records, I wouldn't say there's a whole lot of difference.

In a way Lee is in the John Hammond tradition of production. He actually gets people record deals and attaches himself as a producer, which is a perfectly reasonable, smart way to proceed. In fact, I get calls from people all the time about producing, where I realize they're actually calling me because—I don't mean it in a negative way—but they're thinking I might also be able to get them a deal, or that I have connections with people who will listen to them. I don't have time for that, because I'm trying to play my own music. It's also kind of ironic. I'm barely able to get a record deal myself. I keep saying to these people, "Okay, I'll get you a record deal, and then you get me one."

ROBIN HOLCOMB, *ROBIN HOLCOMB* (1990, ELEKTRA MUSICIAN)
Wayne Horvitz

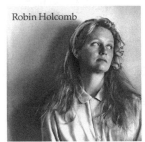

Even though I'm better known for producing instrumental music, I actually prefer to produce song-oriented music. The reason is kind of simple. It doesn't necessarily mean that I enjoy playing or listening to that music more. There's simply more for me to do.

Robin's record was really great because I got a chance to do what the producers I admire got to do. Those producers tend to be more in the pop field. In fact, when I think about the records I admire the most from a production standpoint, it's interesting: *Music from Big Pink* or *The Band*. Neither of them are slick records. They were produced by John Simon. He was sort of an extra member of the Band. He played on the records as well. He was sort of part of the group; halfway a musician, halfway a producer—which is very much the way I like to work.

Robin and I live together; we worked in our house. We had the time to go in the studio, to get away from the tunes for a few days, and then back in and try out ideas, which you never get to do with most instrumental records. It was also a case in point where I did what I think is part of the real pleasure of producing. That's get in early.

Robin sat down at the piano and played the songs for me. Just her. There was no drummer, bass player, or guitar. So I got involved from the very beginning. That makes it so much more interesting. You may not be playing the instrument, but you still feel like you're making music. It's very different from going in and recording a band that's already really well rehearsed, where you're basically there to make sure that things go smoothly.

Once you worked on the tunes, the two of you discussed personnel and how the record should sound?

That's hard to discuss: how you want to make things sound. One of the myths of producing is that you have sort of a strong image ahead of time. Production is a very improvised art. Things are done on the fly. So many things that you can't even predict have to do with how things sound. The studio has a sound. Sure, in an ideal world, you could fly around all over the place and check out studios, but of course you pick studios for all sorts of pragmatic reasons. Things you thought might work don't. Then you have to find things that do work. Sticking too much to your plan can really work against you in a lot of ways.

Give me an example of how an idea emerged in the studio in the process of working.

I'll give you one that I like a lot that did not emerge in the studio. Robin played a song. It's called "Electrical Storm." I love her songs, but it's one of my top-five favorites. On the recording, she plays just the chords, basically, on the downbeat. When she played the song for me, I watched her tapping her foot. She was playing only the whole notes. In other words, she was playing just the beginning of each bar. I turned away and listened. I heard the song in three. She heard it in four. That's as fundamental as you can get. We're not talking about how much reverb there is on the snare drum. We're talking about I heard it as a waltz. I don't think she'd even thought about it. But that's the kind of thing that's really exciting to me, much more exciting than getting that killer bass-drum sound or something like that. That's the kind of production that I really enjoy.

KIP HANRAHAN, *TENDERNESS* (1990, AMERICAN CLAVÉ)
Kip Hanrahan

 I had the words beforehand. I had the music. I had the general mood of it. I had the tones, and I actually had the pitches, the sequences of pitches, pretty much in my head. I definitely had the rhythms in my head. One driving thing for starting *Tenderness*, for describing a kind of emotional complexity, was Giovanni Hidalgo. If you allowed Giovanni to play [congas and quinto] without framing him in a short solo—which nobody else was doing—in his mistakes you'd come up with something unbelievable. You have to work hard to get the right mistakes.

As an aside, when Giovanni stopped being in our band and he was with Dizzy, Don Pullen and I kept going out to hear him. Dizzy would allow Giovanni to do the same solo, two sets a night, every night. Don and I were furious. In our band you can't do the same solo twice. "Hey, I've heard that! I heard that last set! What the fuck are you doing?"

One benefit of me not playing in the band live is that, while onstage,

I can go over and say, "If you add a seventh at the end of that phrase, fuck you! I heard that already!" While the guy's playing. Actually, I do that on my own records, too—I talk into the headphones all the time. If they go into chromatics, I say, "Stay away from that Turkish music!" Turkish music, because at that moment the player is being too lazy to invent another melody.

I wanted to open the record with a long *guaguanco* [a rumba rhythm on "When I Lose Myself in the Darkness"]. I wanted to ride Giovanni so he wouldn't be lazy and hide that creativity and intensity inside himself, so he'd keep dragging it out. We played this guaguanco for a long time, and I kept coming up with other patterns for the trap drums to make it more intense. In the headphones I kept riding Giovanni. I'd say, "I hear you pulling back! Go ahead. Lean into it!" He didn't want to lean into that solo because he was afraid he'd sound bad—he'd make a mistake. I said, "Make the mistake. Ride through it. Keep going." Hearing Giovanni and his guaguanco unframed is one of the intensities that I wanted on *Tenderness*. It's actually what started that record.

Though I'm sure it sounds it, the song ["Faith in the Pants, Not in the Prick"] took under sixteen minutes to write the words and music and under half an hour to record all the parts. That was one of the quickest. I woke up—it was in the summer of '88—and I had this burning thing to go make something that day. I called Fernando [Saunders], Andy Gonzalez, Robbie Ameen, and Cecilia Engelhardt into the studio. In the cab on the way up there, I wrote "Faith in the Pants, Not in the Prick." Once you come up with the words, melodies are easy. (Fernando replaces my vocal tracks with his, as Jack [Bruce] did.) That was the quickest thing. I needed that at the beginning of *Tenderness*, because the rest of the stuff, as casual as it seems, was not. It was intense and uncasual—almost everything. I wanted to get rid of complex voicings and changes, because I wanted to rely on something being as intense and rough as possible.

Our working band—a band we'd taken on the road—formed the core. Sometimes we go into the studio and ask other people to be in on it, when I think they can take the music somewhere further. If they're on, they're there for a particular section.

Aesthetically, I like going in and doing something live. I like the piece breathing, and if I feel critical about it, I like to go back in later and redo it. There are whole sections where we try a piece—I'll come up with an interesting percussion section and the changes on top are double-boring—and afterwards I go back and listen to it, take the changes off, go back in and put different changes over it.

CHARLES MINGUS, *EPITAPH* (1990, COLUMBIA)
Sue Mingus

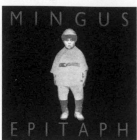

Charles covered the spectrum [of emotions]. He was reflective and very internal. He spent a great deal of time at the piano composing. That was where he found his center, his peace, and his expression. In many cases, he felt the music was waiting for him on the keys. There's a certain mysticism in many musicians who don't take credit for their gifts. They feel a lot of it is just passed from somewhere through them. He didn't feel that way about his virtuosity on the bass, but he did feel that way about the music and the melody.

Anyway, Charles was a very spiritual person. He did what he had to do in the society in which he lived to write the music he had to write and get performed. Duke used elegance. Charles used whatever he could use, the scene-making and everything. It wasn't that he enjoyed doing that at all. It was a tool.

With *Epitaph* some of the most complex stuff was written when he was seventeen years old. In fact, if he could have gone on ... He started out with classical music, and Gunther Schuller was surprised to hear somebody from the West Coast in Watts familiar with European avant-garde composers from the thirties and forties that most people in the United States didn't know about at all. Charles was fully aware of Schoenberg, Stravinsky, and Ives—the American and European avant-garde composers. But he took the route he had to take. The symphonic world was not one in which he was allowed at that point because of his color.

Joel Dorn (Atlantic)

Sue Mingus has done an absolutely stunning, brilliant job of shepherding Mingus's lifework. Her stewardship of his work is brilliant. I don't know anyone who's ever done that in jazz.[19] Lots of people take care of the estates and stuff like that. There's nobody like her. First of all, she really understands what it is. Second, she doesn't let anybody fuck with it. She's in charge of that. You do it her way, or you don't do it. That's great as long as somebody understands it. Most people who have control don't. I respect the shit out of her.

I always thought that Mingus's music, as recorded by Mingus, was a

---

19. Laurie Pepper—widow of Art Pepper—springs to mind.

function of him being there with those specific people. But the first time I went down to catch the Mingus Big Band, I saw that a lot of the madness was written into the music. It wasn't that it was Eric [Dolphy] and Dannie Richmond. Obviously, who played made a difference. But when you listen to Mingus's music now, it sounds like Mingus's music. The levels of solos, the passion, it was written into the music. That blew my mind. Also, I have a much better sense that, if you look at him only as a bass player, you're missing him as an arranger. If you look at him as a composer, you're missing him as a leader. If you're looking at him as just a leader, you're missing him as a player. You need to look at Mingus as a totality.

RONALD SHANNON JACKSON, *RED WARRIOR* (1990, AXIOM)
Bill Laswell

Shannon is a very powerful drummer and always expresses a lot of force, power, and confidence in what he plays. In the way that rock records are recorded and sound, he has that same sort of power. I don't think that translated to a lot of the early albums because people were dealing with a much smaller dimension in terms of the size of the sound and the depth of the low end. The overall picture was much more linear, much smaller. I thought of Shannon's efforts as being much more powerful.

On that record, I certainly encouraged the idea of volume, the idea of electric guitars, and definitely the idea of a much heavier drum approach. That direction, I'm sure, shaped the end results of that record. Then we worked with engineers who have had experience doing metal and other extreme music—and not the safe approach of people trying to reduce jazz records to almost a whisper. I thought his thing should be in a heavier style.

And coming from him, he wanted that as well. We talked about it a lot. None of these guys prefer to sound as bad as they do. Everybody would like to sound a little more focused and a lot bigger and powerful. At the time he and I had already worked together for years. It was very much people come in to work, and do the work. He was there the whole time. It wasn't a manipulation of the artist in any sense, that here's a jazz drummer, let's make him sound like a rock drummer. Let's change it. It was very much coming from him and very much in his best interest. He was there for the duration. It's not always like that. A lot of people don't care. And a lot of people sabotage their own work. A lot of people sabotage others. Which goes into this whole circus.

4

RECORDING TO HARD DRIVE
Producing Digitally,
1991–2013

....

EXEMPLARY RECORDING—ABBEY LINCOLN,
ABBEY SINGS ABBEY

Beginning in the 1950s, the widespread use of magnetic tape meant that record production no longer had to be concentrated exclusively in the phases of preproduction (A & R) and production (recording). What happened after basic tracks were committed to tape—postproduction (editing, mixing, and mastering)—could define an album. That's why rock musicians, in particular, began to rely on independently owned and operated recording studios. They afforded almost limitless control and freedom. You could do what you wanted, play what you wanted, and take as much time as you wanted (or could afford). Think about Brian Wilson's work on The Beach Boys' *Pet Sounds*. That album was virtually all a work of postproduction. Or consider the endless remixes of contemporary dance tracks. With multitracking, postproduction became an increasingly complicated and protracted process. It's no wonder that, in the world of pop, today's record producers frequently start as engineers.

Nowadays, when digital audio workstations (DAWs) are not multiplying options to unthinkable levels of overchoice, they have simplified and automated tasks that were exceedingly difficult and time-consuming to execute on analog tape. That's their most significant contribution to recording. They've informed jazz production most profoundly in the smallest sorts of ways. Fixing the little stuff that once marred otherwise stellar performances is now very quick and easy. Read between the lines of Jay Newland's description of *Abbey Sings Abbey* (2007)—this chapter's exemplary album—and you'll discover a marvelous recording of great integrity made possible by digital recording.

A number of the recordings discussed in this chapter were not recorded digitally, and when they were, many of their producers merely treated digital tape and hard drives as the new, perhaps "improved," analog tape. Or they shrugged and acceded to the inevitable and unavoidable. Or they didn't. They continued to use analog equipment. Nowadays, you could probably find a studio in Los Angeles that would let you record straight to wax cylinders.

Finally, recall that the on-screen look of multitrack digital recorders—whether the "interface" of ProTools or the audio-editing programs preinstalled on laptop computers—adopt and only slightly modify the distinctly linear model of tape recording. (Digital audio files could be visualized in any number of different ways.) The point is, a new medium for recorded music does not automatically or even necessarily replace old means and practices of recording. Most of the time, the new is understood in terms of the old. A potentially revolutionary technology is just added to—and conceptualized in terms of—what was already available. And so, options accrue.

SONNY SHARROCK, *ASK THE AGES* (1991, AXIOM)
Bill Laswell

We were on tour in Germany. I knew, obviously, that he'd played and worked with [saxophonist] Pharoah [Sanders] in the past, and I thought that was always a strong point for him, a strong point of reference. Pharoah was one of the people that Sonny admired. We suggested the idea of trying to do a project where he could do that again, go even further in that direction, and bring in [drummer] Elvin Jones. Then Charnett Moffett [double bass] was a logical choice. He was recommended by practically everyone I asked when I mentioned the other players in the group.

Over time, Sonny had developed his own sound, by using certain amplifiers and by deciding on a particular guitar. But he was open to processing the guitar. He was open to different effects. I worked with that until everyone was happy, including him—especially him. He was quite easy to please. You could always push it a lot further and he wouldn't object.

He'd somewhat famously said that he wanted to sound like a saxophonist.

That was more related to a comment he made in the seventies or the late sixties. At that time he really was trying to sound like a saxophone; I'm sure he was trying to get out of sounding like a guitar. He wanted to play saxophone, but for some health reason he switched to the guitar. I think he was always trying to move the sound away from the guitar. Sometimes, melodically his guitar would remind you of a certain horn player, not necessarily the tone, but maybe the phrasing or the attack or the approach. But I never heard him play the guitar where he sounded like another guitarist. Which means he had a gift, an original voice. He found it by avoiding the clichés that were given to the instrument by people who were repetitious.

CARLA BLEY, *THE VERY BIG CARLA BLEY BAND* (1991, WATT WORKS/ECM)
Carla Bley and Steve Swallow

BLEY: I decided to write for big band because it was a testing ground for my talents. It had been done by the greatest writers. So I thought, "Well, if I can just write straight big-band music—every town, every college has a big band—then I'll be very happy. I won't feel that I'm a fluke. I'll feel like I'm an important part of the music world, and I'll earn my place in history."

SWALLOW: This big band period gained momentum when you taught for a semester at William and Mary, and got to hear Fletcher Henderson, early Duke Ellington, and the history of the big band, maybe, for the first time as a coherent line of music.

BLEY: I had to. I had to teach the stuff. Every night before the class, I listened to the next two hours of important jazz recordings. I learned a lot. I thought maybe I could do it; maybe I could be as good as they were. I did the big band for that reason, also because I *could* do it. That's not an easy thing to do. Who would want to do it anyway? It's not easy, and I can do it. So why not?

Becoming better at playing the piano made it unnecessary for me to make jokes about the way I played. Getting better musicians in the band all the time made it unnecessary to cover myself just in case some idiot played something dumb. Binding the parts together better made it unnecessary to cover myself in case somebody's part fell on the floor.

All these things I used to do, expecting the worst, trying to pretend I didn't care. Instead of having someone who could sing well do something—probably out of fear, someone might say—I'd let the worst guys in the band sing. I'd cultivate the worst things, so that when they happened, as I was sure they would, I wouldn't look stupid. I got better and better through the years. Now I'm so good I'm not even interesting anymore!

SWALLOW: From my perspective—as a long-time sideman in your bands—I can see that sort of sea change. In the days of the band that played on *Live!* [1982]—around that period of time—the running joke was that Carla loved us for our faults. In a way there was a kind of wonderful permissiveness that sprang from that knowledge, the feeling that if we did something terrible, she would just smile benignly at us and carry on. That is no longer the case within the big band or within the duets or trios. There's that opposite sense: we all have to grow up someday, and that that day has come.

JAMES BLOOD ULMER, "BLUES PREACHER" (1992), *BLUES PREACHER* (DIW/COLUMBIA)
James Blood Ulmer

I've been trying to get the sound of a live band and still be a little up-to-date with the sound. I rehearse the band real good before we go into the studio. We go in as a trio. All I'm looking for the first time through the song is the drum sound. We all play to get drums. Once they're all perfect and lined up—meaning the drum track is kicking 'cause we were playing live—then we abolish everything, except the drums. Then I re-put everything on: first the bass, then the guitar. I let the bass nail down that drum sound—even if it's not on a click-track. We synchronize the bass with the drums. And then I add my guitar chords. After I get the basic guitar track locked down, I put down my rhythm guitar track. [Guitarist] Ronnie [Drayton] he comes in totally wired with his foot switch and synthesizes my sound. His guitar makes my guitar sound like I'm using something, even though I don't have anything but a wah-wah pedal. Then I place his stuff on my stuff, and it sounds like we're both using some electronic devices. It updates or sweetens the sound that I'm playing. That's the way I produce those kinds of songs. I've done it many kinds of ways, but now it's kind of a system with me to do it like that.

HANK JONES, *TIPTOE TAPDANCE* (1992, GALAXY)
Ed Michel

Hank said, "What do you want me to play?"

"You're a kind of well-behaved guy," I said. "You go to church, right?"

"Yes."

"Why don't you play some hymns or spirituals?"

He said, "What!"

"Think of them as God's ballads."

"Oh, okay," he said. That's what led to that album. I thought it would be interesting to do a bunch of holy ballads. Some of my favorite Trane is God ballads: "Alabama" and "After the Rain." Why, with all the jazz singers there are, why hasn't a bunch of singers sung the "Psalm" from *A Love Supreme*? I'd think eighteen choirs in New York would be doing it. That's the jazz fan talking. If they did it, I wouldn't listen to it, but I'm surprised they haven't done it.

KENNY DREW JR., *KENNY DREW JR.* (1992, ANTILLES)
John Snyder

Jerry [Wexler]—[who is listed as coproducer on the album]—called me up on the phone and said he'd found this piano player in Sarasota [Florida] of all places. He thought Kenny Drew Jr. was really great. But he said, "I am not in this business anymore. I don't want to shop him."

"Send me something to listen to," I said. He did, and I thought Kenny was great. I shopped him around and finally sold it. I think one of the reasons I was able to sell it was I could say, "Jerry Wexler thinks this guy is great, and he'll coproduce the record."

Jerry showed up. He was very nice, but he wasn't involved in any of the preproduction. I treated it like I usually treat a record. Jerry came in and added a certain authority. Once in a while, he said, "That's really nice," and he said, "Give it more bass." That was basically it.

He knew where the best restaurants were and what was on the wine list. In that sense, he was more an inspiration. I mean everybody knew Jerry Wexler was sitting there, and that had an effect. It made everybody play a little bit better, be a little more professional about their jobs, including me.

MEL TORMÉ, *THE GREAT AMERICAN SONGBOOK*, *LIVE AT MICHAEL'S PUB* (1992, TELARC)
John Snyder

That record was made under adverse circumstances. The guy that ran that club was the biggest jerk I've seen in my life. I finally told him off. I wrote one of the most perfect letters. I laid into him because he was genuinely bad and fucking with my record, and I just couldn't have that. Mel was great, the quintessential gentlemen. He had a great manager. They were extremely professional. I knew most of the guys in the band, or did

soon after we started recording. I had played in those situations myself, and I had recorded a lot of situations like that.

I knew the game. I'd seen Mel's show. He had a certain structure, and we were kind of stuck with it. I knew what I liked about his singing. Basically, I thought the show was a nice version of Mel Tormé.

We recorded maybe two nights. Between technical and musical problems, I didn't feel like we had it. Mel thought we did. After the second night, he and I listened to the playbacks. I said, "Mel, I hate to say this, but I don't think you've given your best performance yet. I've heard you do better on these songs."

"Like on what?"

And I thought, "Oh God, here we go." I gave him a few examples.

He said, "Well, you're the producer."

"Thank you very much," I said. I arranged for everybody to do it again the next night. We weren't going to record that night, but I'd kept everybody over. We did it, and he hit it. We got two really good sets, and we put out a record we were happy with.

ROBIN HOLCOMB, *ROCKABYE* (1992, ELEKTRA MUSICIAN)
Wayne Horvitz

Robin has strong opinions, but she doesn't have a lot of ideas up front about what to do with songs. It's interesting, too, because I'm often kind of shocked. The material she did for the New York Composer's Orchestra was amazing. Her sense of arrangement is fantastic. I'm in awe of it, and jealous of it.

We have a home studio, but she doesn't use it. It might have something to do with that. She basically sings just her own songs. If I say, "We need a backup harmony here." Or if we get going on an instrumental idea, she starts to hear things. Her ears are much better than mine. She hears lines much more quickly, and she's able to sing them to people. She's also like many composers. She thinks her songs are terrible.

I've told this story before, but it's so amazing to me. The song "When I Stop Crying" on *Rockabye* is almost like a soul tune. It has this repetitive ostinato in the piano and bass. It's one of my favorite pieces of music, bar none.

With *Rockabye*, her second record, Robin had a hard time coming up with songs. She had a lot of incomplete pieces. We were sitting in her room one night, where she has her piano, and she was playing me these songs. I was getting depressed, too. We were under the gun. I asked, "Do you have anything else?"

"Not really," she said. Then she added, "I've got this thing."

I'm not kidding. She walked over to the trash can and pulled out a piece of paper, and it was that song. I was in tears by the middle. It wasn't a sketch. It was pretty much complete. She had thrown it away, thinking that it wasn't any good. That completely kills me.

RANDY WESTON, *THE SPIRITS OF OUR ANCESTORS* (1992, VERVE/POLYGRAM)
Jean-Philippe Allard

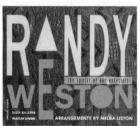

Spirits was definitely Randy's idea, and it was his idea for [arranger] Melba [Liston] to work on that very ambitious project. At first, we were supposed to record the album in Morocco. That's what he wanted. All the musicians were supposed to fly there, because Randy wanted to do it with Gnawas in Morocco.[1] But the first Gulf War happened, and none of the American guys wanted to fly. People are sometimes confused about the situation. I mean, Morocco was safe. Randy and I knew it was no problem, but we realized we had to record in the U.S. We found a Gnawan musician in San Francisco. So it ended up less about Gnawas and African music, and more about New York musicians with the spirit of Africa.

Working with Melba, Randy had ideas about the musicians he wanted to work with. With Brian Bacchus working with me on the project, we suggested additional musicians Randy had never worked with, but who would be great with him, like Pharoah Sanders and Dewey Redman. We also got Billy Harper, but of course it was Randy's call. It was very collaborative. A friend of Randy's suggested that Dizzy Gillespie come to the session as a guest artist. We ended up with a little bit of everything.

---

1. Jazz musicians are drawn to Gnawa music for at least two reasons: the rhythmic interplay between two- and three-beat rhythms, and a harmonic language that recalls the blues. Post-Coltrane and post-Coleman improvisers have found its long trance-inducing songs (which last for hours, not minutes) particularly alluring.

Brian Bacchus

When I was at Polygram, we put out three [Randy Weston] records: *Portraits of Thelonious Monk* [1989], *Portraits of Duke Ellington* [1990], and *Self Portraits: The Last Day* [1990], Randy doing his own compositions. They were produced by Jean-Philippe Allard in France. When I moved over to Antilles, Jean-Philippe called me and asked, "Would you be interested in doing this project in Morocco? Because it's really expensive, I can't do the whole thing, and Polygram U.S. isn't interested in putting up the money for it."

I knew Randy and said, "I'd love to." We worked out a deal, the two of us coproducing. Because the Gulf War had started, we said, "Let's do the project in New York. We'll bring in a Gnawan—Yassir Chadley." He was based out of the Bay Area. (You've really got to look for Gnawans!) So we brought in Yassir, who was actually a friend of Pharoah's. That's how we got hooked up with him. And we did the project. We were very happy with it.

Obviously, I wish we'd been able to do it in Morocco. We were going to drive a remote truck down to Essaouira in southern Morocco: drive it from France, through Spain, and take it across. The Gnawa don't have any real recording facilities. I think we were going to record in a plaza. We wanted to have the [American] musicians for two weeks so they'd get a feel for what was going on: eat the food, rehearse the music, and then record as part of a performance.

Weston had been there a number of times, right?

He owned a club for, I think, nine years in Casablanca.

How did you figure into the project? What was the give-and-take like?

A lot of it was scheduling, getting everybody, flying in people, taking care of everybody. Also, getting the rehearsals down, listening to that. I happen to read music. Sometimes, it helps for me to look at the arrangements. I worked with Melba, got the band together so they understood the arrangements, and made sure they had all the right parts. In terms of the actual recording, it was the sort of thing where you get takes and then Jean-Phillipe, Randy, and I decided which takes we liked the best—what held and what didn't. It was kind of a magical session. There wasn't a lot of stress there. The music just flowed.

The three of you listened to playbacks?

Actually, the whole band. Melba's arrangements were really tricky. Melba and Randy went back many years, and even though she'd suffered a stroke, Randy wanted to bring her back in. A lot of people had said—for example, Dizzy and Quincy—that Melba was really one of the best arrangers of that period. Because she's a woman, she didn't get the proper respect that she deserved. She had a band for years and then when she had the stroke, she was unable to play [trombone] any more. One of the things she could still do—with the use of a computer—was write. That's how she came to arrange the compositions, writing specifically for the players.

Randy is a very spiritual person. Nothing was contrived or overthought. One of the things I remember him doing—it was "African Village Bedford Stuyvesant 2"—starts off solo piano for one chorus, then a trio, and then a soloist from each of the band's sections. I remember we recorded four takes, actually, two complete takes and two breakdowns. The first time Randy played, it was amazing; then there was a breakdown: someone didn't come in on time. I thought, "I probably won't hear an introduction like that again." The second one was even better than the first, and the third one was better than the first two. For Randy, it's a gift, but it's always there. It's always going to be something different.

Jay Newland (Engineer)
I was working at RCA Studio on Forty-Fourth Street. It was a pretty awesome place. Now, I think it's the IRS or something. The first record that Jean-Philippe did with Abbey [Lincoln], I wasn't the engineer. I was the studio second engineer. The thing goes by, and Jean-Philippe says, "I'm doing sort of a large-band record here in a few months. Can you recommend somebody?"

I said, "Yeah, you're talking to him." That was *The Spirits of Our Ancestors*. That was a pretty amazing session. Randy had so much spirit and energy it was incredible. He's a Bösendorfer [piano] guy. You have to get one brought in. With all of his records, part of the production meeting is to make sure we get a Bösendorfer sent over and tuned up. He really knows how to make that low octave become like an earthquake or volcano. It's amazing.

PATRICIA BARBER, *A DISTORTION OF LOVE* (1992, ANTILLES)
Brian Bacchus
My thing is to put the whole thing together: try to get a realistic budget; deal with all of the musicians; put the right people together; book the studio; be there and set up; understand the recording process, what the tunes are going to be; help choose tunes, whether it's standards or working from originals; make everyone comfortable and relaxed, which is really important. I don't think, "I'm the God of it; it's my creative thing."

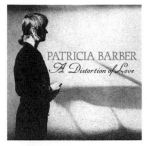

Especially with certain musicians, the way you learn things is to hear what they're thinking.

It used to be that someone—say, Quincy Jones—would come in, when he was an A & R person and in-house producer, and write material and bring arrangements. Very few producers do that anymore, but I do have ideas about things, and what I have to offer comes out.

A lot of producers like to work with certain engineers. I'm pretty much the same. I'm not an electronic genius, but I know how the board works, the recording process. It's good, though, to find someone that understands you.

Let's say it's a session where you're mixing down. You've recorded multitrack. Maybe Billy Higgins is the drummer on the date, and you know the sound he has. He sits there; he's bouncing in his seat; his cymbal sound, it's not overpowering, but it has this real happy sizzle. And you're not getting it. The engineer's job is to get that sound. Sometimes, you need to be able to talk in his terms, but you also might want to give him more of a painting and have him deliver that to you. There are a lot of inexact things to describe. It's not like, "You need to have this at so many dBs with this type of EQ." That way the engineer can play around with all kinds of different ways.

Working with the engineer Jim Anderson on a Patricia Barber recording, we were trying to get a certain type of reverb, echo reverb. We were at Power Station, and he ended up running one of the vocals through plate mikes they had in the stairwell. He played it at the top of the stairs, and the plate mike picked it up at the bottom. That gave us this really different reverb without using anything artificial. So I had an engineer who was willing to try things: "Let's do something a little freaky here."

[The Temptations'] "My Girl" was something that, on a break, we were just joking around with. We were laughing a lot because [guitarist] Wolfgang [Muthspiel] didn't know the song at all. He didn't grow up here. He started playing along, but had no real context. I told Patricia, "That would be a great tune for you." We sent somebody out to get sheet music so Wolfgang would know the song form and the lyrics. And so Patricia would know all of the lyrics as well. We did the song on the spur of the moment. The natural reverb was added when she was playing piano.

HAL RUSSELL, *HAL'S BELLS* (1992, ECM)
Steve Lake

I started writing about music in 1973, when I was twenty-one. That was for the *Melody Maker* in England at a time when they still had a lot of jazz coverage. My attention was split between different types of music. I was already interested in jazz, but I also liked rock, blues, folk, country, contemporary classical music, and the broad area they now call world music. I left the *Melody Maker* in 1977, and I freelanced for a year. Then, I got a call from Manfred Eicher who invited me—I was living in London—to come and work for ECM in Munich in 1978, which I did. I worked for them for about three years. One main responsibility was looking after the Japo label, which was an ECM sublabel. At that time, I produced half a dozen records for them. That was my first run of doing this work.

I quit and spent another ten years freelancing as a writer. Did that full force for a decade while living in Germany. Then it was seeing and hearing Hal Russell and the NRG Ensemble at the Moers Festival in 1990 that made me feel strongly, "This music has to be documented. It's not enough for it to be scattered over a few obscure labels." I went and talked to Manfred Eicher to try and persuade him, actually, to record them for ECM. He said, "Why don't you get the project together?" So I did that, compiling and mixing the live album *The Finnish/Swiss Tour* [1991]. The next thing I knew I was back at the ECM office, which is more or less where I've been since, doing a bunch of different jobs in the production department, as well as developing a line of productions of my own.

From my perspective, record production is criticism in action. Instead of talking about the music after the event, you can help to shape it. For me it has often been more enjoyable and more challenging than sitting behind a typewriter and giving marks out of ten to the finished thing. As a journalist and listener, I'm grateful for the improvised music document if that's all that is available, but I also know that free-improvised music can benefit from controlled production circumstances. That's an area that's still largely unexplored. What happens if you don't make these records more or less on the run—as most free-jazz records have been made?

To see what Hal could do in a solo situation, which he had never attempted before, working with overdubs, was just amazing. The Berlin Jazz Festival, 1991, was when we started talking about that, and then we recorded it half a year later. My wife asked Hal if he ever played solo gigs. He thought that was a very interesting idea, and he began to consider it. He hadn't thought about an overdubbed record at all. Because Hal's different selves, if you like—as drummer, vibraphonist, trumpeter, and saxophonist—had belonged to different historical periods, I was curious how they would relate to each other if you used the magic of multitracking. The way he finally went about it really surprised me.

I've been at rock recording sessions where you lay down a drum track and then you do the rest. But Hal put down the horns first—he'd play some of his furious saxophone—and leave these big holes where the other instruments would be filled in. In every instance on the record, he put the drums down last. Sometimes you couldn't grasp the whole picture until the drums appeared. It was very, very weird to see him doing that.

But by this time, Hal's health was failing. So they were tough sessions for him. The physical challenge of playing the horn took a lot out of him. For his solos he'd push as much air through the horn as he could to shape his solo, and then he'd gesticulate, indicating where the vibes were going to be or the drums afterwards. Then there'd be a hole, and you'd get the next burst of post-Ayler sax. Layer by layer the thing would fill up. He knew exactly what he wanted.

It doesn't happen very often that you meet a musician who turns your ideas around or makes you think about music in a new way, but he was definitely one of those men.

HAL RUSSELL NRG ENSEMBLE, *THE HAL RUSSELL STORY* (1993, ECM)
Steve Lake

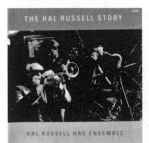

The Hal Russell Story was a project I suggested to Hal and the NRG Ensemble. Probably people don't know about the extended writings of Hal Russell at all, but he had several longer conceptual pieces in his repertoire. There was a suite for Artie Shaw, for instance, and one for Fred Astaire, and a sort of mad deconstruction of *The Sound of Music*. We were talking about doing some of those things, but then I thought, "Hal's own story is so interesting. Why don't we try and make an autobiographical album?"

Hal charged into the project with gusto. The band sent me rehearsal tapes every week. Wild, hilarious tapes. In between the music, Hal tried to do an improvised monologue holding his life story together. When that didn't work, he asked me to write some kind of connecting text. So I did that for him. We had a little back and forth, six months of fascinating correspondence.

I booked a short European tour for the group so they could road-test the material, and then we went into the studio and had a ball, basically. By this point, the music was pretty well prepared, but it still changed. We ended up not using the finale that Hal had written because the previous movement had built up such a head of steam that there was no way to top it at all. That was a fantastic band. The NRG Ensemble with Hal has my vote as one of the great under-acknowledged bands of jazz history.

There is certainly more than one "ECM sound." If you listen to the catalog, there are so many different approaches taken. A lot of things that I've done had to do with directions Manfred initiated on ECM in the first place. The recordings with Circle, or the Art Ensemble records, the Music Improvisation Company. These are things that were tremendously influential to me. Manfred follows his very broad enthusiasms, and I guess I follow mine. We're two different people, but often enough the interests overlap. Manfred, of course, has vast experience that I don't have.

BERN NIX TRIO, *ALARMS AND EXCURSIONS* (1993, NEW WORLD)
Wayne Horvitz

He sent me tapes, and we met once, since I live out here in Seattle. It could not have been simpler. I tried to get him a really nice studio [Sear Sound]. I got Joe Ferla to engineer. He's engineered on quite a few things I've done. We recorded live to two-track. So that's a whole different scene.

One thing you try to do is get a lot of takes of each tune, and keep it flowing. But with a lot of takes things can start to feel dead. You have to keep it jumping. Instead of doing four takes of one tune, I like to do all the tunes and then do all the tunes again. Take two of piece number one happens three hours after it was first recorded. You're sort of back at it again, fresh.

The real production role with that kind of record is making sure that sounds go down well and everything sounds good. Also, afterwards, there's the postproduction job of listening to all the takes, getting together with the artist, and choosing the ones you like the most. Particularly on a jazz record, if an artist likes one take and I like another, then it's the artist's choice. A lot of producers might not agree, but I feel like, "It's their record. What's the big deal? How did my opinion get to be so important?"

ART PEPPER, *THE HOLLYWOOD ALL-STAR SESSIONS* (1993, GALAXY)
John Snyder

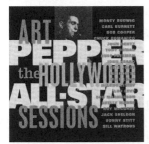

Art Pepper could be doing every drug under the sun, except heroin but including methadone, and think he was straight because he wasn't doing heroin. That's just the way it was. Art was a wounded person. He'd been scarred, and he was not going to change, but he was a beautiful person. He was funny, and he was kind. He was also a manipulator and a con man, but those were survival skills. The fact that somebody maintains those skills doesn't surprise me.

One time, Art was at my house. His nose didn't work anymore, and so he turned to me and said, "Hey man, where is your kit?"

"What?"

"Your kit." He made this motion—hypodermic thing to the arm.

I said, "Art, I don't have a kit." He thought everybody had a kit! That's Art. In a way, he thought everybody was like him. Not me. I'm with you to a certain point but not to that point.

But you know what it was, I didn't judge him. I wasn't moralistic about it at all, although in my heart I felt he was destroying himself, but I wasn't getting on his case, because it wasn't about that. I thought if I can just show him love and respect. Other people were on his case about the drugs. I didn't have to do that. It made me different if I didn't and, also, he trusted me.

RANDY WESTON AND MELBA LISTON, *VOLCANO BLUES* (1993, VERVE/POLYDOR)
Jean-Philippe Allard

The blues album was my idea. I suggested it because I love the creative way Randy plays the blues. To me, he's a real blues player, and it was my suggestion to bring in Johnny Copeland. Randy loved the idea.

Brian Bacchus

Randy loves the blues, and Jean-Philippe thought he had that deep feel. Jean-Philippe and I talked about who we wanted to use in the band. Randy had heard Johnny, and because Johnny recorded for Polygram in France, they were on the same label.

It was an interesting session because [on "Blue Mood"] you get to hear Johnny Copeland on acoustic guitar, which is unusual. "Harvard Blues," a Basie tune, was the other track he did with the band. Randy had always loved it, loved the lyrics. It was just a matter of getting the tune, finding what key Johnny wanted to sing it in, and learning the music. Randy was trying to show the blues in a lot of different forms, and Johnny got right down to the grit of it.

Were players isolated on different tracks?

It depended. We recorded Johnny Copeland separately from the band. His solo piece was just by himself. But no, basically it was out in the open, though using some baffling. That was in the old RCA Studios. They're beautiful and have quite a history—really huge, open rooms.

VARIOUS, *MUSIC FROM AND INSPIRED BY THE FILM "SHORT CUTS"* (1993, IMAGO)
Hal Willner

Joel Dorn taught me to create a framework. You'll get the best performance from artists if you make them feel a certain way. Sometimes that's even making them uncomfortable, putting them in with people they normally wouldn't be with. You've got to get that performance. It was really exciting for me to witness and work with Robert Altman on *Short Cuts* because that's the way he works on film. His scripts and what he wants provide such a strong foundation that he can let you loosen it: people that he trusts. If he hires you, he knows who he's hiring. He knows what you do, and then he lets you loose within that framework. That's why an actor, appreciating that, will give 200 percent.

Altman gave me the script, and often I almost had to force him to listen to material early on, because he was waiting to see what we would do. I was like, "Tell me about this character and what she sings." Meanwhile, it was all exactly what he wanted. The script was so strong—with Annie Ross. And being around the set: everyone comes to the dailies, from the caterers on. We knew what kind of thing he wanted. I spent three months working night and day, and it wasn't like work.

That's the atmosphere I've always wanted to create on my records, but I haven't had a *M.A.S.H.*, which can, of course, open up new doors. But I'm very lucky to have seen a lot of stuff. Through my *Nino Rota* album, I got to know Fellini. He was supportive of that. I took Joel to meet Fellini, when he was on the *Dick Cavett Show*. I said [to Fellini], "This is the man who taught me."

CASSANDRA WILSON, *BLUE LIGHT 'TIL DAWN* (1993, BLUE NOTE)
Craig Street

When I first moved to New York, it was kind of because I wanted to put combinations of musicians together: to try different things, to interpret material. I started doing that, and that's how I met more musicians.

The first record I ever did for a label resulted when people started coming up to me and saying, "We know you've been in the studio, and you know how to talk to engineers. So come help us." But nobody called it production. I didn't know what it was.

I happened to live in a huge apartment building in Harlem. Cassandra Wilson lived there as well. At the time, I was a construction worker, and I was also doing a bunch of live music projects. With money from the city, I had assembled groups of musicians who toured as a project, pretty radically interpreting Hendrix. Cassandra had done a couple of things as a vocalist with me. I put together a project for the city in which an interesting group of musicians I'd been around did a personal take on a bunch of songs that were performed in films. That was how Cassandra and I got to know each other.

I was around the apartment one day, and I went down to get the mail. I ran into her. She told me, "I got signed to Blue Note. They want to put me with all these big, fancy producers. They all make me nervous. I don't know what to do." She started talking, "I want to do a record that's about the R & B records that influenced me as a kid. I want to do a jazz version of R & B songs."

We knew each other. "Cassandra," I said, "that's stupid. That's like being in a box. Why would you do that?" Because we had worked together, because we had talked about music, I knew that she had a deep love of Joni Mitchell. Her dad was a bass player and a blues musician. She loved country music. We used to argue about seventies pop. She liked Seals and Crofts—stuff that I couldn't stand.

We talked about her record all the time. I said, "Don't conceptualize it.

Don't put it in a box. Look at it more as a group of songs that you could sing." We talked about tunes, and I started giving her samples of songs. We started going through them.

She went to the label and said, "I found the guy that I want to produce my record. He's a construction worker who lives in my building." But [Bruce] Lundvall [president/CEO of Blue Note] knew who I was. At one point, Blue Note had been poking around with what I was doing with those projects. He gave Cassandra and me a small amount of money to go in and record demos. Those first three demos became the first three tracks on *Blue Light 'til Dawn*.

What happened was Cassandra and I talked about all the songs she could do. I said, "You don't have anything to lose. I don't have anything to lose. I have a great job, plastering rich people's houses on the Upper West Side. Let me do what I feel might really work with you."

Still, Cassandra and Lundvall were both willing to take a chance on a complete unknown. She did, literally, risk her career going into the studio with somebody who had pretty wacky ideas for a jazz artist. And a guy at a label had enough vision to allow an artist to do what she was feeling and to take the risks that she wanted to take. Having them both do that allowed me to step into an arena where two years prior to that nobody wanted to look at me as a producer.

At the time Cassandra had a band, all from the jazz world, and it was obvious they were the wrong instrumentation. She has that lush, gorgeous contralto, which I thought was fighting for space among all those so-called jazz instruments. All the instruments were in that same range: [Hammond] B3, low brass, upright bass, a jazz drummer playing a lot of ride cymbal. Everything was in the same frequency range as her voice. You could not hear what her voice could do.

That speaks to my influences. Some of the most influential things to me, for voice [recordings], are R & B records, where the voice is so loud it's just voice and bass. Everything else is secondary. I like to hear the vocal. It sounds good to me when you can hear and you can feel the voice. And you could not do that with her band.

Cassandra is very creative and very generous. She was like, "Try what you want to try." I put together a group of people that I knew. I was starting to find people who were straddling different worlds. I brought in acoustic instruments.

Sometimes, I give myself a particular beacon. If I start drifting, "Ah yeah, there's the beacon. I see it. I remember. Okay, that means we don't want this straight organ tone; we want this tone, because the beacon is there." With Cassandra's first record, the beacon was a visual image—an image that I knew as a kid from a record my dad had. There was this beautiful picture of an early twentieth-century black string band: five guys holding fiddles and mandolins, sitting in a field under a tree. It was this thing: "People don't think of us like this. They don't think of us as sitting in a field, wearing suits, playing mandolins and violins. So let's do this." It was a visual thing, but it was a sonic thing, too. The acoustics against that voice, I knew, would set the voice in a different way. And then Cassandra was very clever and very collaborative about the songs that she went for. The musicians were phenomenal, even though she had some safety nets in there—musicians that she felt comfortable with.

Quite often what somebody is afraid of is where the best stuff is. Like if somebody says, "I really don't feel comfortable playing guitar and singing, but I do play guitar." You say, "Hey, what's there?"

A lot of what I learned dealing with Cassandra was that. I knew she played guitar. If there were songs that she'd written or if there were songs that we'd ultimately agreed to do, I had her invent some version of that song with her playing guitar and singing into a cassette. Then I gave that cassette to the musicians and said, "Here's the foundation that we're going to work from." So instead of letting them hear a Robert Johnson song or a Hank Williams song or hear a Joni Mitchell song, I'd let them hear Cassandra's interpretation of that and then I would let them expound on it.

Jazz in its ideal sense is a balancing act, a tightrope kind of performance, where somebody is way up in the air doing all these astounding feats on this narrow little wire. Skill alone keeps them on the wire, but it's their emotion that draws you into the situation. With that forming my primary definition of what jazz is, anything that requires rules to be established around the music is, to me, not jazz. It's therefore perfectly jazz to have pedal steel and violin, and it's also perfectly musical. If I have pedal steel and violin, I can make a string section, depending on where I place the pedal steel against the violin. If I add an accordion to that, I can practically have an orchestra. If I add a Chamberlain—which is this sort of antique electronic instrument that plays tapes when you press the keys—it opens up completely other doors. If I can mix it, if I don't have to go straight to two-track, then we're talking about a whole other thing. It opens up numerous possibilities.

Likewise with recording, what's really interesting is the notion of all the things that can exist on a soundstage. When I'm talking about a soundstage, I mean the space in between two speakers: how you choose to place things from left to right or from front to back; how you have dry things against wet things—that is, a track that has nothing on it except for room sound (or maybe not even that, if it was close-miked) against something with massive amounts of reverb, like you drenched it in something. Through the contrast between all of those different things, you can come up with something you didn't even think about.

I'm always trying different things, shifting things—particularly, if I'm doing something where overdubs are involved. Maybe I've got to do a piano. What I'll do is shift the speed of the tape slightly, record the piano, and then when it's brought back to normal, the piano is maybe lower than it would normally be. Or it's a little bit out of tune, not much, but a tiny bit, so that it sounds a little more real. It's a little fatter. I might play around with different types of reverb or miking things in different ways. Sometimes you mike a piano, and it's really lush and traditional. Other times, you stick a weird, squirrely little microphone inside there and get the most spastic sound imaginable. To me, that's part of the fun, though it shouldn't ever sound gimmicky. It shouldn't ever detract from the song and the person singing the song.

CARLA BLEY, *BIG BAND THEORY* (1993, WATT WORKS/ECM)
Carla Bley and Steve Swallow

BLEY: There's the kind of producer that oversees every note. I guess it's more in the popular music scene where the producer chooses everything and writes the arrangement. That's a kind of producer that jazz doesn't have and doesn't often need. Then you go to the self-production thing, which is very hard and lonesome.

SWALLOW: There isn't much that I do for you as a producer. It's the closest you could get to not having a producer.

BLEY: Well, jazz musicians don't usually need a producer.

SWALLOW: I just mix the records very carefully, and do whatever I can to facilitate getting it onto tape the way you want it in a way that's very close to the environment you worked in. With Kip [Hanrahan] or Hal [Willner], both of them are utterly permissive. They find the money, assemble the cast, officially begin the date, and then step back. With Kip [on the *Conjure* albums], it was like going to a Freudian analyst.

BLEY: The music wouldn't even be written.

SWALLOW: You'd get everybody in the room; we'd mill around and wonder what was going to happen. Finally, somebody would get impatient, usually me, and say, "So Kip, what are we going to do?"

Invariably his response was, "I don't know. What would you like to do?" And so you're off, like that. Every question was answered by a question. He had immense patience. Sometimes six hours would go by and that question would never get answered and nothing would get done. Sometimes the project would assume a momentum that would lead to some really wonderful music. What I'm saying is there's not so much difference between self-production and working for Kip and Hal. In a way, they're at the same end of the spectrum. The inmates have control of the asylum. The other end of the spectrum is the rock 'n' roll producer, who does everything.

BLEY: When I get a band together—like for *Big Band Theory*—my gripe is that we'd only played the songs for a week and a half when we made the record. We had to record early in the tour, because Alex [Balanescu, violin] had to go to Japan. By the end of the tour, we were playing really good, but when we started, it was all new music. I kept thinking of Count Basie with his guys, all there on the bus. "Drive them to the recording studio. Okay, let them out. Close the doors quick! One of them's trying to escape." He had them! They were sitting ducks all those years. I get the very best guys, but I have them for like one week at a time.

KIP HANRAHAN, *EXOTICA* (1993, AMERICAN CLAVÉ)
Kip Hanrahan

The band was working really well live; we were taking a lot of chances. We wanted to try that in the studio. I didn't want personal lyrics on the record as much as political lyrics. I rewrote them in the studio as we were sitting there working. The band had to be as immediate and live as we were live onstage. It had to have that same feeling of both roughness and understanding each other. That's what we were trying to get. In some ways the record was liberated by grunge. It was a band record, and we could be sloppy in the way that some grunge things are. And there was a hip-hop influence. You're influenced by everything you see. I don't think there were intentional formal innovations, but it was supposed to be the band's record with the new words—not personal, but political.

KEITH JARRETT, GARY PEACOCK, AND JACK DEJOHNETTE, *BYE BYE BLACKBIRD* (1993, ECM)
Jay Newland (Engineer)

I did a record with Keith Jarrett called *Bye Bye Blackbird*.[2] Whoever ECM's regular guy [in the States] is, he wasn't available, and somebody else also wasn't available. I got the call. Maybe Jean-Philippe [Allard] steered them to me.

I got a phone call from Manfred [Eicher]. He says, "I want everybody in a separate room—total isolation."

"Sure, no problem."

Half an hour later, I get a call from Keith. He goes, "I don't want any of that separate room thing. I want everybody right in the same room, like we're in a club—no headphones."

I'm like, "Whoa, okay." The drums were right next to the piano like you'd see in a club, and the bass was a little bit behind Keith's shoulder. He [Gary Peacock] actually had an amp, just a little speaker to magnify the sound of the bass, but I didn't mike it. I just miked the bass. That's how we did it.

We started at noon or at one o'clock, and we were done at six. At the time, I'd run a DAT, back when it was the really cool thing.[3] I recorded a DAT of the session, a rough mix kind of thing. Plus, I recorded to a multitrack digital.

This is the story I heard. I guess Manfred had mixed the multitrack a few times to do the ECM thing, which is that kind of ambient sound. It didn't really work out because there was leakage, and Keith didn't like it. So the DAT, the board mixes, were what became the record. It was a tribute to Miles, and Keith wanted it to sound like Miles at the Five Spot or something. It was just this very live sounding thing.

MARILYN CRISPELL WITH REGGIE WORKMAN AND GERRY HEMINGWAY, *ON TOUR* (1993, MUSIC AND ARTS PROGRAM)
Marilyn Crispell

I wanted to do this for a long time because I'd had this trio together for years. The year the recording was done I was the touring artist for the

---

2. Manfred Eicher is this album's producer, but Newland's anecdote reveals the flexibility of that designation.

3. ADAT (Alesis Digital Audio Tape) was introduced in 1992.

New England Foundation for the Arts. I had six to ten concerts. We recorded every one, and then I listened to them and picked out the stuff that I wanted to be on the CD. When I listen to it, I hear the results of having played with Reggie for several years, and playing with [Anthony] Braxton had a tremendous impact on me, his sense of space and composition. Braxton talks about pulse feelings as opposed to a time: one-two, one-two-three-four kind of thing. It's like a repeating wave. With Reggie I felt, particularly, a kind of rhythmic grounding—which might sound strange if you know my music—but I hear it in there.

How did the digital revolution, for example, the long form of CDs, affect your work?

I like that actually. Something in me balks at having to organize things into an LP format, because in a live performance you can get into something. If you're recording and thinking, "Well this has to be a length that can be played on the radio," another whole element comes into it. You're controlling something that, maybe, you don't want to be controlling that way. I like the longer format, because it gives you more of a chance to stretch out.[4]

PAUL BLEY, EVAN PARKER, AND BARRE PHILLIPS, *TIME WILL TELL* (1994, ECM)
Steve Lake

Evan's one of the great saxophone players and a great musical mind. I had been talking with Manfred Eicher about avenues that could be pursued, and what kind of context we might try to put Evan Parker into that would not simply duplicate the many records that had already been made on Incus, FMP, and so on. We thought about Paul Bley, and I knew that Evan had greatly admired the Jimmy Giuffre 3 recordings, and so we were thinking that there was something to be done that might not exactly update that tradition but offer a contemporary parallel.

It started with choosing the participants. All three musicians were surprised to be asked to make this session. They hadn't played together as a

---

4. *On Tour* is composed of highlights from Crispell's U.S. summer tour of 1992.

trio. Parker and Bley had never played together at all before. But Barre Phillips had played with both men and, like Bley, had worked extensively with Giuffre. There was a lot of talk between the four of us about what should be explored or not be explored. We ruled out the idea of having a lot of solos, which Bley had done on a previous session with John Surman for ECM.

The first piece they played is the first piece on that record. It's called "Poetic Justice." That was a voyage of discovery on the basis of no discussion. After that, it was clearer what might be attempted. For example, there was the suggestion that we could record a piece that started with a sort of archetypal Evan Parker circular-breathing episode, but instead of using it as a solo element, as it usually is in the Alexander Von Schlippenbach Trio, the other guys should be right in there from the beginning, working with the dynamics of this and seeing what happened. There were small ideas like that. Still, I wouldn't overestimate my role in the making of that particular recording, beyond the fact of instigating it. Sometimes that's all there is to do, allowing the dynamics encountered to shape the album.

Paul Bley has often said his dream is to keep the taxi waiting while you do an improvised session. As a producer, the idea is to slow him down a little bit, not let that be the reality. But it was a session that happened really quickly and very easily. In a way there was more discussion than there was playing. A lot of coffee and classic Bley anecdotes. Almost everything that was played was a take. I think we ended up leaving out just one piece from the two days of recording. On the third day we mixed, without Paul, and I finished the session with Evan and Barre. I was glad that Bley liked the result enough to want to take the trio on the road.

Manfred does many of his Norwegian recordings at Rainbow Studio in Oslo, and that is a good, large room, with a church-like feeling, and natural daylight. I did the [Paul] Bley record there, and Hal Russell solo, Raoul Bjorkenheim with Krakatau, mixed the John Surman Brass Project there, and so on.

With Russell's solo project, Hal's Bells, did you know you wanted to work at Rainbow from the beginning?

Yeah, with that kind of multitrack record you're very dependent on what the musician can actually hear through headphones. [Engineer] Jan Erik Kongshaug's headphone mix is widely admired, so Rainbow was a good place for that.

ETTA JAMES, *MYSTERY LADY: SONGS OF BILLIE HOLIDAY* (1994, RCA)
Jay Newland (Engineer)

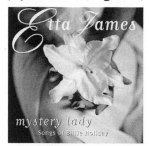

One of my favorite records ever is one John Snyder produced, *Mystery Lady*, by Etta James. I was the engineer on that one. It was her first jazz record. The really amazing thing was it was recorded all live with the horn section and everything.

John and I had flown out to Los Angeles to work in a studio out there. They had assured us that the piano was in great shape. Cedar Walton was the pianist/arranger on the session. He gets in and goes, "John, I can't play this piano. It's terrible."

We were all, "Now what?" Amazingly, John said, "We're going to cancel today. We'll get a new Steinway brought over here." They couldn't get it done in the next five hours or something. We canceled the first day and did the whole record the second day. It was amazing.

John had this great idea to get a really big, comfortable chair and put it in the booth for Etta, like she was queen. Everything that came out of her mouth was awesome. I always think of that as one of the greatest things John and I ever worked on together. The arrangements are so hip and so subtle. The trumpet solos are perfect.

BILL FRISELL, *THIS LAND* (1994, NONESUCH)
Lee Townsend

I'm naturally drawn to hybridized music. I like combining acoustic and electric instruments. I like combining different effects that are obvious with more naturalistic tones. Where those worlds meet is what's interesting to me. And I'm interested in technology as a service to bringing out the humanity of the music.

Bill Frisell This Land   Since I work in both jazz and, for lack of a better word, more pop- or rock-oriented music, I somehow try to meld those worlds together. The records which were influential to me growing up span the range from jazz to rock. I can't divorce those types of music. What I try to do is to bring the attention to detail, arrangements, and sound of rock production to the jazz area, and I try to bring the jazz interest in spontaneous creativity and in musicians truly playing together and reacting off each other into the more rock-oriented productions that I do.

For the purpose of optimum sound quality down the road while mixing, I like to have the instruments isolated from each other so that there's not intended leakage of sound into microphones. That means the whole setting up in one room and everybody playing together is not really the way I go about it. Still, I really like for people to play together as much as possible, at least during the original tracking. And so I like to work in studios where I can achieve that isolation and still have people physically close with good eye contact through glass. There's nothing earth-shattering about what I'm saying. It doesn't seem at all abnormal, but I'm kind of a stickler about that because it gives me maximum flexibility down the road if I want to put a certain effect on a certain instrument without it affecting the others. I suppose that reveals a little bit greater preoccupation with pop-oriented producers than with jazz-oriented producers.

On *This Land*, the horn record I did with Bill, we had all the separation that I just described, but the horns were a little bit closer together. There wasn't any pretense that there was going to be separation. That worked fine.

In postproduction were there things not typical of stock-in-trade jazz recordings?

Probably, but they were subtle. Changing drum reverbs in the middle of a song to get certain effects, that was employed on the record. There was a time when we cut part of a trombone solo and put on a little delay to make a dub-reggae moment. But there was no big, beat-you-over-the-head, pop-production technique. I kept it so the intent of the music wasn't eclipsed. It was really a fun mix. [Engineer] Joe Ferla and I did a lot of exploring and saying, "Oh yeah, this sounds really cool," or "Nah, this doesn't work." We had the time to come up with things that we felt good about. Then, of course, we always checked with Bill. If he didn't think it was too strange or whatever, I felt confident in going ahead and not being shy.

You've worked with quite an array of guitarists.

There's variation about what people are satisfied with. John Scofield is definitely the kind of guitarist who feels that he's said what he has to say after two or three takes. In a certain way, Bill is also like that. If he feels like it's not happening after he's done three takes, he thinks there's a deeper reason why it isn't working. "Let's move on." Pat Metheny is somebody who feels that he's just getting inside the music, just getting started, after that many takes. Sometimes it takes him a few extra takes to arrive at something he's comfortable with. In his case it's really not something that anyone not inside the music would even notice. He's his own toughest critic. He's very demanding. Things he might want to address or change in a solo are so subtle that a lot of people might not notice or care. He'll go back in and fix things that really bug him, though it's not as if he's aiming for clinical perfection. There are things—miniscule glitches—that he lets go if he thinks it enhances the humanity of the music.

BILL FRISELL, *MUSIC FOR THE FILMS OF BUSTER KEATON: "GO WEST"* AND *MUSIC FOR THE FILMS OF BUSTER KEATON: "THE HIGH SIGN"/"ONE WEEK"* (1995, WARNER BROS.)
Lee Townsend

Those sessions were interesting and fun. For many years, Buster Keaton was a major figure for me. And when I look at Bill Frisell's band [a trio with Kermit Driscoll (bass) and Joey Baron (drums)], I think they had the same kind of importance and impact as some of my biggest heroes: the John Coltrane Quartet or Miles Davis's Quintet. So the marriage of Buster Keaton and Bill was like a dream come true.

We synced up three-quarter-inch videos of those films, hooked up video monitors, and the band played along with the sequences. We did it in a way that was kind of live and ensemble-oriented. If we didn't get what we wanted, we went back and did it again. Then we took some days of overdubs, went with each musician and did various colors and effects on bass, drums, and guitars to help bring out details that couldn't be cut in during live action.

To us, it was important not to telegraph every little event that happened with a drum crash or whatever—although we did enough of that for sure—or to make a document of every crazy event that happens in the films, but rather to let Bill's music bring out the underlying emotional truth of the actions and the dilemmas that Keaton's characters dealt with. For my tastes Bill really accomplished that in a way that made me understand the films in deeper ways than I ever had in the past.

From the start we thought of the project as a one-record set. We'd combine and edit things, and make it tell a story in one record. Then, if we could ever get the clearances, the full issue would have the videos. But when he finished recording, Bill had a hard time with the editing ideas I came up with. He had a hard time giving up his attachment to the whole overall context in which he created the music. He really felt like the pieces should remain as complete units. The people at Nonesuch were very supportive of that once we told them, but then came the debate whether we should release the titles as a package or as single albums so that the discrete projects would have lives of their own. That final decision was a collaboration between Bill and the record company.

ITALIAN INSTABILE ORCHESTRA, *SKIES OF EUROPE* (1995, ECM)
Steve Lake

Why does one do this at all? I guess, for me, it's about waving a flag for music that you feel needs to be heard. In this way writing and producing are very similar. There's this feeling of wanting to shake people by the lapels and say, "Hey, you have to listen to this!" To be able to instigate projects and then to follow that through is, to me, like taking it to the next level.

The Italian Instabile Orchestra is an eighteen-piece big band that I first heard at the Noci Festival in south Italy in, I think, 1992. I really wanted to do something with them. The album is two long suites by Giorgio Gaslini, the pianist, and Bruno Tommaso, the bassist. It goes into a lot of different areas. Gaslini's piece has allusions to everything from Erik Satie to Fellini's film music and Ornette Coleman. [Bruno] Tommaso's piece has a lot to do with Sicilian folk music and Charles Mingus. In both cases there's a wide spectrum. We were lucky enough to have Ornette Coleman write some liner notes for us. It's a good project. There's a nice energy.

This is a band that's comprised entirely of soloists. So the first thing was that ECM said they'd take on this project if these two guys—Gaslini and Tommaso—were the featured composers. The orchestra had to accept that, with some grumbling in the ranks. Also, Manfred Eicher had some input here. He likes, very much, Gaslini's writing for cinema, and in particular for Antonioni's films. This was one consideration. Gaslini has a long suite on this record of about forty minutes.

And then it was a question ... This is, mostly, very written music. The improvised sections kind of take care of themselves, but I had to carefully monitor all aspects of the playing. It was not a case of turning on the mikes and hoping for the best. With an eighteen-piece big band there's also the practicality of doing it. How do you make it cost-effective and all of these things? We recorded, finally, in a theater in Florence for a few days. We had a reciprocal arrangement with the people who ran the auditorium that we'd give them a free concert for the use of the place. Then we had two days of recording in the auditorium. We recorded it on ADAT, took the tapes to Winterthur; meanwhile I was going through the many takes of this material, marking out splice points so that Martin Wieland, an excellent engineer, could edit. We went into the studio in Winterthur and pieced it together like a jigsaw puzzle. If you record Globe Unity you might do it different, but this one was done like that.

CASSANDRA WILSON, *NEW MOON DAUGHTER* (1995, BLUE NOTE)
Craig Street

By the time we got to the second record, there was some trust there, and so we pushed it even further. Dougie [Bowne] and Kevin [Breit] completely smeared any boundaries whatsoever.

Cassandra wanted a good environment, an environment for her that was comfortable. We went up and recorded in the barn at Bearsville [Woodstock, New York]. It was a rehearsal studio. It didn't have a control room. We had to bring things in and set it up—just open up the barn doors.

At that point, I had come to understand that many of my favorite records were not recorded in studios: whether it was the Robert Johnson stuff, or the Led Zeppelin stuff done at Headley Grange, or *Exile on Main Street*. So all I did, going into that record and through the entire recording process, all I listened to was *Exile on Main Street*. I didn't play it for anybody else—just for me. Every time I listened to music outside the sessions, it was *Exile*. That record was my tip of the hat to Glyn Johns: "You're the man. I can't even touch you. But here." I was thinking about people being in a room together—sonics being not necessarily perfect; outside noise getting in—and how that creates a physical presence that the performer then responds to. The performer then delivers the performances of a lifetime, and everybody can believe it. You can feel it, and it's not anything other than, "Yeah, there's somebody in the kitchen cooking gumbo and clattering pots and pans, and we are doing a take."

T. J. KIRK, *T. J. KIRK* (1995, WARNER BROS.)
Lee Townsend

I guess the birth of that band was late '93. They got together and did a gig. I was in Europe recording. I got a call from Will Bernard, one of the guitar

t.j. kirk

players, saying that this new band sort of instantaneously had been a hit. He wanted me to hear what was going on. When I got back, I listened to a tape they'd had made and went to a gig.

I got really excited about the chemistry of people involved, the unbridled fun in the group, and at the depth and seriousness with which they explored these composers' material [Thelonious Monk, James Brown, and Rahsaan Roland Kirk]. It was a great palate to work with. All three composers have been important to me.

It was a dream come true: strong guitarists [Charlie Hunter, Will Bernard, and John Schott] with interesting sounds, playing over fat beats by an amazing drummer [Scott Amendola]. Why not do it? I sent out a few tapes, shopped them to a few people, and we decided to go with Warners.

I got involved with the album pretty early when we started to do the recording. I went to rehearsals, put in my two cents' worth about the arrangements and the grooves, and tried to encourage a certain musical economy to it all, so that it didn't get busy and unfocused. We all came up with something that we felt was pretty fresh. It was definitely a group effort.

The recording was the kind of thing I might have been a little skeptical of if I'd just heard about it. But it took eight bars to realize that there was something deep going on with those guys. I came up with a sequence [of songs] and made a tape for everybody. After a discussion, we had a couple of little refinements. Basically, with sequencing, the best-laid plans might be close, but you never know until you put it on a tape, listen for a while, and see how things strike you.

Dealing with the label's A & R guys was not hard at all. They were tremendously supportive. They're fans. They wanted us to make the record that we wanted to make. Pleasing all four members of a cooperative band was the challenge. Regardless of how in tune everybody is with one another, there are always going to be differing opinions. After a lot of deliberation, negotiation, and accommodation, it worked out for all five of us.

Discussions about the arrangements went smoothly. In rehearsals it was easy to decide what worked best. After recording, it was also easy to decide—although it was sometimes painful to cut out a song—which songs should make up that first record. One thing I always try to do is have a record tell a story in some sort of way, especially if there are no lyrics. It was also easy to decide with the band which pieces would be the best introduction to the group. What took a lot of deliberation, however, were certain mix issues, what it needed in mastering, and stuff like that.

With that record, even though basically it's a groove record, there were lots of different styles of music employed, from metal to ting-a-ling-a-ling swing, not to mention reggae, funk, et cetera, et cetera. That meant we had to create a world that would serve each song. Sometimes it was very different than the previous song we'd mixed. Yet the record had to have continuity in sound. It was a balancing act. It was a challenge to deal with that stylistic range in a fresh way that had integrity.

GERRY MULLIGAN QUARTET, *DRAGONFLY* (1995, TELARC)
John Snyder

The first time I worked with Gerry was in the seventies at CTI, and I convinced Creed to record the Gerry Mulligan/Chet Baker Quartet [*Carnegie Hall Concert*]. I was trying to get Creed to buy Chet, which he did, but he said, "You should work on the project."

There was a concert at Carnegie Hall, and so we recorded it. Essentially, that was the reunion of that quartet, plus other people. Then, when I went back to A&M, we talked about what artists to sign. "Call him," they said.

"Coincidentally," Gerry said, "I'm finishing up something."

I said, "I'd love to hear it, but I'd also love to make a new record."

"You should hear this first," he said.

I heard it and thought it was great. We finished it [*Lonesome Boulevard*, 1989]. We got along so well he asked me to be his manager, which I shouldn't have done, but I did it, and it ended unpleasantly. Not irreparably. Let's say, I realized that was not my forte. A few years later, I convinced Telarc to sign him.

We finished a classic record. Gerry was so thorough in his preparation you wouldn't believe it, enough to make you pull your hair out and never want to grow it back. As a result of all that angst and preparation, the record was exceptional: all new material; Gerry's arrangements, though Slide Hampton wrote and arranged some things. Gerry and Grover Washington Jr. played beautifully, as did Dave Grusin.

HENRY THREADGILL, *CARRY THE DAY* (1995, COLUMBIA)
Bill Laswell

I don't have too many positive things to say about most of the ways people were doing certain kinds of music—the kind of music we're talking about. I think it had suffered a lot because of people's lack of adventure. Soni-

cally, everything was so squashed, so small and timid. I can't really listen to that kind of music at this point.

I didn't really research his earlier albums. I probably imagined what they sounded like, and it wasn't good for him, because there were a lot of dynamics in what he was doing. There were lots of possibilities to work with size of sound. Like a tuba really needed to sound like a tuba. If you were listening to it closely, you should've felt the low end. There was no bass in that music; the tuba was the bass.

The way Threadgill wrote, in terms of frequencies, the registers of instruments, he might put a high instrument playing in the low register and a low instrument playing in the high. The way it was written, it was one of the best examples, I think, of using frequency ranges in a positive way in terms of composition. You really got to hear the voice of every instrument. But that had a lot to do with how you balanced things. It meant writing things on tape, manually. It had everything to do with the way sounds were EQed. You didn't want one sound to cancel out another. That was all a feel. You had to hear it as music. It wasn't about following the charts or being familiar with the tunes. It had everything to do with being able to hear sound fit together and to know when it didn't.

With Threadgill, I pretty much agreed with what he said about performances. And performances of the same chart could differ drastically in that kind of music. Performances could sound almost like different compositions, depending on how a tempo got started, how someone phrased, or soloed.

JIMMY SCOTT, *HEAVEN* (1996, WARNER BROS.)
Craig Street

When Joe McEwen at Warner Brothers approached me, I hadn't done anything for them yet. He came having heard the Holly Cole and the Cassandra recordings. He asked, "Would you like to work with Jimmy Scott?"

"Man, yes! In a minute."

"He wants to do an album of spirituals."

To cut to the chase, I met with Jimmy at his apartment over in New Jersey. We started talking, getting to know each other. We actually talked about architecture. After a while, he gave me a stack of sheet music, some old, standard gospel tunes. I told him I'd go through them and pick some material. In turn I said, "I'm going to go and find some songs. I'll bring them back to you in a couple of days. We'll sit down and talk about stuff."

I went through his material, picked out the songs I thought were really great. Then, to get a sense of where he was at, I went through and found some songs that to me were spirituals, without applying any particular rule to them. I got songs from Bob Wills, Emmylou Harris, and Bob Dylan to more traditional material, songs from Paul Robeson and Mahalia Jackson.

I didn't know what I was going to do. The label probably thought, "Oh, he'll go in with some wacky instruments and make a really cool-sounding, weird record." I was a little nervous, because it was Jimmy Scott, and the two previous records were wonderful. Mitchell Froom had done one, a standard sort of jazz thing, and Tommy LiPuma did the other one with orchestrations, a fantastic Sinatra kind of record. Both of those guys are producers I admire.

I went in and played Jimmy a cassette I'd made with all these songs. We started choosing: "Yeah, this song. That song." In the end, he picked all of the songs that I never would have imagined he'd choose. He was every bit as open to what spirituality is as I was, and he was ecstatic that somebody was looking at material in a different kind of a way.

We settled on the tunes: a combination of songs from the sheet music and my cassette. I knew that I wanted a piano to be the central part of the recording, and I was thinking, "I'll probably have to do lots of overdubs." People kept telling me, "His voice is shot." I figured, "I'll do this basic thing and then add some colors here and there." I wanted to keep whoever was in the room fairly simple. There were two pianists I was thinking about, and it just so happened that Jacky [Terrasson] was the first one I brought over to meet Jimmy.

We got to his apartment. Jimmy opened up the door, and his eyes got real wide. He said, "Man, I've been wanting to play with you for five years. I saw you in Paris. I saw you in Los Angeles."

I knew right there, "This is it!" The other pianist is wonderful, but I couldn't bring him over. When they sat down in Jimmy's living room, and Jacky started playing through the material, I knew, that's the record. Basically, the whole thing should be either piano and voice—like some of those Robeson recordings or other classic spiritual things—or there should be minimal accompaniment.

Jimmy said, "I'd love to use my bass player. The last two records the producers wouldn't let me bring him in." I'm like, "Cool, let's bring him in on a couple of things." And I needed a percussionist.

We finished the record. We did everything we'd planned, and some more. Jimmy called me up from L.A., "Craig!"

"What's up, man?"

"I've found another song."

"What is it?"

"'Heaven.'"

"You talking about David Byrne's song?"

"Yeah, I want to do it."

I called the label and said, "I know we're done, but Jimmy really wants to do this song." What are you going to do? You've got Jimmy Scott, and he wants to cut "Heaven"?

He came back in the studio. He and Jacky sat down, and we did it right then and there. Between the two of them, they came up with what you hear on the final take. That was Jimmy's idea, but I think he knew there was an openness to whatever material he found. He loved the sense of humor in that song—if you look at it in the sense of it being a spiritual. A lot of those tunes were ambivalent. The Bob Wills tune is extremely moving, but it's downright sarcastic in a way. The Louvin Brothers' song, "The Christian Life," the one Gram Parsons covered: it's about as sarcastic a song as you can get. Listening to it, you get the sense that this guy is trying to convince himself that he really does like the Christian life, when in fact he'd rather hang out and carouse with his buddies. That was what I was looking for in a lot of those songs: the ambiguity that exists in spirituality, or the wide range that it covers. And that's what Jimmy came back with when he picked that song.

BILLIE HOLIDAY, *LOVE SONGS* (COMPILATION, 1996, COLUMBIA/LEGACY)
Steve Berkowitz (Columbia/Legacy Reissues)

Billie Holiday is somebody who was popular as soon as she started to make records for Columbia in the thirties. By the forties, they were already reissuing her records from the thirties. The masters were acetates, and acetates were not built to last. They were built to be used, basically once: to be listened to, duplicated once onto a mold and then a stamper, and then that's it. By the time magnetic tape and tape heads started to be good in the mid-fifties, those original acetates were just about on their last legs. A lot of original transfers that were done to tape really don't sound all that great.

A few years ago, I did a Billie Holiday project and found out that, out of the one hundred and sixty-four or so tracks that Holiday did for Columbia Records in the thirties and forties, there are only six acetates left. A couple of them sound incredibly great; the others are scratched or used up. Then I went through what ended up being a horrible situation, listening to the original tape transfers from the late forties to the early fifties. Tape recording quality wasn't perfected yet. As I moved from the early fifties into the mid-fifties, I could hear a tremendous advance in tape and tape-head technology, but I also clearly heard the decay of the original acetates as I went along. They sounded worse and worse every time they were played. It was a ghastly process.

In its early days the record business was cash and carry, except in the case of a few artists. It was like, "We're going to make a new record. We're going to put out the record, and then we're going to move to the next one." They didn't realize they were building this incredible library, museum, vault, and cache of precious American musical gems. That wasn't realized until later. They were corporations first and foremost. You put in x dollars and hoped to get y dollars as a return. Parallel to that, of course, there were people who worked at the companies who were really great musical people.

So what did we do with Billie Holiday, even though the acetates were gone? The first method was to work with the Library of Congress, who seems to have about ten of every single one of the released Billie Holiday records, [and composite or comp a master]. Record the records in parallel in digital form—straight, flat transfer to digital. Go through each song and pull out the bits that sound great and perfect. Have all ten of them. When you get all of the parts that you like the best, press enter and get one perfect record.

Fortunately, in the case of Billie Holiday, we did have a lot of the original, metal pressing parts. For many years, common wisdom was to play these metal pressing parts—just like a record—with a special needle and a heavy-duty turntable. Problem was when you play the metal, you end up with a high-frequency squeal that you then had to eliminate through noise reduction.

What we did instead, our second method with Billie Holiday, is a wonderful story. The person who's pressing the best 78s in the world is Harry Coster. He works out of his garage in the Netherlands. Piece by piece, we shipped our metal stampers to this guy in Holland who will only work in the spring and the summer, because he doesn't have heat. We've offered to get him heat or even to build him a new building. He said, "No, I don't want it. I only want to work then." So we get him to press like crazy. He makes us brand new, not shellac, but vinyl 78s where the surface is much quieter.

We discovered that there's a lot more information in the metal parts, that you can get out now, than you ever could through the various means of playing back shellac records. To some degree, you hear stuff you've never heard before that was actually part of the original recording session. Contemporary listeners get to hear what the musicians heard. There's much more depth and clarity to the recordings. A lot of the [original] recordings were done really well.

Get a copy of the Billie Holiday *Love Songs* record that I did and listen to either "All of Me" or "Until the Real Thing Comes Along." That's the best sounding Billie Holiday music you've ever heard in terms of sonic reproduction. You can close your eyes and figure out, "She's there. The drummer's there. Oh, the bass player's . . . Wow, I didn't even know there was a guitar player."

ARCANA, *ARC OF THE TESTIMONY* (1997, AXIOM/ISLAND)
Bill Laswell

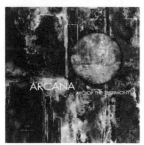

It was recorded live in a way that gave you the option, in a lot of cases, of separation. But it was done in an old-fashioned way in terms of everyone in the room playing instruments.[5]

Separation is obtained by how you set up the room. By where you put the drums. By who's next to whom. How things are miked. By checking things as you go. Also, it's down to the performance. From my perspective, everyone plays it best the first or second time. You've got to be ready to capture that performance, and that's really down to the relationship between an engineer, an assistant, and a producer to capture it sonically, making sure that everything is perfectly in place. If you miss the first or second take, you might not ever get that back. They're there to play that piece and move on.

A lot comes down to the setup and being able to do it quickly: to being spontaneous, to being able to judge performances, and to encouraging

---

5. Personnel on this album are Nicky Skopelitis (guitar), Bill Laswell (bass and synthesizer), Tony Williams (drums), Pharoah Sanders (tenor sax), Byard Lancaster (alto sax), Graham Haynes (cornet), and Buckethead (guitar).

people that something was great or that something was a little suspicious. Once you've done a lot of production, it can be more of a subtle science. The best way is to set up a right environment. If you set up the right feeling among people, then music can happen. If there's anything outside of that, there can always be trouble. If there's not the right environment, if you know there are problems between certain people, if technically there are problems, a lot of things can lead to something not happening.

CHARLIE HADEN AND PAT METHENY, *BEYOND THE MISSOURI SKY (SHORT STORIES)* (1997, VERVE)
Charlie Haden

I sent Pat a tape of the Delmore Brothers singing "The Precious Jewel" [Roy Acuff]. On the same cassette was "He's Gone Away" [traditional] and, I think, the "Cinema Paradiso (Main Title)" [Ennio Morricone] and "The Moon Is a Harsh Mistress" [Jimmy Webb]. We recorded all four of those. I had three songs of mine, and he brought two songs.

I always strive to play beautiful melodies that have character. I think I was influenced a lot by country songs in that respect. A lot of country musicians play very melodic, and I was singing all the time. From when I was two until I was fifteen, I sang every day on the radio. You develop a melodic sense when you sing. That went into my playing, I hope. The tunes that we chose for this record are very melodic and very beautiful.

There's a special challenge for anybody who plays in a duet, but I really like playing duets because you can hear. You can listen more intensely and complement the other musicians. I like playing in my quartet and I like playing with Ornette and a lot of other people. I love playing with drums, but playing with one other person is different.

Pat Metheny

The duet playing was done very quickly. That seemed to be the appropriate way to approach what we were trying to achieve, which was to get a spontaneous documentation of us playing together: two guys who have known each other for a long time and played together a lot. The basic recording of that album was done in two days. Then we started this process of filling the record, something Charlie, in particular, wanted to do. I was quite happy with it as a straight duo record.

Johnny Mandel's "Moon Song"—in particular Charlie wanted me to treat that song the same way that I've done stuff with my band, where it's almost orchestral in nature. I honestly resisted. "Man, this is so beautiful just as it is!"

But he was like, "There's that thing that you do—there're those chords that you use—that thing."

I knew what he was talking about. So I said, "Okay, you mean like this." I did a little.

"That's it! That's it!" He got me going. About half of the tunes wind up with that kind of treatment. The filling in was quite hard and very time consuming. The music was very exposed. There were no drums, and it was all acoustic. It was like doing a very delicate water coloring of a Japanese single-stroke pencil drawing. The actual playing was maybe 5 percent of the time that I spent on the record. The rest of the time was spent on doing the details. The mixing of that record was quite involved. It's a really good-sounding record because of some technical stuff that went on. But it's funny that the least time-consuming part of it was what most of the record is, which is just playing.

"Spiritual" [Josh Haden's composition] required a big chunk of time. It's kind of the odd tune on the record in the sense that I actually did cross the line and put a little bit of percussion stuff on there, expanding it way past what it originally was. It's what the tune was asking for. Again, Charlie was there on the sidelines, totally egging me on. It seemed like, if we were going to do that, the only place to put that tune would be the last thing on the record. So that's where it is.

Jay Newland (Engineer)

Charlie and Pat had two different styles. We'd start around eleven in the morning, and by seven at night, Charlie was ready to go back to the hotel. Pat was like, "Okay, see you later Charlie." Then he'd say, "Okay, Jay, let's get to work." He'd work on his stuff.

I had the most overdone microphone setup on Pat, but it sounded great. His sound [on that record] is really a combination of all that stuff. Charlie, pretty much I miked him the same way as always, with a ribbon mike and a condenser mike. He'd say, "Hey, Jay, you got the mike?"

"I've got the mike." He was really partial to using an old RCA 44. When I first used it, he said, "That's the one." I had gotten the idea from Walter Sear, the owner of Sear Sound. With John Snyder, I'd done a record there with Frank Morgan, Kenny Burrell, Grady Tate, and Ron Carter. Walter was always peering around. He kind of walked up behind me and went, "Have you ever tried an RCA 44 on the bass? It has incredible transient response."

"Cool! I'll try it." So I did.

"Man," Charlie said, "nobody has ever gotten my bass to sound like that."

When Charlie passed away, I went back [and counted]. I did twelve records with him. You kind of lose track over time. But *Missouri Sky*, to this day people come up and say, "Man, that record!"

ANDY BEY, *SHADES OF BEY* (1998, EVIDENCE/12TH STREET)
Herb Jordan

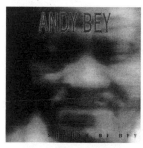 I wanted the record before this one [*Ballads, Blues, & Bey*, 1996] to be kind of minimalist, just the human voice and a piano. It's kind of scary to be out there, walking without a net on a tightrope. The philosophy was that, if you have great compositions and a master vocalist/musician, you could distill things down to their essence and still make a great record. You didn't need to dress it up, with all manner of props and supporting players.

Having done that, we felt the need—and it was very much a collaboration—to move forward, still basing the record on great compositions. Everything we try and do with Andy starts with a great song. But here we wanted to stretch out a little bit and explore some songs that weren't in that American songbook mode, opening up the field to any- and everything. That's how "Drume Negrita" found its way onto the album. It's a song that I knew of, for many years, as an instrumental coming out of Cuba. It's a simple, beautiful guitar piece—a lullaby. We came up with a guitar part that really puts the song in a different place than previous versions. My great love of Nick Drake led me to "River Man," which was kind of a risky move, because it's cross-pollination. Here, you've got Andy, who has this great history as a jazz vocalist. This is a song that, as a composition, it has some jazz elements, but it's not a jazz piece. But it was so well written and such a poignant piece that I thought we might just be able to pull it off. Andy nailed it.

My approach in making this record was, first of all, Andy has one of the most beautiful voices you could want to hear. I tried to work with songs and arrangements that would set it up so he didn't have to push it. I wanted the beauty of his voice to shine through without a lot of vocal gymnastics. We saved that for the up-tempo songs.

Phrasing was crucial to this record, that and allowing other vocal qualities to come through: the timbre of his voice, his ability to explore nuance in a note and in the delivery of a phrase. A lot of singers have a tendency to show everything they know in one song. Sometimes they forget that people have to listen to it. People generally listen to things that please them and aren't like the Olympics of vocals. There's always space for that. Andy can set it out there. He's brilliant. But at the same time, on the other end of the spectrum, he has the ability to explore nuance and understatement. We spent a lot of time on the selection and delivery of material.

REGINALD ROBINSON, *EUPHONIC SOUNDS* (1998, DELMARK)
Bob Koester

[Pianist] Jon Weber had produced a tape of Reggie, just for local consumption. We wound up buying the tape, and then Reggie wanted to redo some of the tunes. We added others, and that became his first album. I produced three albums [*The Strong Man* (1993), *Sounds in Silhouette* (1994), and *Euphonic Sounds*].

Normally we don't offer exclusive contracts. We don't want to stand in anybody's way. Our attitude with an artist is, "We're going to pay you *x* thousand dollars. We're going to pay all of the studio rental, the sidemen, the travel costs to get people in for a day if they come from out of town. And we have an option. We'll do it again next year. But in the meantime, if you go cut a record for five hundred bucks against 5 percent, don't expect us to pick up the option. We may be foolish, but we're not silly."

Against my better judgment, I did an exclusive contract with Reggie and paid a lot of extra money. It was the only exclusive I'd done in years and years, but when I had Reggie, I felt, "If I don't have an exclusive with him, he'll be making the same record for six little Dixieland labels and the whole thing will dissipate and nothing much will happen to him. He'll become at least as popular as David Thomas Roberts." Have you ever heard of David Thomas Roberts? No? Well, my point is well taken.

But I think Reggie is a phenomenon. Here's a guy from a neighborhood that has produced more drug addicts and dealers than musicians by an outstanding ratio. He's a very intelligent guy, but he's not a well-educated guy.

On his third recording there were more traditional numbers than formerly. Did you sit down with Reggie and discuss direction?

Oh, hell no. We don't do things that way. We asked, "What do you want to record?" And we let him record it. The only reportorial direction I gave was, we did some vocals we didn't put on the record, and we're very glad because we didn't think they were that good. He wanted to include the Joplin etudes.

Over the years, our communication with Reggie hadn't always been real good. There were things that frustrated us that Reggie did. Reggie's problem was, and I certainly hope that he's gotten away from that now, he felt he could make a living as a composer without becoming a performer. He actually resisted any kind of live-action work.

LOUIS ARMSTRONG, *THE COMPLETE HOT FIVE AND HOT SEVEN RECORDINGS* (REISSUE, 2000, SONY LEGACY; ORIGINAL RECORDINGS, 1924–1929, COLUMBIA AND OKEH)

STEVE BERKOWITZ: Because of the original medium, there were no sources to go to. There were, however, old parts made from the original sources. They remain, and they were utilized again. We started, then, by asking: What have we got? What can we borrow? What can we get from the Library of Congress, from collectors in Belgium, Massachusetts, or out of Michael Brooks's living room? That means every single one of these ninety recordings had a journey. They're all different.

MICHAEL BROOKS: Basically, the original records were made to be played and thrown away. They were popular records for a minority market—six month's life and move on. No one ever thought these things would be listened to years afterwards. That's why source materials vanished. They were expendable products.

Columbia Records went bankrupt in '34, and I know a huge amount of [metal] parts were thrown out then for their scrap value—and then a lot more in World War II for the scrap drive. Also, I think very often people looked at sales figures. "Guy Lombardo? We'll keep this. It sold x amount. Robert Johnson? A thousand copies? Forget it." Then, John Hammond and George Avakian were on leave in the forties. They came back, and they found this massacre going on. They managed to save blocks of Duke Ellington, Louis, Benny, and some other people. But by then the damage was done. Still, we've got a lot more than, say, American Decca, who threw out an enormous amount of stuff—and that was in the sixties, I believe.

Plus, early on, the real money was in publishing. Recording was the handmaiden of publishing. That hierarchy was reversed at a certain point.

STEVE BERKOWITZ: Some of the Armstrong records that we had previously worked on [in the first, mid-eighties wave of reissue CDs], it turned out Mike had better copies. But it's an ongoing process. Something comes out. Someone calls and says, "I have a better copy of that." We could have gone on forever.

MICHAEL BROOKS: Columbia introduced electrical recording in September of '25. Okeh was still doing acoustics in '26, but it was an "improved" technology. They called it True Tone Process on the label. I don't know what the process was, but it really was an improved acoustic. Records had much more range and depth.

Brass instruments were one thing that did come across well in acoustic recording. It's singing that came into its own with electrical, because you didn't have to shout. And Armstrong's singing was really soft. He, as much as Crosby, relied on the microphone. He was no belter.

STEVE BERKOWITZ: My question is whether or not Armstrong was fully aware at that point how his singing would record. Another point, though, is that the reproduction of records has improved by leaps and bounds. The reproduction equipment they used then could not hold a candle to what we're able to do today. So the entire nuance and the entire content of the recordings were not perceivable until recently. Which makes my original question moot. Record buyers weren't able to hear what had actually been recorded.

MICHAEL BROOKS: Armstrong certainly sensed it [the possibilities and limitations of the medium] enough on some level that what comes out is magic. He had some sensibility about what was going on there. But I doubt that he was doing anything for history. He was a southern Negro in the twenties. I think it was just sheer professionalism. He wanted to do the best that he could because that was his job. Then, late '26, early '27, Okeh introduced electrical recording. Armstrong's first electric recording, I think, was September '27.

KEN ROBERTSON: It's astonishing how much depth those very first electric recordings have compared to the acoustic. There is a quantum increase in terms of overall quality, and it's really because of signal-to-noise. You're able to make a louder recording in the groove, and that helps to overwhelm the natural noise which was created as a part of the recording process. After all, you were carving a furrow in this material, and that process itself introduced noise.

MARC KIRKEBY: When we first reissued the Hot Fives and Sevens on CD, we had maybe three or four styli we could use to play recordings. Now we've got a tackle box full.

STEVE BERKOWITZ: That represents a fortune right there. Thankfully, there's a company in England that still makes styluses. When you do a transfer to digital, a disc might require one needle on one part of it and a different needle on another part of it. That's because the records didn't wear evenly. Then the parts are digitally edited back together.

KEN ROBERTSON: We often intercut from different specimens in order to assemble a total. We might go from metal A—when a section of the metal is damaged—to pressing C and then to metal B. We assemble a transfer out of a pastiche. We pick and composite the best surfaces possible. Because our recording mechanism is stereo [and the source materials are mono], we were able, in many cases, to get a far superior result by determining which wall of the groove held the cleanest data. We got a phenomenal improvement in quality because we were able to reject the noise and damage on one side of the groove.

MARC KIRKEBY: The stylus that's chosen puts you deeper into the groove. A bigger stylus may go down only so far. A small stylus will go all the way down to the bottom—which you do not want. At the bottom of the groove there's nothing but garbage. So it's an ear-training exercise to decide where you want to place the stylus. Hopefully, it will emulate what the people who made the recording thought you were going to hear.

STEVE BERKOWITZ: With more sophisticated transfer equipment, we discovered what engineers did with very limited technology. We found that what was in those old record grooves was amazing. If you have a clean copy and the right stylus, stuff comes out that you've never heard before. We're hearing more now than perhaps anybody ever did. In converting this music, though, we had to be really careful not to convert the music into a sound that we thought we needed to hear now.

MATT CAVALUZZO: We didn't bring out anything that wasn't in those grooves. We didn't add; we didn't pull anything out of the electronic ether.

STEVE BERKOWITZ: A degree of noise has to be tolerated if you want to hear the nuances between the players and the sound in the room, and especially when you get to electrical [recording], where the sound of the room was captured. To some degree, the acoustic recordings were much easier to work with because we had fewer available choices. There wasn't as much to go in and find. That whole recording process was flatter, less dimensional. And we didn't have as many sources to choose from. Still, I'd venture to say we gathered about the best collection of source material ever in one place at one time.[6]

6. To anyone who doubts the importance of recordings to jazz history, observe that, except for two appearances sponsored by Okeh Records, Armstrong's Hot Five and his augmented band, the Hot Seven, never played outside the recording studio.

DIANA KRALL, *THE LOOK OF LOVE* (2001, VERVE)
Tommy LiPuma

I had just taken over GRP Records. Someone had sent Larry Rosen and Carl Griffin, the A & R man, an album of Diana on a small label named Justin Time from Canada. "There's this girl," they said. "We think she's pretty good." They played the album for me. They were thinking of making a deal to pick up the album and put it out. Quite frankly, I wasn't that enthusiastic. It sounded a little bit like a Holiday Inn group or something. It didn't strike me.

Later, when I went back and listened to it again, it wasn't quite as bad as I thought at the time, but it didn't really impress me. But thank God, I said something like, "Do you have anything else you can play that she's done?" And as I said, thank God, they had a video she'd done for the BET Channel. It was Diana sitting at a piano solo, playing and singing "Body and Soul." It knocked me on my ass. I couldn't get over it. "This girl is something." So I was very enthusiastic. We signed her, of course.

I said, "We can buy the album, but let's put it out at another time just as a catalog item [*Stepping Out*, 1993]. I don't want that to be the first album of hers that comes out from us. I think we can do better than that."

We didn't have that much money to spend at the time, and Diana was totally unknown. I decided to do a direct-to-two-track. I had Al Schmitt come in. He was a master at catching things, being able to mix them on the spot. So we did the first album, which was called *Only Trust Your Heart* [1995]. We did pretty well with it. It sold about seventeen thousand, which, for a jazz album, is not bad.

Diana had been playing with a great guitar player by the name of Russell Malone. Her bass player was Paul Keller. She had the idea to do a takeoff on the Nat King Cole Trio. So that's what we did. The song "All for You" had been the first thing that Nat recorded for Capitol. So that's what we called the album [*All for You: A Dedication to the Nat King Cole Trio*, 1996]. We did very well with it. Maybe we sold thirty-five or forty thousand, something like that. We were going in the right direction.

Around that time, we recorded all the artists on GRP doing Beatle songs, because it was the twenty-fifth anniversary of the Beatles. That was the first time I went in the studio with Diana where we weren't recording direct to two-track. I had a great rhythm section: Lewis Nash on drums and Christian McBride on bass. Russell Malone was back on guitar. Diana did "And I Love Her," which she changed to "And I Love Him." We spent time, as I usually do when I go in the studio, messing around, figuring out the best way to approach the tune, and then she dropped this performance that, again, knocked me on my ass. I couldn't believe it. "We've got to check this out," I said. "We've got to listen to it."

During my time as a producer, I've always had a problem with having glass between me and the band. They'd say, "What do you think?"

I'd hit that talkback button, and it was very difficult for me to communicate. At one point, sort of by accident, I wanted to explain something to the band, and I said to the second engineer, "Do me a favor. Put a chair and some earphones for me out in the studio. I want to be out there as we're going through this thing." I found out I felt much more comfortable being in the room with the musicians and the artist than I was in the booth, for many reasons: the glass between us, not being able to communicate as well as I'd like to; the other thing is there are a lot of distractions in a booth—the phone rings, people talk, people walk in and out. It's distracting. When I'm recording, I don't want to lose my concentration. So it turns out, I'm in the room with the musicians and the artists when we record.

When this happened with Diana, I said, "We've got to listen to this." She and I went in the other room and listened, and I'm telling you, by the way she listened to the playback, you could tell that she got it. She realized this is the way you do it. You work on something for a while. You get to a point where you think you're close to a take. And that's the other important thing. When I'm running something down, I get to a point where I start feeling like the shit's happening, something's going on here. I've got this signal that I do between Al and me that tells him to start recording.

Other than all of the preproduction, trying to get the right material and casting the right players, as a producer you have to recognize when the magic is ready to happen, and then, obviously, when it does happen. There are a lot of times when the artists or the musicians don't necessarily recognize it. They're dealing with detail. I'm already beyond the detail. I'm listening for a take.

After that, Diana and I did *Love Scenes* [1997], which was her breakthrough album. She found this great song, which was "Peel Me a Grape." We did about eighty or ninety thousand on that album.

Diana loved Johnny Mandel, and I was a friend of Johnny's. I said, "Let's do something with John [who earned arranger, conductor, guest artist, and producer credits]." We did a full-blown thing with strings, the whole deal. That was called *When I Look in Your Eyes* [1999]. We sold about two million albums. Diana got nominated for Album of the Year. So that was really the big breakthrough.

The next album was *The Look of Love* [2001], and that's where I convinced Claus Ogerman to come out of the shadows so to speak. He was interested in writing piano concertos, symphonies, and stuff like that. He didn't want to do any more pop things. But I was able to convince him to come back. He did the arranging. That was Diana's biggest album. We sold about four and a half million albums. These are all worldwide numbers, by the way.

Did the two of you record vocals and piano at the same time?

Ninety-nine percent of the time, it was all live. There was a song here or there, where we redid the vocal. "The Look of Love" was one of them. But there weren't many. Most of what you hear with Diana Krall is live as we did it. Al came up with this idea. He had the piano wide open, meaning the top would be open so we'd get the full sound of the piano harp. But he put a wooden plank in front between where she put her music—the music stand on the piano—and the harp, so that her vocal leakage wasn't going into the piano harp. We put a cover over the top of the opening of the piano. We were able, pretty much, to isolate piano and vocals. Let's say we got a great take, but there was a phrase in the bridge or a verse that we thought we could do better, we could replace that phrase instead of the whole thing. There was something about getting that live vocal with the musicians; everything happening at the same time, that's part of the magic.

NORAH JONES, *COME AWAY WITH ME* (2002, BLUE NOTE)
Brian Bacchus (A & R, Demo Producer)

I was the A & R guy at Blue Note. Norah was singing with a group called Wax Poetic, which was signed to Atlantic. They were also interested in her. We had a woman, Shell White, working in royalties who was managing some artists. She knew Norah, because Norah had come in and sung on a session for [folksinger] Victoria Williams, who Shell's husband had produced.

Shell brought Bruce [Lundvall, president of Blue Note] and me three songs. Two were actually from a publishing demo of Jessie Harris's. Jessie was using Norah as a singer. And then, there was a standard. We listened, and we were, "What's not to like?" We loved her voice, and started paying attention to her. I went to all of the gigs. First, she was doing standards and then she started to do a lot of gigs where she sang Jessie's material. When we decided to sign her, she started writing her own material.

We did a demo deal, basically, so that we'd have sort of first rights to her. We could add matching rights to anything Atlantic offered. We went to Sorcerer Sound, which is now closed. I pulled in Jay Newland to engineer, because he'd worked on a lot of country, blues, and jazz stuff. Jay is also a great producer. He's an incredible engineer and a great personality. There's no drama. Everything is always calm and collected in the studio. I thought Norah needed that because she'd actually never really recorded before.

Jay Newland (Engineer)

We did thirteen songs in two days, including rough mixes which I did in, like, three hours. I had gone to a rehearsal. Shell White or somebody else had an apartment in Brooklyn. I showed up, and the guys were all there, playing this stuff. I thought, "Wow!" I was really knocked out by Norah.

I selected a studio where I'd done a blues record with Shemekia Cope-land for Bruce Iglauer and Alligator Records. The studio was Sorcerer Sound, which was a really funky place, but it sounded great. That's what made me pick that studio to do Norah's demos.

We started up live. She played and sang at the same time. "Don't Know Why," the one that's on the record, the big hit, was cut at that demo session.

I understand you did very little to it and to some other songs later added to the album, but what did you do?

I think we added a second rhythm guitar, maybe a second acoustic guitar. I think that's pretty much it. There may have been a harmony vocal added, too. It pretty much was a moment in time.

Brian Bacchus (A & R, Demo Producer)

Because it was going to take over a year to get out a record, I talked to Shell, who was managing Norah, about putting together six tracks from the demos so they'd have something to sell at gigs. We did that, and those six tracks from that original thirteen became the nucleus of the first album. The six-track demo was also a springboard, because a lot of radio stations started picking up on it. When they played it, they were getting such great *cume* [as in "cumulative audience"] that by the time the album came out we were already rolling.

For the album, Norah really wanted to work with Craig Street. We had a relationship with Craig. He had a producer deal at Blue Note, meaning he got a certain amount [of money] to do a certain amount of records. He'd produced the Cassandra [Wilson] records for us.

Initially, we went up [to Allaire Studios, in Shokan, New York] with

Craig, but in the end, it didn't quite work out in terms of what it was. I think Craig had a vision. He knew where he wanted to take Norah, but when they finished, it wasn't where she was comfortable. We scrapped most of that. At the same time Bruce [Lundvall] was trying to get Arif [Mardin] to come over and resurrect Manhattan Records, which Arif had run. Bruce succeeded, and then I, basically, sold Norah on Arif. She was a little bit hesitant: one, because he was so established and, two, because he was older. But they got along fine. It was the perfect match. He obviously is great with singers but especially singer-pianists.

Did she know his history, for example, in reinventing the Bee Gees?

She knew most of it. She knew as much as she could know for someone who was into music and twenty years old, but yeah, she knew who Arif was and who he'd worked with, from Roberta Flack to Aretha. She was quite aware.

He ended up bringing back Jay Newland, and they returned to Sorcerer Sound. A lot of the finished album was stuff they'd recorded during the original demo recordings [eleven of fourteen tracks]. They were that good. Arif combed through the vocals. He had a little box that he used to go back and forth between takes. Every syllable had to be clearly heard. Sometimes, you know what the lyrics are, but you're not thinking that people are going to listen who've never heard the song before. Arif's attention to lyrics was what I really learned from him.

Jay Newland (Engineer)

Arif approached sessions as a producer, but he was also an arranger. I think he did a couple of string charts for the sessions. To me, that made him a little bit more personally involved in musical decisions. He'd make suggestions, but when he came onboard, Norah pretty much had her musical thing as she wanted it. We did the rest of the original record in the style of the demos.

The piano sound on that album is particularly distinctive. Is that accomplished during mixing or is it a function of miking?

It's the way she played the piano. She has this touch that is special. I mike the piano pretty much a standard—well, I don't know if there is a standard—but something I would normally do for a jazz recording session would be a couple of mikes pointing at the hammers. Also, I had one extra mike on a piece of foam in the piano, just to give it a little darker sound, if I needed it. But the way that piano sounds on the album, it's her touch that creates it.

For Norah's vocals on that record I chose to use a Neumann M49, because I'd heard it was a Barbra Streisand microphone. "If it's good enough for Barbra, let's try it." It sounded great. Norah ended up buying that microphone when the studio went out of business. Now that's my go-to mike. I used it on Gregory [Porter].

I notice a line or two where there's some coloring—maybe a vocal is doubled. I'm curious how and when that comes into the recording process.

Norah had a nice idea where she wanted to put harmonies. So there might be one line that has a harmony part. She was a minimalist in a way—in a really great way. She totally didn't want to overdo things. It was not, "Here's the chorus. Let's load it up with backgrounds." She had the spots picked, and Arif went through on other songs that we did later. He was pretty gifted at that. He was great because there was this aura around him that made everybody feel like everything was going to be cool. That was him personality-wise and the incredible experience that he had. I think we all felt pretty lucky to have been able to work with him.

While mixing, Arif sat in the control room. I'd work on the mix; he'd be doing something else. When I felt it was time for him to sit and critically listen, he'd sit between the speakers, listen, make a few comments, or highlight a few words on a lyric sheet that, maybe, we needed to dig out.

NORAH JONES, *FEELS LIKE HOME* (2004, BLUE NOTE)
Jay Newland (Engineer)

Half was done at Allaire and half was done at Avatar [formerly known as Power Station]. Norah had done some of her "alternate" first record up at Allaire. She liked the place. It's a pretty amazing studio. So we spent a week up there, working on stuff. Then we took a few months off and decided to finish up at Avatar. Norah and Arif produced that record. I was the engineer.

Arif said something somewhere about the challenge of getting Jones's vocals at Allaire. They bounced off the peaked roof or something?

It's an enormous room. We actually had to build a kind of cloud thing over Norah so it wouldn't be so spacious sounding. She likes to play and sing. And so in this big room the voice sounded ambient in a way that you wouldn't really want.

I built this thing to go over the piano so she could sing, and her vocals wouldn't get into the piano mikes. Later, if she wanted to change something, she could change it.

I don't understand compositing vocals with jazz-oriented musicians, who are constantly altering their performances. Is comping really possible with jazz guys?

With jazz it's a little more trial and error. Like if you're trying to comp three different solos together, you might have to try a few spots and see where you can connect the dots, so to speak. With a pop song, the lyrics are pretty much timed and sung in pretty much the same way each time. There are subtle variations, but it's easier to take a line from a verse in a pop song than a phrase from a jazz solo.

The first two albums I did with Norah were both recorded to tape. I think everything she does is probably analog. We never went to computer or anything. It was mixed on a board, mixed to ½-inch tape. So we'd do edits, but it's a little easier now [than it used to be]. It's easier now to try it out and see if it works. There was no autotune, ever, on those records. It was just her doing what she does.

CHARLES MINGUS SEXTET WITH ERIC DOLPHY, *CORNELL 1964* (2007, BLUE NOTE)
Ed Michel (Fantasy)

I stopped [producing records] from the end of '88 until the beginning of '94. I came back because I'd built a house. Like everybody else, I ran over budget. There is zero economy on the big island of Hawaii. There's no way to make a living there. I'm back here to pay for my house and pay for some more time. At the moment, I am on a two-year project to catalog Fantasy's vaults.

Is that exciting?

I'll give you an honest answer. The real answer is "no." It's dull. It's drudgery. I'm a musical janitor. The upside is that there's all kinds of amazing shit sitting in those vaults. There's stuff that makes my heart go pitty-pat—fantastic stuff. As a jazz fan, yeah, I am excited. As a producer, I'd rather make cassettes of all this stuff and go back to Hawaii and listen to it. I'm glad I've got the work. Mostly, I'm looking at what the boxes say and writing down what it means and entering it into a computer.

At the moment, I'm working on the Debut Records story. [Debut was founded in 1952 by Charles and Celia Mingus.] It starts with some horrendous recordings. I mean just dreadful. And they're moving from dreadful to poor, which is a big step forward. But that's as far as we can take them at the moment. Hopefully, in my lifetime, they'll move from poor to pretty good, but it's going to take more control tools than exist now [fall 1995]. The best choice is to record it right the first time. But in a lot of cases you couldn't do that, and there's some magnificent music that wasn't very well recorded to begin with, but the performances are killers. You try to make them as accessible as possible and remove the distraction of whatever it is that's between the listener and the music. That's part of a producer's job, and it's part of an engineer's job. It's the place where they interact.

Do you find that you have to choose, "Am I going to please this or that group of listeners?"

No. I figure I've got the job. I've been hired to do this. That means I've been hired to make decisions. And I'll make the decisions that I think are right. I may have to go back to the guy who hired me and point out that doing it the right way is going to be very expensive, and if he wants it done the wrong way, maybe somebody else should do it, because I don't know how to do it the wrong way. The right way is going to cost him more than he's planning to spend. I've done that before. I've been told, "Can't you do it not so well?" My answer is, "No. I don't know how to do it badly." I can do it badly by accident, but I can't set up by design to do it badly.

P.S. Very soon after my 1995 conversation with Ed Michel, he discovered a 1964 Mingus concert that no one knew existed. I later [in 2014] asked him, "How did you know the recording's provenance?

I knew that period of Mingus fairly well, because I was interested in the band when Dolphy was in it. There were lots of recordings once they got to Europe, but this was before they left the country.

I told Ralph Kaffel [president of Fantasy Records] about it. "We probably don't have the rights," he said. "The tapes probably belong to Sue Mingus." He took the very correct position, which I figured out later, that Sue was hard to do business with. I sent her a copy of the tapes and stopped worrying about them.

ABBEY LINCOLN, *ABBEY SINGS ABBEY* (2007, VERVE)
Jay Newland

Jean-Philippe and I produced that record together. I'd produced a record for him by an artist named Ayo. She's this incredibly talented Nigerian-German singer/songwriter. I had the idea for her to cover an Abbey Lincoln song. We selected a song called "And It's Supposed to Be Love." We did it, and Jean-Philippe was at the studio. He heard her singing an Abbey song in a nonjazz context.

He had the idea, "Wow, wouldn't it be great if we did a record of Abbey Lincoln singing her songs that really showcased her as a songwriter, as

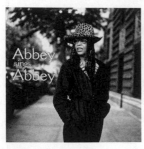

opposed to a jazz artist." Everything she had done was streamed for a jazz context: upright bass, piano, horn solos, vibes. So he came up with the idea to do this singer/songwriter version of Abbey's stuff.

The guitar player I chose was Larry Campbell, a guy I'd worked with on Ayo's record. The drummer was Shawn Pelton, and the bass player was Scott Colley. Larry, one of the greatest musicians I've ever met, plays all kinds of instruments: guitar, mandolin, fiddle, pedal-steel.

All of a sudden these sound colors were showing up on Abbey Lincoln songs. It created this incredible vibe. There's a song on that album called "Music Is the Magic." Larry heard her original version and came up with an idea for the guitar riffs. It's got a little bit of a room sound to it. It's great. Same thing with Shawn. He'd hear something and say, "I've got this idea for this vibe here." [We'd] let those guys create.

It was really an interesting record because we had Abbey in the studio for only six hours: two hours, three different days. She was in her late seventies. If we started at one o'clock in the afternoon with her, by three she was ready to be done. We had to do four songs each day in that time.

I got the guys in the studio early. We'd rehearse the songs. They'd worked out whatever they were going to do on each song. Then she'd sing live with the band, and that was it. She'd leave, and we'd do whatever overdubs or pickups we had to do.

It was an old-style recording. As needed, you did a little sweetening.

Exactly. But with Abbey, she was in the vocal booth singing with the band. She might stop halfway through a take. We'd go back and start another one. In postproduction I might have grabbed a line from a take that wasn't used or something. But that's the magic of what we can do now.

While it's pretty common in the rock world for engineers to become producers, it's not all that common in jazz. When you do produce, what do you bring to projects as a consequence of having been an engineer?

It allows me to have a better understanding of what I think the record can, potentially, sound like. I know how to get there quickly. The great thing about working in jazz is you have to learn to be fast. Jazz never has the budgets of rock records. You don't have two days to get a drum sound. The engineering thing really helps me figure out how the pieces need to fit together.

Jean-Philippe Allard

The idea came from discussions, Jay Newland [producer and engineer] and I very often talked about songs and songwriting. We felt that Abbey was almost like a writer of folk songs. In a way she was like Odetta, but in the jazz world. To generalize, singers do a composition by Cole Porter or Michel Legrand. The song exists already in a classic, original, or Broadway version. The musicians reharmonize the song; singers change a little bit of the melody or alter their phrasing. They interpret songs. In a jazz context, it means that you never hear the songs by themselves. For me that was a kind of frustration. I thought sometimes that the focus wasn't enough on the songs, simply on the melodies and the lyrics.

Jay and I had in mind to do the album in, let's call it, a nonjazz context, even if that's not exactly what it was. We had recorded with Stan Getz, J. J. Johnson, Hank Jones, Jackie McLean, Bobby Hutcheson, Steve Coleman, Pat Metheny, and Charlie Haden. We'd had some of the greatest jazz soloists in the world. So our idea was to do it with Larry Campbell. He was working with Bob Dylan and other songwriters. His focus was on songs, on playing the chords of songs. At the same time he's as great a musician in his style as the musicians I just mentioned. Larry was the reason we thought we'd be able to do the album.

I talked to Abbey about the idea, but at the time she was already not stable, psychologically speaking. She could forget things. It wasn't like it was before. She couldn't be in control of everything, but she had total confidence in me by this point. She'd always wanted to keep maximum control over everything, but we were close enough—working together for so many years—that she trusted me.

So we spoke to the musicians that Jay cast. Also, I wanted to do an album without piano. I think that, sometimes, the piano clashes with the voice. With a lot of singers, the piano, as a tempered instrument, doesn't really fit the voice, but the guitar, for some reason, blends much better with the voice. I wanted to hear that.

With Abbey, we established a list of her songs. Then at the studio she discovered the musicians for the first time. "Jean-Philippe," she said, "I don't know any of the guys." She was surprised.

I said, "Yeah," and I introduced her to the players. As soon as they started to play, she started to sing. She was so happy because she was so comfortable. She didn't have to fight against new chords, new differences.

For jazz singers that's part of the art form, but it's very difficult. When nobody plays the "right" chord, when they change everything, when they play a solo behind her, Abbey loved that. But in this context she was relaxed and comfortable because she could hear the songs the way she wrote them. She sang naturally. I really wanted to do the album well, and she loved, loved, loved it. She said that many times. For the first time she could hear her songs in the most simple way and realize they were great songs. Of course, there were some solos, some improvisation, but it was more like a Bob Dylan album than a Sarah Vaughan album.

CHARLIE HADEN QUARTET WEST, *SOPHISTICATED LADIES* (2010, EMARCY)
Jean-Philippe Allard

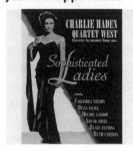

Charlie was very creative in terms of projects and concepts. When he came with ideas, I tried to make it possible for him, to encourage him to do them, and to extend his ideas. He had great ideas—film noir, singers from the forties, nostalgia—except I gave him the idea for *Sophisticated Ladies*, his last album with Quartet West. It was something we'd already started with *The Art of the Song* [1999], which was his idea. I called him with the idea to do something with different singers. I thought he'd love Melody Gardot, even though he didn't know her, and I thought that Norah Jones playing with the Quartet would be a great idea. I said we should call it *Sophisticated Ladies* and do something very elegant. He knew so many songs—"If I'm Lucky," things like that—and he had the best ideas for songs.

GREGORY PORTER, *BE GOOD* (2012, MOTÉMA)
Brian Bacchus

Gregory came to me via Al Pryor, a friend at Mack Avenue [Records], who's also an A & R guy and producer. Al was supposed to do Gregory's record, but it became a conflict of interest. He recommended me. Gregory and his manager had met with a few producers. I sat down with them, and we hit it off. I'd seen Gregory sit in with somebody, and I was impressed. I heard *Water* [2011], which was the first record he did. Then I went to see him live, and it was, "Okay, this guy, he's got it." That's how his second record from Motéma came about.

GREGORY PORTER, *LIQUID SPIRIT* (2013, BLUE NOTE)
Brian Bacchus

Before even starting the third record, I went to my old friend Jean-Philippe Allard. He was running Universal Music Publishing in France. I said, "You should really sign this guy. He's a great songwriter." They definitely wanted to sign him, and then, at the same time, Universal Worldwide was reorganizing its whole jazz program. They realized, "We should sign him as well," because his deal was up at Motéma. So they ended up signing him to a publishing and also to a recording deal.

When you say the two of you hit if off what do you mean?

You'd have to ask Gregory, but I think, generally, he liked where I was coming from. I think he heard that I heard the right things about him. I understood the soul aspect of his singing, where he was coming from vocally, and I also got his songwriting.

The other thing was that I went up to see his band. Everybody was telling him, "You've got to get a new band. You've got to get the best piano player, the best drummer, the best bass player." It went on forever. They were basically saying, "Hire all-stars to do your next record." I listened to the band, and I was like, "They've been doing this gig steady. They know his music." He'd done a lot of soul gigs. He was with the Four Tops for a while. He knew that church thing and R & B thing, as well as the jazz thing. I thought, "It's not like these guys can't play. They can definitely play." It was really a matter of focusing them in the studio in terms of what the songs were and the mood we wanted to set.

To me, the recording went pretty smooth. It wasn't like I had to crack a whip or anything. We sat down and discussed what we were going for. Also Kamau Kenyata, who acted as the associate producer on both the records I did, was an old friend of Gregory's from San Diego. He'd gotten Gregory initially involved in music and in jazz. Kamau also arranged the horns. He was really helpful in pulling things together. He got it. We got along fine.

Was Porter writing on the record date or was the repertoire already together?

Gregory has a backlog of songs. The first meetings we had was, mainly, going through songs, demos and things, stuff like that. We had seventeen songs. "We're not going to record all seventeen," I said. "Let's have a meeting." This was about four days out, before we went into rehearsal and, then, recording. "Let's sit down, go through the songs, and get it down to a manageable list of thirteen, fourteen, maybe even twelve songs."

Gregory came into that meeting with another four songs, and all four were great. He made our job even more difficult, but that's the thing. He's prolific, as far as I can tell.

I don't know many other artists, outside of a very special few, who have done three albums in a row where they wrote the majority of the material, and the material is, for the most part, terrific. You don't have many jazz vocalists who are great songwriters. Being a musician and a jazz artist, that takes a certain skill set, but writing songs, to me, is the magic. There are people who are great songwriters who don't have super skill sets as musicians, but they can deliver some incredible songs. Gregory's got that, and he's a great musician.

On the two records I've done with Gregory, there are, usually, two or three standards that he wants to do. He's chosen some interesting songs. He pulled the theme from *Imitation of Life*, and he wanted to do Billie Holiday's "God Bless the Child" acapella on the *Be Good* album. He did also "The 'In' Crowd," as well as "Lonesome Lover," the Abbey [Lincoln] and Max [Roach] song from the Impulse album [Roach's *It's Time*, 1962]. He picks straight-up-the-middle standards here and there, but also some stuff from left field. It mainly has to do with his palate, what he listens to, what really moves him, what gets under his skin.

Jay Newland (Engineer)

He's got one of those oh-my-God voices. That guy is incredible—very strong but very relaxed. The main vocal mike for him was a Neuman M49, and then I would set up a second mike—the emergency mike—just in case something happened to the first mike.

I actually started doing that when I was working with Etta James. John [Snyder] and I did a bunch of Etta James records together. She was singing along great, and then she just opened up one time, and it completely saturated the tape. I was like, "Oh, wow!" With her, I'd put up a second mike and record it 10dB softer than the main mike so that if she surprised me ... I used a compressor, but I didn't want to use it very hard. Anyway, that's the kind of the thing I did with Gregory.

A lot of that record is just him doing a take with the band, and that's it. He might do two or three takes until it seems to feel right to him: the vocal sets in right, and the band is right. Then, if we need to do any fixes, we can do that. It's not like, "Let's do a take, and then I'm going to go in the booth and do ten passes with the vocal." That's not him.

That's an amazing record. I've let a lot of different people hear it who don't consider themselves jazz fans, and they're all like, "Man, I can't get enough of that Gregory Porter record." One nice thing about Gregory is that he doesn't oversing. He's fun to listen to.

I suppose the new default—to blast away at a vocal—came from The Voice *and* American Idol.

Let's oversing, and let's reward people for oversinging. Let's train America to think that's what it's about. Which it isn't. When you hear the subtlety of Abbey Lincoln, Gregory Porter, or Norah Jones, you go, "That's what it should be like."

CODA

....

John Snyder (Artists House)

Up until recently, I would say my role was to take the artist, his concept, and his point of view and put them down on tape—not really fool with it too much. Now I'm more particular. I think if somebody is choosing a piano player who is not especially good or there are ten guys who are better, I am going to say so. "I am okay if you want to use this guy because he's in your band, but is he in your band because he'll work for three hundred a week? You can do better." I know the argument about loyalty, and I know the argument about closeness. I buy them. I think they're good arguments, but you can also make records with musicians that are not quite up to the job, and you are not going to sell as many of them, I don't think. The idea is to speak up and be more back-and-forth with the artist. Then again, some guys—especially jazz guys—know what they want.

I've always thought the major role of the producer is to be the first audience. An audience is a group of people who react in a kind of a pure way. The producer goes in the studio. You sit and you wait. Whatever happens is going to affect you in one way or the other. You know yourself, when you go to hear music, you can feel satisfied, or you can feel excited, or you can feel sleepy, or you can feel pissed off, or whatever. The music is going to have an effect on you—even if it is "ho-hum." That's an effect.

Then, the question is, "Why?" The audience/listener may not have to answer that question, may not give a shit. "I don't know why this went wrong; it just wasn't right." The producer has to have that initial feeling— a very open sort of receptiveness. In the midst of all the political mayhem and chaos in a recording studio, it's not easy. After you hear the music and feel it, you've got to be able to express what you heard and felt, and then even take it further: "How do we now change it? How do we make it better?" Or you have to know, "That was perfect." Identifying first takes that are right is an acquired ability. I am with producers a lot who are not that experienced. They hear something great, and they think they can get it greater. One of the things you have to learn is that when it's right, you leave it alone.

Jazz records in the past have suffered because they were made so haphazardly. I think one reason they don't sell well or that more people don't find the music more accessible is because most of those records aren't very good. They're not very interesting. I think that's due to lack of preparation or perhaps to a cloudy vision on the part of the creator, the artist. The producer can often help clarify the vision of the artist by asking questions and pointing out things that the record company is concerned about.

Joel Dorn (Atlantic)

Where are you calling me from?

York, Pennsylvania.

You've got a strange accent for there. Where are you from? No, I'll tell you. You're from Georgia.

Atlanta.

Come on, how many guys know a Georgia accent from a fucking hillbilly, that shit? When you write whatever you're doing, put in that I nailed your accent—by the state. I deserve something for that. I don't give a shit what you say about me or the records, but I caught your accent out-of-the-box. There's something very bebop about that. Now, what do you want?

ACKNOWLEDGMENTS

....

Most of all, I want to thank the fifty-seven artists who agreed to speak with me. They made this book conceivable and a pleasure to write. Even more important, without the records these folks produced, I can't imagine my life at all. I don't know who I'd be. I certainly wouldn't be able to recognize myself. And so talking with people who contributed significantly to my identity was, to say the least, a dream come true. I wouldn't trade the experience of interviewing George Avakian, Joel Dorn, Michael Cuscuna, Ed Michel, Don Schlitten, John Snyder, Ornette Coleman, and Bob Belden for three wishes from a genie. One more time then, with feeling, thank you.

It took so long to write this book that I've unfortunately lost track of most every record-company person who helped me along the way. There were many. I couldn't, however, forget Brian Bacchus, Tom Cording, Terri Hinte, Arthur Levy, Marilyn Lipsius, and Don Lucoff—publicists extraordinaire. I appreciate all of the leads and phone numbers you gave me. In 1995, I wrote a feature story on jazz record producers for *Pulse!*, Tower Records' magazine. It gave birth to this book. As he did with lots of my stuff, Marc Weidenbaum edited the article with great care and skill. For fifteen years, the editors at *Pulse!*—Marc, Ned Hammad, Jason Verlinde, Jackson Griffith, and Peter Melton gave me one terrific assignment after another—a lot of them weird and beautiful. In the process, these guys unwittingly taught me (or led me to discover) more about music and writing than grad school or my day job ever did. I also wrote producer-related pieces for Michael Fagien and Roy Parkhurst at *Jazziz* magazine, for Daniel Fischlin and Ajay Heble (*The Other Side of Nowhere*), and for Simon Frith and Simon Zagorski-Thomas (*The Art of Record Production*). I interviewed Sonny Rollins for Bob Rusch at *Cadence* magazine and James Blood Ulmer for Columbia Records. Will Kinnally generously let me interview Ornette Coleman—the chance of a lifetime. Many others, whom I've sadly forgotten, lent a hand or encouraged me. My thanks to all y'all.

Penn State University granted me a sabbatical, a paid leave of absence that allowed me to sneak off to Costa Rica in the middle of the winter (not part of the official deal) and, when I returned refreshed, enabled me to finish writing this book. Though I am counting the days until retirement—12:00 A.M., December 10, 2018—I do love my day job.

This book ended up at the University of North Carolina Press largely be-

_____

cause of Steve Weiss, curator of the Southern Folklife Collection at the Wilson Library, UNC–Chapel Hill. I am indebted to him for introducing me to Mark Simpson-Vos, editorial director at the press, who supported my work without the slightest hint of reservation. Thank you, Mark. Alex Martin copyedited my manuscript with the eyes of a musician (he's a guitarist). Mary Carley Caviness served as project editor and with Rich Hendel turned it into the sort of book I'd want to read. Gina Mahalek handled initial publicity. I am grateful for the care and creativity shown by this team. Making a book, very much like making a record album, is a group project.

Finally, I appreciate the constant support (and tolerance) of my closest family and friends. Greg Seigworth has, for years, listened to stories that record producers told me. Now that I think about it, I'm constantly trying out new material on him. Pamela, the love of my life, deserves a producer credit for everything I've ever written that's worth reading.

INDEX